Preaching & Reading
the Lectionary

Preaching & Reading the Lectionary

A Three-Dimensional Approach to the Liturgical Year

O. Wesley Allen Jr.

CHALICE
PRESS
ST. LOUIS, MISSOURI

Cover image: GettyImages
Cover and interior design: Elizabeth Wright

Visit Chalice Press on the World Wide Web at
www.chalicepress.com

10 9 8 7 6 5 4 3 2 1   07 08 09 10 11 12

Library of Congress Cataloging–in–Publication Data

Allen, O. Wesley, 1965-
  Preaching and reading the lectionary : 3-dimensional approach to the liturgical year / O. Wesley Allen Jr.
      p. cm.
   ISBN 978-0-8272-3006-4
  1. Lectionary preaching. 2. Preaching. 3. Church year. I. Title.

  BV4235.L43A45 2008
  251'.6—dc22   2007037171

Printed in the United States of America

CONTENTS

ACKNOWLEDGMENTS

This book is written by a seminary professor who is a perpetual guest preacher, but it is written for pastors who stand in the same pulpit Sunday after Sunday trying to offer a glimpse of the gospel of Jesus Christ to the same people sitting in the pews week in and week out. While for many the distance between the academy and the church is as far as Athens is from Jerusalem, for me the journey is no longer than shifting my weight from one foot to the other. I try to live and work with one foot in both worlds of ministry. Indeed, my experience of ministry in congregational settings informs much of what I do in the classroom and in my writing. This book is an example of that.

I have spent most of my pastoral life as someone who follows the lectionary in homiletical and liturgical planning. For me the lectionary is a great gift. It saves me time from scanning the canon looking for texts for Sunday's sermon and helps me focus the various elements of the worship service around common scriptural texts and themes. It invites me into ecumenical dialogue with other preachers and congregations who are exploring the same texts on the same Sunday I am. It reminds me that my task is to preach on more than just those theological themes and biblical texts with which I am familiar and comfortable by pushing me into parts of the canon through which I might not naturally journey. It nourishes me by giving concreteness to the liturgical themes and practices that shape so much of what I offer to God in worship.

However, I also struggle with the discipline of following the lead of the lectionary. I struggle to be true to the predefined texts while also being relevant to current, constantly changing, historical and current life situations of the congregation. I struggle to stay fresh, to offer good *news* in the pulpit when returning to the same sets of texts every three years and to many of those texts every year. I struggle to offer a cohesive Christian worldview while jumping from Gospel to First Testament to Epistle to psalm.

Therefore, I developed the material in this book and on the accompanying CD-ROM out of my loving struggle with the lectionary and for those who similarly experience the rhythm of lectionary existence as both a blessing and a bane. My hope is to crack open new homiletical and liturgical possibilities by taking a step back from our usual practice of focusing on the weekly lections in order to bring into view a bigger, yet still manageable, sweep of the lections. In this process of studying how the lectionary texts function season-by-season, I have been reminded of many things I had forgotten, have found new potential in elements that I had taken for granted and glossed over, and have learned things that I should have known long ago. I wish I had had this sort of resource when I was preaching to the same congregation week-after-week, year-after-year, and pray that those who do so now may find it as meaningful to employ in worship planning and sermon preparation as I have found it to be in writing.

One of the reasons writing this material has been meaningful is I have not worked on it in isolation. I am thankful to a number of people who have been willing to be sounding boards for my ideas. While I take responsibility for whatever shortcomings are to be found in the work, I cannot deny that there would have been many more deficiencies were it not for the support, critique, and advice offered by friends, family, and colleagues. Bonnie Cook, Robert Cueni, Bill Kincaid, and Steve Monhollen read early drafts of portions of the work, offered serious feedback, and helped me focus the project better. The library staff at Lexington Theological Seminary, especially Barbara Pfeifle and Charlie Heatherlin, found for me some well-hidden yet much-needed information and resources. Lisa Davison and Jerry Sumney, my colleagues who teach Bible at the seminary, have been open to many a doorway conversation about this or that lectionary text. Students at the seminary and various clergy groups have allowed me to work through different portions of the book in oral form and have provided invaluable suggestions. Daisy Machado, who arrived as dean at LTS after I was well underway in writing this material, has been quite supportive of the project and the requirements of meeting publishing deadlines. Kerry Moore has been an invaluable student assistant. She read through the bulk of the text found in both the book and the CD-ROM—not only noting typographical and grammatical errors, but also extensively commenting on the content.

Finally, I am especially grateful to Pablo Jiménez, Trent Butler, and their colleagues at Chalice Press for their support of this work. The publishing market is filled with commentaries on the Revised Common Lectionary, journals offering homiletical aids for each week's texts, and liturgical and musical resources related to the weekly lectionary choices. These works have established a standard expectation of how lectionary resources are to function. In taking on this project, Chalice Press has been willing to stray from, indeed has been enthusiastic about, moving beyond this Monday to Sunday approach of using the lectionary in shaping worship practice. They have sought ways to shape the work so that it might combine a serious look at the complex layers of the Revised Common Lectionary with an ease of use for worship planners.

PREFACE

Cumulative Preaching

Most books about and resources for preaching deal with the individual sermon. It is little wonder that texts written by homileticians, who are perpetual guest preachers and who spend most of their time in the classroom trying to introduce beginning preachers to the task of developing and delivering sermons, focus so much energy on what "the sermon" is (theologically speaking) and what it is supposed to do (in terms of rhetoric). From the perspective of pastors who read these texts, however, this focus on the individual sermon has led to many blue Monday mornings as we fret over questions like, "Why did this sermon change no one's life or even their theology? Why was no one moved to make a decision for faith? Why at the rear door of the sanctuary did no one speak of the sermon as if they had truly engaged its content at the level I offered it to them?"

While we have much to learn about preaching from works discussing the sermonic event, all pastors know (or at least hope), deep in their hearts, that the great power of preaching lies less in the individual sermon and more in the cumulative effect of preaching week in and week out to the same congregation, to the same community of believers, doubters, and seekers —and, by the way, these labels can usually all be applied to any person instead of separate groups. In other words, we need to find a way to celebrate that, while the individual sermon that profoundly changes lives is a wonderful exception to the rule, sermons offered Sunday after Sunday, month after month, and year after year weave together to have an immeasurable, cumulative influence on individuals' and the congregation's understanding of God, self, and the world.[1]

Although there is no excuse for ill-prepared, boring sermons, it should rarely be the primary goal of preachers to create and deliver sermons in which parishioners remember "the word" offered on that particular day. Instead, pastors need to find homiletical techniques that intertwine their sermons over the course of their preaching ministry within a congregation in order to reinforce the laity's faith formation. This does not mean that preachers need to resort to offering multi-part sermon series. While such series may at times be appropriate, they can also hinder the cumulative process of faith formation in worship if individual sermons in the series are so tightly connected that previous sermons must be lodged in the memory for later sermons to make sense or have an impact. For assimilation of the Christian worldview to occur, individual sermons dealing with narrow topics and specific biblical passages need to stand on their own as an isolated sermon at the same time that they reinforce the glimpses of the broader Christian worldview offered in other sermons.

In other words, I am arguing for a cumulative understanding of the preaching ministry. Instead of building sermon series, preachers should approach the sermon development process in a manner similar to scriptwriting for a television series. Most weekly dramas or sitcoms strike a balance between the two sorts of demands with which we are concerned. On the one hand, each individual episode is complete in and of itself—it has a story with a beginning, middle, and end. On the other hand, there is also a level of continuity from episode to episode. Even though new situations arise each week, the scriptwriters use a supply of regular main characters, settings, themes, subplots, and running jokes that recur show after show. (See Table 1.)

TABLE 1: Cumulative Nature of Television Series

Characters ⟶ *Setting* ⟶ *Themes*

EPISODE 1	EPISODE 2	EPISODE 3	EPISODE 4
Beginning	Beginning	Beginning	Beginning
Middle	Middle	Middle	Middle
End	End	End	End

⟶ *Subplots* ⟶ *Running Jokes* ⟶

While first-time or occasional viewers who tune in to a series mid-season will miss nuances of the continuing elements of the series, they can usually follow the storyline of the episode and "get something" out of or enjoy the show. If the continuing elements are too strong and overpower the individual nature of the episode, the first-time viewer may never tune in again. However, if new or occasional viewers are able to follow the individual story, can easily get to know the main characters at a basic level, and are stimulated or entertained by what they watch, they are more likely to start watching regularly. As they become loyal viewers, they will gain more enjoyment from the series because they will become familiar with continuing themes and developments. They watch as characters grow, relationships between characters develop, themes and issues repeat, and underlying subplots evolve. They will develop relationships and identify with characters in some depth. They may, at times, even find connections between their lives and the storylines, issues, and dialogue on the show.

To write a television series that meets the demands of creating a narrative world with coherence and gradual development over the course of the series and of creating an individual, complete narrative for each episode, television writers must constantly have their eyes focused on the details of the individual episode and maintain a consistent vision for the broader sweep and flow of the series. Moreover, they must be attentive to how each influences the other, how each dictates limits and offers potential for the other. Were they in one episode to write action or dialogue for a star of the show that is "out of character," change the setting of the show for a single episode without sufficient explanation, or change the tone of the action or dialogue radically, they would break the coherence and stretch the credibility of the narrative world that the series has created over time. In contrast, slight changes in characterization, small shifts in setting, and little plot twists in individual episodes open up new directions for the series and are more easily accepted by the viewers.

As with script writing, preachers must have a bifocal approach to developing sermons in order to preach effective individual sermons that cumulatively influence the congregation's and individual hearers' meaning-making processes. That is, they must move beyond the task of individual sermon preparation to the task of developing their extended preaching ministry (of which preparation of the individual sermon is a key part).

This book is meant to assist lectionary preachers in achieving such a cumulative approach. The Revised Common Lectionary indeed represents a specific (yet broad and suggestive) cumulative approach to working through representative portions of the canon in the context of worship over the course of a three-year period. As such, it invites the pastor to shape sermons over time that reiterate but also revisit from different views core biblical and liturgical themes and stories.

The *Introduction* that follows this Preface provides an overview of the Revised Common Lectionary in terms of the three dimensions of its cumulative nature: the relation of the various lections assigned to any given Sunday (width), the relation of lections from week to week (height), and the relation of reading from year to year (depth). This wide-angle look at the Revised Common Lectionary will help preachers keep the whole in view even while focusing on the parts as they plan their preaching season by season.

The *main body* of the book offers a variety of potential cumulative strategies for preaching through each of the liturgical seasons of the three-year cycle of the Revised Common Lectionary. These homiletical strategies deal primarily (but not solely) with the height dimension of how the flow of readings week to week presents opportunity for preaching cumulatively Sunday to Sunday. The list of strategies is not meant to be exhaustive but rather suggestive of the range of possibilities that preachers can develop in different ways. Indeed, the examples are specifically intended to be helpful for defining the *starting point* of sermon development for each season without determining the end, i.e., individual sermonic content.

To clarify, I envision something like the following process for using these resources to choose a cumulative preaching strategy before the season under consideration begins. Such a process can be done by an individual or by a group responsible for planning worship:

1. A number of weeks or months in advance of a liturgical season, read through each set of Sunday lections for the *whole* season. Make short notes about initial impressions of the texts and various ways they are interrelated. (Use the charts at the beginning of each season and the materials on the CD-ROM noted below to help in this process.)
2. Read through all of the strategies suggested for the season. Reflect on the possibilities they suggest, evoke, and miss. Consider as well how they fit with and build upon cumulative strategies employed in the liturgical season(s) prior to the season for which you are planning.
3. Choose a basic cumulative strategy (from the book, adapted from the book, or developed on your own in conversation with the book) to follow during the season. Write this out to help your memory when the season draws near and you begin working on the individual sermons.

4. Since many of the suggested strategies allow for focusing on different lections for a given Sunday, choose an individual text to preach on for each Sunday during the season. Write the list on the notes you made for Step 2.
5. If you have been doing this process alone, share these choices with others responsible for planning various elements of worship or other arenas of congregational life (such as educational ministries) that utilize the Revised Common Lectionary.
6. When the liturgical season draws near, review your notes, and confirm or revise your choices. Consider ways to integrate/publicize your cumulative direction or the cumulative connections of the Revised Common Lectionary for the season in advance.
7. When the season arrives, work on the individual sermons with an eye to your cumulative purposes.

Finally, a *CD-ROM* is included that complements the cumulative preaching strategies by offering introductions for reading each lection during worship throughout the three-year lectionary cycle. With the dominance of television and the near absence of public reading in North American culture, worship leaders cannot expect that worshipers hear that much of what oral scripture reading has to offer. Moreover, in today's fragmented, cacophonous world, it is certainly too much to expect worshipers, on their own, to see any more than the most obvious connections in the lections on a given Sunday, much less from Sunday to Sunday, season to season, and year to year. If we want congregations to see the three-dimensional character of the Revised Common Lectionary in a way that enhances their experience of worship, the Bible, and the Christian faith, lectors and preachers need to name the interconnectedness of the lections explicitly. The introductions are intended to help in this naming.

The CD-ROM includes brief introductions for each liturgical year, season, and individual lection. Copyright permission is granted for use and/or adaptation of the introductions for worship and free congregational publications (e.g., bulletins and newsletters). The introductions have been written in such a way as to help the congregation view the larger biblical, liturgical, and lectionary contexts and connections of each individual reading, Sunday, and liturgical season. But church leaders may well need to edit the language in the introductions so the wording does not seem artificial or stilted when a specific reader presents them in worship, to better fit the tone or style of the worship service or congregational publication, and to reinforce the particular cumulative homiletical strategy chosen.

The Three-Dimensional Lectionary

The Revised Common Lectionary was primarily designed as a liturgical tool, with homiletics being a secondary concern. For most Protestant pastors, however, it has primarily been used as a homiletical tool, with liturgical import being secondary. As a pastor I would consult the lectionary on Monday morning to choose a single text from which to preach for the coming Sunday, but do little to design a worship service in which all of the lections would be read effectively in the midst of the congregation. The problem with this pastoral practice is that while I gained some sense of the cumulative nature of the lectionary over time, the connective tissues of the lectionary (and thus to some extent of the liturgical year) were completely lost on the congregation.

The practice is also problematic in theological terms. Choosing one text from the lectionary to use for the sermon and discarding the other three shows that we have subordinated the reading of scripture to the sermon. Yet surely when asked, most of us would claim, theologically and ecclesiologically, that preaching should be in service to the reading of scripture, not that the reading of scripture should serve the preacher.

Before turning to the practical aids of introductions to the lections and cumulative preaching strategies, it is important to obtain a broad view of the way the Revised Common Lectionary functions cumulatively itself. The best entryway into understanding the cumulative nature of the Revised Common Lectionary is to recall a little of its historical evolution.

A Brief History of the Revised Common Lectionary[1]

Prior to the mid-sixteenth century, practices concerning the liturgical calendar varied to a great extent from region to region, which meant that lectionaries varied as well. In 1563 the Council of Trent established a liturgical calendar and a corresponding lectionary that was authoritative for the whole of the Roman Catholic Church. This Tridentine lectionary varied greatly from the denominational and ecumenical lectionaries of today in two major ways. First, there were only two lections assigned for each Sunday—an Epistle and a Gospel reading. On a few occasions, a reading from the First Testament was substituted for the Epistle reading; otherwise the only part of the First Testament that was used each Sunday came from the Psalter, with portions of a psalm used as the gradual hymn. Second, the lectionary followed an annual cycle, so that the same lections were used year after year. The same lections were used for five hundred years...until Vatican II.

During the Second Vatican Council, the Constitution on the Sacred Liturgy decreed, along with other sweeping changes, that "the treasures of the Bible be opened up more lavishly so that richer fare might be provided for the faithful at the table of God's word and a more representative portion of sacred scripture be read to the people over a set cycle of years."[2] So, beginning in Advent 1969, the Roman Catholic Church initiated use of a new *Lectionary for Mass*.

Although the liturgical calendar still dictated the ways choices of lections were made for each Sunday, some broader principles were brought into play that made the lectionary function cumulatively. First, the *Lectionary for Mass* moved from an annual to a three-year cycle, with each year focused on one of the Synoptic Gospels (with John used each year during Lent and Easter). This dominance of the Synoptic Gospels affects not only the shape of the lectionary year, but also the tone of most individual Sundays. Second, the number of readings for each Sunday was expanded to include a selection from the First Testament. During the liturgical seasons (Advent to Epiphany and Lent to Pentecost), the lections from the First Testament and the Epistles are almost always subordinate to the Gospel reading. (The choice of a psalm is usually derived from the themes and language of the First Testament reading.) A third principle was developed for Ordinary Time. During the Sundays after Epiphany and after Pentecost, the *Lectionary for Mass* utilizes a modified *lectio continua*. Semicontinuous readings from the Synoptic Gospel of the year and from the Epistles are used, instead of the two readings being connected thematically.

This new lectionary marked a major shift in liturgical and homiletical practice for Roman Catholics. Moreover, it quickly began to attract the attention of those outside the Roman Catholic Church as well. And why wouldn't it? The melding of biblical texts and liturgical calendar, the focus on the Synoptic portrayal of the Christ Event, the exploration of much of the canon, and the interplay between a thematic approach and literary approach to choosing texts make the *Lectionary for Mass* a potentially powerful cumulative liturgical tool. Most mainline North American Protestant denominations had adapted some version of this lectionary by the mid-1970s. Use of these adaptations marked as radical a change for Protestant liturgical practice as had the lectionary revision for the Catholic Church, for, prior to the 1970s, most Protestant denominations had no such guiding lectionary.

These new adaptations of the *Lectionary for Mass* became so popular among Protestants that in 1978, the Consultation on Common Texts, an ecumenical group that works to create English liturgical texts, formed a group to develop a consensus concerning the liturgical calendar and an accompanying lectionary. The resulting *Common Lectionary*, published in 1983, was a monumental success. It remained very close to the *Lectionary for Mass*, but made two significant adjustments. First, while the dominance of the gospel readings was retained, the reins were loosened a bit. This allowed for a few changes here and there in the First Testament and Epistle choices during the liturgical seasons (Advent through Pentecost). But during the Season after Pentecost (Ordinary Time) the First Testament selections were radically revised so that they were no longer preparing for the Gospel reading but instead followed the same principle of semicontinuous reading that was used for the Epistle and the Gospel lessons. Second, the lections overall (and especially those from the First Testament and the Psalter) were expanded in length. Growing out of the decreased control of the Gospel reading for any given Sunday, this change allowed each passage to be heard better in terms of its original literary context and function.

The *Common Lectionary* was published and widely tested for two cycles—i.e., six years—and then feedback was sought from denominations and congregations, scholars and preachers. More changes were called for and made in the *Revised Common Lectionary*.

For example, the relative absence of biblical women from lectionary choices was corrected by replacing a number of readings (especially the readings from the First Testament for the season after Pentecost) with narratives involving women characters (although more changes in this direction should have been made). Another change was an attempt to offer the option to return to the dominance of the Gospel over the First Testament reading in Ordinary Time without letting go of the advances made in developing a pattern of semicontinuous readings for the First Testament. Thus the full version of the Revised Common Lectionary published by the Consultation on Common Texts in 1992 offers an alternate reading for both the First Testament lesson and the responsive psalm. In many mainline Protestant publications utilizing the Revised Common Lectionary, however, the choice for semicontinuous readings is the only one provided, and indeed this is the option followed in this book.

This sense of how the Revised Common Lectionary evolved from the cumulatively structured *Lectionary for Mass* prepares us to explore the cumulative character of the Revised Common Lectionary itself in more detail.

The Three Dimensions of the Revised Common Lectionary

We can grasp the Revised Common Lectionary's cumulative structure by thinking of the three-year lectionary as three-dimensional, that is, as having width, height, and depth. (See Table 2 on next page.)

Width: the connection between the four lections on any given Sunday or feast day

As we have noted, during the liturgical seasons (Advent, Christmas, after Epiphany, Lent, Easter), the Gospel reading is usually the anchor of the other two readings and the psalm. The Revised Common Lectionary thus offers a Gospel passage that is appropriate to the themes and narrative memories associated with a particular day or season. From the choice of the Gospel lection proceed the choices of readings from the Epistle and First Testament, with the Psalter reading proceeding from the First Testament lection. At different times, this procession is based on obvious intertextual relations, common theological themes, related imagery, or shared vocabulary.

During the liturgical seasons, many preachers unwisely attempt to preach on the width dimension instead of simply using it as one way to help focus their attention on one of the individual lections. The result is too often a sermon that at best preaches on the lectionary instead of scripture, or at worst uses the lections in proof-text fashion to preach a thematic, instead of biblical, sermon. Preachers or lectors should certainly point out the width dimension of the readings for the day during the reading of the lections. However, when preaching the sermon, the preacher should choose one text and do exegetical and homiletical justice to it, while at most using the width dimension to help shape the way she or he approaches or focuses on that text.

TABLE 2: Three Dimensions of the Revised Common Lectionary

WIDTH

	ADVENT, YEAR C			
1	Jer. 33:14–16	Ps. 25:1–10	1 Thess. 3:9–13	Lk. 21:25–36
2	Mal. 3:1–4	Lk. 1:68–79	Phil. 1:3–11	Lk. 3:1–6
3	Zeph. 3:14–20	Isa. 12:2–6	Phil. 4:4–7	Lk. 3:7–18
4	Mic. 5:2–5a	Lk. 1:47–55 or Ps. 80:1–7	Heb. 10:5–10	Lk. 1:39–45 (46–55)

	ADVENT, YEAR B			
1	Isa. 64:1–9	Ps. 80:1–7, 17–19	1 Cor. 1:3–9	Mk. 13:24–37
2	Isa. 40:1–11	Ps. 85:1–2, 8–13	2 Pet. 3:8–15a	Mk. 1:1–8
3	Isa. 61:1–4, 8–11	Ps. 126	1 Thess. 5:16–24	Jn. 1:6–8, 19–28
4	2 Sam. 7:1–11, 16	Lk. 1:47–55 or 89:1–4, 19–26	Rom. 16:25–27	Lk. 1:26–38

	ADVENT, YEAR A			
1	Isa. 2:1–5	Ps. 122	Rom. 13:11–14	Mt. 24:36–44
2	Isa. 11:1–10	Ps. 72:1–7,18–19	Rom. 15:4–13	Mt. 3:1–12
3	Isa. 35:1–10	Ps. 146:5–10	Jas. 5:7–10	Mt. 11:2–11
4	Isa. 7:10–16	Ps. 80:1–7,17–19	Rom. 1:1–7	Mt. 1:18–25

DEPTH

HEIGHT

An even worse mistake, which is made all too often, is to try to give this same sort of homiletical attention to the width dimension during the Season after Pentecost. But trying to connect the four lections during this season is a contrived effort. The width dimension during Ordinary Time all but disappears. While on occasions the different readings will connect and while the responsive psalm is usually related to the First Testament lection, there is rarely a connection between the semicontinuous readings from the First Testament, the Epistles and the Gospels. A different dimension becomes dominant during this season—height.

Height: the connection between lections progressing from Sunday to Sunday

During the Season after Pentecost, this dimension is most evident and easily observed. Because the principle of semicontinuous reading is used for the First Testament, Epistle, and Gospel readings, there is a natural literary connection from week to week. Of course, this cumulative pattern applies only for each individual type of reading, not for the set of readings as a whole. During this season, or—better— for parts of this long season, pastors should choose sequences of readings from a specific biblical writing to preach on. This offers the opportunity to dive deeper into the theological perspective of a particular biblical writer, the themes and progression of a particular biblical argument, and the theological plot of a particular biblical narrative. In an age of biblical illiteracy, this approach is a wonderful gift of the lectionary.

During the liturgical seasons, the height dimension is certainly present, but takes a different form. The connection from week to week from Advent to Pentecost is drawn less from the biblical writings themselves (although the dominance of one of the Synoptic Gospels does add to this aspect), and more from the progression of themes and celebrations/remembrances of the liturgical calendar. In particular, the progression is one that loosely follows the narration of the Christ Event: expectation (Advent); birth (Christmas); revelation epitomized in the baptism and transfiguration (Epiphany); temptation, facing Jerusalem, passion (Lent); resurrection and exaltation (Easter); and gift of the Spirit to the church (Pentecost). Within the individual seasons, the height dimension of the lections grows out of the range of themes associated with the season along with specific events from the Christ narrative associated with particular days (e.g., John the Baptist, the baptism, the transfiguration, and the ascension).

While the height dimension during the liturgical seasons is fairly easy to identify for the group of readings as a whole, it is difficult to use this connection for cumulative preaching without focusing on the Gospel lections to the exclusion of the rest of the canon for nearly half of a calendar year. This is a problematic habit, and one into which the lectionary invites us to fall. While it is certainly appropriate for the stories of Jesus to receive special attention, it is a mistake to send congregations the message that the gospel (i.e., God's good news) should be equated with the Gospels. Preachers must work to bring the fullness of the canon to bear on the congregation's Christian worldview.

Depth: the connection of lections from year to year

When one examines the three-year lectionary cycle as a whole and reflects on the repetitious patterns of readings utilized during each of the three years of the Revised Common Lectionary cycle, the depth dimension is obvious. But in the slow moving, week-to-week experience of worshipers sitting in the pews, this dimension is nearly invisible. If pastors and lectors want Christian lives to be informed by the liturgical cycle, they must be intentional about exposing worshipers to this dimension (both in their sermons and in other venues) by repeatedly offering them broad views of the liturgical calendar and the lectionary. This dimension is evident in two main ways.

First, while the lectionary is a three-year cycle, the Christian liturgical cycle is annual. Therefore, each of the three years follows the same sequence of liturgical events and its pattern of thematic progression. So while the primary Gospel lections that anchor the Revised Common Lectionary each year rotate among the Synoptic Gospels, the readings that are chosen from each Gospel during its year will echo the readings chosen from the other Gospels in their years on days and in the seasons when the liturgical themes and remembrances dictate what Gospel text must be read. Likewise, the First Testament and Epistle readings will often support the Gospel reading in similar ways on the same liturgical day of each of the three years.

Second, following the original intent of the *Lectionary for Mass,* the Revised Common Lectionary offers a great span of readings from across the whole of the canon. Of course, it is undeniable that the Revised Common Lectionary has a canon-within-a-canon, and most preachers are frustrated with the omission of key (and sometimes some of their favorite) biblical passages. This problem is especially troubling when considering the First Testament, since the thirty-eight, often quite lengthy writings of the first part of the canon (excluding the Psalms) are assigned one reading per Sunday while the twenty-seven, often quite short writings of the New Testament are assigned two. Nevertheless, if we are honest, the lectionary's canon-within-a-canon is much broader than the canon-within-a-canon from which most individual preachers choose preaching texts when left to their own devices. This is not only due to the fact that the Revised Common Lectionary provides four lections for each Sunday, but also due to its efforts to touch on as many parts of the canon as possible in the three-year cycle. So, while from Advent to Pentecost liturgical themes dictate the range of choices and at times (especially on the highest liturgical days) the same readings are used for multiple years in the three-year cycle, the Revised Common Lectionary offers a fair amount of variation each year during the liturgical seasons. Especially over the course of the three years of Ordinary Time, the Revised Common Lectionary carries congregations into the narrative, wisdom, and prophetic literature of the First Testament; into most of the epistolary literature of the New Testament; and through significant portions of the Gospels.

The Liturgical Year

Knowing the history of the Revised Common Lectionary and recognizing its three-dimensional character gives us a broad view of the cumulative nature of the Revised Common Lectionary. To fully appreciate this character, however, we need to put down our wide-angle lens and zoom in our focus upon the cumulative tendencies of the Revised Common Lectionary as they get played out in the annual liturgical cycle.[3]

Liturgical Time

As noted above, the liturgical year presents two types of time—liturgical time and ordinary time—that divide a calendar year in half. Liturgical time, the first half of the annual cycle, is devoted to remembering, celebrating, and liturgically experiencing the Christ Event in a basic narrative order. The two foundational stones of this liturgical arch are Christmas and Easter. Advent to Epiphany moves toward and grows out of the celebration of the *nativity*. Ash Wednesday to Pentecost moves toward and grows out of the celebration of the *resurrection*.

ADVENT

The liturgical year begins with the four Sundays before Christmas known as Advent. While Advent prepares the church for Christmas, it is not simply a pre-Christmas season. Advent (from the Latin, meaning "to come to") is a season of expectation of and waiting for the coming of Christ, or, better, for the coming of God-in-Christ. Originally the season was a forty-day period of fasting and penitence leading up to Epiphany, similar to the Lenten preparation for Easter. But as the liturgical cycle evolved and the celebration of the nativity was separated from Epiphany and designated for Christmas (see below), Advent was shortened to the four Sundays leading up to Christmas. Thus the season prepares for the coming of God-in-Christ in the nativity, but not only in Jesus' birth.

Indeed, the emphasis of the season is more on our future than on the past. For instance, while the First Testament readings for Advent are almost all from prophetic passages that the early church interpreted as predicting the coming of Christ, they are thoroughly eschatological and invite modern hearers to think of God (and Christ) as being in our future. The Epistle readings for Advent often share these eschatological tones.

This future-oriented emphasis also serves to highlight the eschatological nature of the Incarnation. Consider the pattern of the Gospel readings during Advent:

Advent 1	Reference to the *parousia* in Jesus' eschatological discourse
Advent 2 Advent 3	Presentation of John the Baptist as the one who prepares for the coming of Jesus
Advent 4	Announcement of Jesus' coming birth

In Christian terms, the liturgical year begins apocalyptically at the "End" with announcements of the second coming. It steps backwards then to John the Baptist preparing for Jesus' adult ministry with language that highlights the eschatological significance of Jesus' person and work (e.g., the one who will come to baptize with the Holy Spirit and fire). Finally, on the Sunday before Christmas, an angel tells Mary or Joseph that Jesus is to be born as God's Son, or Elizabeth exclaims that Mary will give birth to her Lord. The reverse chronology of the season represents a correctly ordered theology: in order to look to God in our future, we must search for God in our past so that we remember what we are to be looking for.

CHRISTMAS

As mentioned earlier, the celebration of the nativity anchors the first set of liturgical seasons. Although worship attendance might imply otherwise, this celebration comprises not a day but a season. A serious problem with which liturgical congregations struggle is that the contemporary American church has lost the battle to define the season of Christmas to secular culture, which defines it as the shopping period between Thanksgiving and Christmas. But the "twelve days of Christmas" of the liturgical year actually extend from Christmas Day (on December 25) to Epiphany (on January 6).[4]

To be more precise, in a manner similar to the Easter Vigil (which few Protestant congregations observe), the first service of Christmas is on Christmas Eve. Many churches have services on Christmas Eve, while their doors are closed on Christmas Day due to our giving in to culture's view of Christmas as a family holiday instead of a religious one. Nevertheless, the practice of celebrating the nativity on Christmas Eve also reflects the ancient Jewish understanding that the day begins at sundown (instead of at sunrise). Thus when the angels come to the shepherds at night, it is not at the end of the day but at the beginning. So, Christmas Eve is the liturgical beginning of the Christmas season and Epiphany is the end.[5]

With this understanding of the season in hand, let us consider the pattern of readings provided by the Revised Common Lectionary for the Christmas cycle. On three out of the four days (the First Sunday after Christmas is the exception), the same readings are used for all three years of the lectionary cycle; and the Gospel lessons are the focal point. The pattern is as follows:

Christmas	The birth story in Luke 2 in which the angel reveals the birth to the shepherds.[6]
Christmas 1	A story from Matthew or Luke concerning Jesus' childhood (A: the flight to Egypt in Matthew; B: the presentation of Jesus in the temple and the witness of Simeon and Anna in Luke; and C: Jesus at age twelve questioning the elders in the temple in Luke).
Christmas 2	The prologue of John in which the Incarnation is described in poetic/philosophical terms of the Word becoming flesh.
Epiphany	The Matthew 2 story of the Magi's pilgrimage to give homage to the king whose birth the star revealed—traditionally interpreted as the first revelation of Christ to the Gentiles.

It is important to recall that since Christmas and Epiphany are fixed dates that rotate through the days of the week year after year, the number of Sundays after Christmas each year varies. (See the discussion of this issue under Cumulative Preaching Strategies for Christmastide, Year A, pp. 34–38.) So not all of these texts will be available each year. Nevertheless, viewing all the possibilities makes it clear how the Revised Common Lectionary has achieved a tight focus for the very short season: the story of Jesus' birth (as told in Lk. 2) anchors the season, the readings concentrate (in terms of narrative chronology) on Jesus as infant / child, and the doctrine of Incarnation sweats out of every pore. Yet at the same time, the readings invite congregations to overcome the harmonization of the birth stories that is burned into the minds of most of us thanks to St. Francis's creation of the crèche by separating Luke's Jewish shepherds coming to the stable on Christmas Eve / Day from Matthew's Gentile Magi coming to the house on Epiphany. So in the course of twelve days, this season, woven so thematically tight, takes Christ from a stable in Bethlehem to the world as a whole.

Sundays after Epiphany

The Roman Catholic Church (and thus the *Lectionary for Mass*) construes the Sundays after Epiphany to be a bridge of Ordinary Time in between the two groupings of liturgical time.[7] For most Protestants who follow the liturgical year and use the Revised Common Lectionary, however, the Sundays after Epiphany comprise a season that flows out of Epiphany and allows its themes to unfold over the course of a number of weeks. This means that the Feast of Epiphany is both the end of Christmastide and the beginning of the Season after Epiphany.

To get a sense of how the Sundays after Epiphany appropriately extend the liturgical emphases of Christmas, it is helpful to understand how the Season after Epiphany evolved. *Epiphany* means "revelation" or "manifestation." Epiphany is the celebration of the revealing of God's divine glory in Christ. This celebration originated in the Eastern Church and is actually older than Christmas (which originated in the Western Church). In its earliest form, Epiphany seems to have been a celebration of the extraordinary revelations of Christ—in the nativity, in the star given to the Magi, in Jesus' baptism, and in Jesus' first sign of changing the water to wine at Cana. As time passed and Epiphany was adopted by the Western Church, which by that time was celebrating Christ's birth on Christmas, Epiphany evolved into the twelfth day of Christmas, completing or complementing Christmas Day. Its emphasis on the nativity was diminished without being eliminated. Emphasized instead was the manifestation of the divine glory in the visit of the Magi. Thus the original unitive feast of Epiphany was broken into a sequence of celebrations. Epiphany was followed by the celebration of Christ's baptism, which was in turn followed by the commemoration of Jesus' miracle at the wedding at Cana.

The Revised Common Lectionary still contains this extended pattern. Because the annual liturgical cycle has been expanded into a three-year lectionary cycle, however, the story of the miracle at Cana is read only on the Second Sunday after Epiphany in Year C instead of every year.

The Revised Common Lectionary expands Epiphany's emphasis on revelation even more dramatically by assigning the Transfiguration of the Lord to the Last Sunday after Epiphany. The Roman Catholic calendar celebrates the Feast of the Transfiguration on August 6, and the traditional lection for the second Sunday of Lent is also the story of the transfiguration. Protestants following the Revised Common Lectionary, however, celebrate Transfiguration of the Lord on the Last Sunday after Epiphany, so that the heavenly voice at the end of the season echoes back to the voice on the Baptism of the Lord. The result of this evolution is that the annual pattern of readings for the season as configured by the Revised Common Lectionary looks like this:

Epiphany	The Matthew 2 story of the Magi's pilgrimage to give homage to the king whose birth the star revealed— traditionally interpreted as the first revelation of the Christ to the Gentiles
Epiphany 1 (Baptism of the Lord)	First Testament reading with calling and water imagery; Psalm 29 with "the voice of the LORD...over the waters"; a passage in Acts dealing with baptism substituted for the Epistle reading; one of the Synoptic versions of Jesus' baptism
Epiphany 2	A reading from the Gospel of John (dealing with Jesus' baptism, the calling of the first disciples, or the first sign at the wedding at Cana) replaces Synoptic Gospel
Epiphany 3–?[8]	Semicontinuous readings from First (and Second) Corinthians; semicontinuous readings from the Synoptic Gospel of the year taken from the beginning of Jesus' ministry, with the lections from the First Testament and Psalter supporting

Last Sunday after Epiphany (Transfiguration of the Lord)	One of the Synoptic versions of Jesus' transfiguration; supporting readings that deal with Moses or Elijah (who appear in the transfiguration stories) and the revelation of divine glory

What this history and the chart of the current cycle of lections demonstrate is that the cumulative emphasis on revelation in the Revised Common Lectionary plays itself out in this season in three ways. (1) The season flows forth from the paradigmatic revelation of the epiphany given to the Magi in relation to Jesus' birth and moves immediately into the celebration of the Baptism of the Lord. (2) The influence of the *Lectionary for Mass*'s approach to the season as part of Ordinary Time is evident in the use of semicontinuous readings from 1 and 2 Corinthians and the Gospel for the year in the middle of the season. But in the context of the thematic emphasis of Epiphany, the readings from the Gospel, which tell of the beginnings of Jesus' ministry, call the church to reflect on the ways Jesus' deeds and teachings manifest God. (3) The celebrations of Jesus' baptism and transfiguration serve as bookends to the season. In all three Synoptic versions of these two stories, a heavenly voice speaks from a cloud declaring Jesus to be God's beloved Son. Thus, by its very structure, the season of revelation extends the Christmas season's emphasis on christology.

LENT

The historical evolution of the Lenten season is difficult to ascertain. For our purposes, however, it is enough to recognize that the season grew backwards out of Easter instead of forward from Epiphany. This historical memory, combined with the fact that the *Lectionary for Mass* views the Sundays after Epiphany as Ordinary Time so that there is a clear break between Christmastide and Lent, accounts for a decisive change of themes and tone from Epiphany to Lent. The somber sounds of, "Remember that you are dust and to dust you shall return; repent and believe in the gospel," that are whispered on Ash Wednesday begin a new phase of liturgical time that sounds radically different from the cymbal crash with which the Season after Epiphany ends on Transfiguration of the Lord. In sum, Lent does not grow out of Epiphany, but leads to Easter.

Lent prepares the church for Easter in two primary ways. The first is biblical in nature, and the second is in relation to the rituals of

Christian initiation. First, the liturgical procession to and through Holy Week with its emphasis on Jesus' entry into Jerusalem, last supper with the disciples, arrest in the garden, trials before the Sanhedrin and the Roman authorities, and crucifixion prepares the congregation to hear the good news of the resurrection in its proper theological and narrative contexts. Second, Lent evolved from the early church practice of preparing adult catechumens for baptism on Easter. This tradition of preparation included fasting, self-examination, and intense biblical and theological study. Today, Lent is still practiced as a time of preparation for baptism and, by extension, confirmation using these same methods. But the fact that the season leads up to the commemoration of the crucifixion and resurrection as the center of the Christ Event means that Lent serves as a preparatory time of penitence, self-examination, study, and remembrance of baptism for *all* those in the faith.

The "narrative" preparation for Christ's death and resurrection as well as the individual and corporate preparation for the "baptismal" experience of dying and rising with Christ account for much of the three-dimensional character of the lectionary choices for Lent. Let us consider a number of significant lectionary patterns.

First, the readings that open the season on Ash Wednesday and the First Sunday in Lent set the tone for the whole season. In all three years of the Revised Common Lectionary cycle, the readings for Ash Wednesday are the same (Joel 2:1–2, 12–17; Ps. 51:1–17; 2 Cor. 5:20b—6:10; and Mt. 6:1–6, 16–21). While the imposition of ashes confronts worshipers with mortality, themes of penitence and religious discipline dominate the lections. On Lent 1 the Gospel reading for all three years is the story of Jesus' temptation (A: Mt. 4:1–11; B: Mk. 1:9–15; and C: Lk. 4:1–13). In all of the synoptics, the temptation scene follows the story of Jesus' baptism. After being baptized, the Spirit leads Jesus into the wilderness where he fasts for forty days and the devil tests him in preparation for the beginning of his ministry. Assigned to the First Sunday in Lent, this Gospel reading establishes the forty-day liturgical season as one of fasting and preparation for Christian ministry into which all believers are baptized.

Second, language and imagery related to baptism fills the readings for Lent. For example, consider all of the references to baptism, water, and anointing over the course of the three-year cycle:

	YEAR A	YEAR B	YEAR C
Lent 1	Ps. 32:6	Gen. 9:11, 15 1 Pet. 3:20–21 Mk. 1:9–11	
Lent 2	Jn. 3:5	Ex. 20:4, 11	
Lent 3	Ex. 17:1–7 Ps. 95:5 Jn. 4:5–15	Num. 21:5	Isa. 55:1 Ps. 63:1 1 Cor. 10:1–4
Lent 4	1 Sam. 16:1, 3, 12–13 Ps. 23:2 Jn. 9:6–7, 11	Ps. 51:2, 7	Ps. 32:6
Lent 5			Isa. 43:16, 19–20 Ps. 126:4 Jn. 12:3

While these images function quite differently in their various literary contexts and while no clear structural pattern emerges from this chart, the number of references to imagery that is often related to baptism is substantial (especially in Year A) and clearly has potential for a cumulative approach to preaching the Revised Common Lectionary.

A third lectionary pattern that is unique to Lent is that the width dimension of the four readings for each Sunday functions differently than in other seasons. While often the same kinds of thematic and vocabulary connections exist between the Gospel reading for the day and the other lections, two other controlling patterns and Lenten themes play a role in the readings as well. One relates to the First Testament lections and the second to the Epistolary lessons.

The First Testament readings assigned by the *Lectionary for Mass* for the Sundays in Lent leading up to Palm / Passion Sunday follow a salvation history schema that involves origins, Abraham, the exodus, the nation of Israel, and God's eschatological promise. As the Revised Common Lectionary modified the readings for Year B, this schema was damaged in places. Nevertheless, the overarching pattern is still evident and can be seen in the following chart. Where the Revised Common Lectionary changed the lections in Years B and C, the original lections in the *Lectionary for Mass* are included in brackets [ ].[9]

	Year A	Year B	Year C
Lent 1 Origins	Gen. 2:15–17; 3:1–7 The tree in the garden	Gen. 9:8–17 God's covenant with Noah	Deut. 26:1–11 "Creedal" declaration associated with first fruits
Lent 2 Abraham	Gen. 12:1–4a God's promises to make a nation from Abram	Gen. 17:1–7, 15–16 God's covenant with Abram and Sarai [Gen. 22:1–2, 9–13, 15–18, Sacrifice of Isaac]	Gen. 15:1–12, 17–18 God's covenant with Abram
Lent 3 The Exodus	Ex. 17:1–7 Water from the rock	Ex. 20:1–17 Decalogue	Isa. 55:1–9 Call to repentance [Ex. 3:1–8, 13–15 Moses and the burning bush]
Lent 4 The Nation	1 Sam. 16:1–13 Samuel's anointing of David	Num. 21:4–9 Moses' lifting the bronze serpent [2 Chr. 36:14–17, 19–23, The fall and rebuilding of Jerusalem]	Josh. 5:9–12 Transition from manna to eating fruits of the promised land
Lent 5 The Promise of the New Covenant	Ezek. 37:1–14 Valley of the dry bones	Jer. 31:31–34 God's new covenant written on the heart	Isa. 43:16–21 Exodus from exile

So while on individual Sundays the themes and imagery of a First Testament lection may be related to the Gospel reading for the day (width), their more significant connection is with the historical pattern shaped over sequential Sundays (height).

Turning to the Epistle readings for Lent, we find a similar situation. They are often thematically and linguistically related to the other readings, especially the First Testament lections. But considered as a group of readings on their own, it is clear that a soteriological orientation dominates the selection of Epistle lections. Repeatedly, the Epistle readings present an interpretation of the new life effected through the cross and resurrection of Jesus Christ in a way that functions liturgically to prepare worshipers to embrace fully the reality to which Holy Week and Easter give testimony.

A fourth lectionary pattern for this season involves less Lenten themes or specific theological concerns and more the problems of having a three-year, Gospel-oriented lectionary when the canon includes four Gospels. It would be difficult to base a full liturgical year on John because, whereas the Synoptics easily break into many short pericopae, John's passages are much longer and thus fewer in number. Lent and Easter are the seasons in which John most often substitutes for the Synoptic Gospel of the year. As can be seen in the following chart, however, during Lent the use of John decreases with each year of the three-year cycle.

	Year A	Year B	Year C
Lent 1	Matthew	Mark	Luke
Lent 2	John 3:1–17	Mark	Luke
Lent 3	John 4:5–42	John 2:13–22	Luke
Lent 4	John 9:1–41	John 3:14–21	Luke
Lent 5	John 11:1–45	John 12:20–33	John 12:1–8

This discussion of John being substituted for the Synoptic Gospel assigned to the year leads us to consider a fifth and final cumulative pattern to be found in Lent. Specifically, our attention turns to the way the Gospel readings chosen for Palm/Passion Sunday stand in contrast to those selected for the weekdays of Holy Week. On Palm/Passion Sunday during the three-year cycle, the liturgy of the palms and the liturgy of the passion rotate among the three Synoptic versions of the final week of Jesus' life, beginning with the entry into Jerusalem and ending with his death and burial. In contrast, the Holy Week readings for each year are the same, with the Gospel lections being drawn from John and culminating in (1) the scene of Jesus' washing the disciples' feet and giving the new commandment on Holy Thursday (13:1–17, 31b–35) and (2) Jesus' arrest, trials, crucifixion, and burial on Good Friday (18:1—19:42). This pairing of the Synoptic version on Sunday with the Johannine version on the weekdays leads to a choice to be made on Easter Sunday.

EASTER

In terms of developing a Christian liturgical calendar, Christianity's first liturgical innovation was making the move from worshiping weekly on the Jewish Sabbath to worshiping on the day of the resurrection. The Church's next major innovation was developing *Pascha* as the first annual liturgical celebration. *Pascha* is the Greek word for the Jewish Passover. Because the Gospels narrate Jesus' passion, death, and resurrection in relation to Passover, the Christian commemoration of those events was initially called *Pascha*. Indeed, as the "Christian Passover" developed in the early centuries of the church, there was a great deal of debate concerning whether it should continue to be connected to Passover in its dating or not. This complicated controversy is not important for us to explore here.

It is important to recognize, however, that originally *Pascha* was not simply a celebration of Jesus' resurrection; it was a unitive commemoration of the crucifixion and resurrection. It was not until the fourth century that the celebration was separated into a commemoration of the passion (which evolved backward from Sunday into Good Friday and back further into Holy/Maundy Thursday) and a celebration of the resurrection with the Easter Vigil (on Saturday evening) and Easter Sunday. Likewise, the celebration of the resurrection and exaltation of Christ separated into Easter and Pentecost (fifty days later, following the Jewish practice of celebrating Pentecost fifty days after the Feast of Unleavened Bread as described in the chronology of Acts), from which Ascension later separated into its own solemnity ten days earlier. Thus Easter Sunday functions as a hinge in the liturgical seasons of Lent and Easter. It is both the climax of Holy Week (or more narrowly of the Easter Triduum, i.e., three days of Holy Thursday, Good Friday, Easter Vigil/Sunday) and initiates the Great Fifty Days of Easter.

With this developmental background in mind, let us consider some of the cumulative tendencies of the Revised Common Lectionary for the season of Easter:

First, we find the depth dimension of Easter Sunday. During all three years of the lectionary cycle, the Gospel readings obviously focus on the discovery of the empty tomb. But the pattern is more complex than just that. Each year the Revised Common Lectionary offers two choices for the Gospel reading for the day: John 20:1–18 and the empty tomb narrative from the Synoptic Gospel of the year. There are two related reasons for this approach. The first is that the choice on Easter allows the preacher to flow cumulatively from either the Gospel readings from Holy Week, which come from John, or from the extended Gospel reading for the previous Sunday (Palm/ Passion Sunday), which comes from the Synoptic Gospel of the year. The second reason comes from the readings for the Easter Vigil on Saturday night. In all three years, the readings for the Great Vigil remain the same with the exception of the Gospel lesson. It circulates each year among the Synoptic versions of the empty tomb story. The results of these two patterns looks like the following:

Palm/Passion—One of the Synoptic versions of the events in Jerusalem including the Last Supper and institution of the Lord's supper, the crucifixion, and the burial.

Holy Week—Johannine readings including Jesus' last meal with the disciples (washing their feet and commanding them to love one another), crucifixion, and burial.

Easter Vigil—One of the Synoptic versions of the discovery of the empty tomb.

Easter Day—Either John's or a Synoptic version of the discovery of the empty tomb.

For congregations that observe an Easter Vigil, it is obvious that the Gospel reading for Sunday morning should be John 20:1–18, since they just read the Synoptic choice the night before. But for those that do not hold a vigil (and that includes most Protestant congregations), the choice to be made is whether the best cumulative approach is to bring to completion for the congregation the Synoptic account of the events in Jerusalem from the previous Sunday or the Johannine account from Holy Thursday and Good Friday.

The decision is often weighted toward John since the Revised Common Lectionary substitutes John for the Synoptic Gospel of the year throughout the remainder of the Easter season (with the exception of the Third Sunday of Easter, Years A and B). This use of John is the second cumulative tendency of the season we should consider. Emphasizing John during Easter in a three-year lectionary cycle is especially appropriate since resurrection is a major theme throughout the gospel. Moreover, Jesus' farewell discourse in John, from which lessons for Easter 5–7 are drawn, repeatedly speaks of Jesus' "departure" in reference to the crucifixion, resurrection, and ascension as a unitive whole.[10]

In terms of the way John is used during Easter, the readings for the season divide into three sections: Easter 1–3, Easter 4, and Easter 5–7. The pattern is laid out as follows:

Easter 1–3 focuses on the event of the resurrection and the resurrection appearances primarily in John 20-21:

EASTER 1–3	
Easter	The empty tomb (Jn. 20:1–18)
Easter 2	The gift of the Spirit and the revelation to Thomas (Jn. 20:19–31)
Easter 3	The Risen Christ revealed in relation to the sharing of a meal (Year A: Lk. 24:13–35; Year B: Lk. 24:36b–48; Year C: Jn. 21:1–19)

Easter 4 focuses on Jesus as the Good Shepherd, and the Gospel readings for all three years are drawn from John 10.

Finally, as already noted, the Gospel lections for Easter 5–7 come from Jesus' farewell discourse to his disciples. Reading Jesus' testament just before his death may seem like an odd liturgical practice for Easter, but it is not if we remember that the Johannine Jesus speaks of his departure and glorification as involving his crucifixion, resurrection, and exaltation. The readings from the farewell discourse for each year follow narrative order and always end with a portion of Jesus' prayer for the disciples in chapter 17. Themes especially appropriate for the church to consider during the Easter season that show up during Easter 5–7 each year include the relation of Jesus and the "Father," the new commandment, Jesus' departure, and the coming of the *Paraclete*.

The third cumulative pattern of the Revised Common Lectionary lections for Eastertide is that the First Testament readings are replaced with readings from Acts, that is, primarily from the first half of Acts. Since Acts is neither a gospel nor an epistle, it does not fit naturally into the normal categories of lectionary readings. While it is somewhat odd to displace the First Testament during this season, it is actually a practice that dates back to the fifth century. Moreover, the substitution is justified given that the chronology of Acts establishes the fifty-day celebration of the season of Easter, and tells the story of the post-resurrection church—i.e., the story of the shift from Jesus' preaching to the church's preaching about Jesus and of the transition from a band of followers in Galilee to an empire-wide movement. Nevertheless, it cannot be denied that there is something uncomfortable about reading stories of the post-Pentecost church before we have celebrated Ascension and Pentecost in our liturgical cycle. The Revised Common Lectionary attempts to deal with this problem by assigning John 20:19–31 (the Fourth Gospel's version of Jesus giving the Spirit to the disciples) for Easter 2 each year.

A fourth cumulative pattern involves the Epistle readings. First Peter (Year A), 1 John (Year B), and Revelation (Year C)[11] are read for Easter 2 7. These texts are chosen because they are thematically appropriate for the season of Easter, and individual readings do at times relate to the Gospel or Acts reading. However, the dominant relational dimension for these texts is that of height in that the Epistles are presented in a semicontinuous manner (although Revelation does not receive enough attention in six Sundays to cover the breadth of the writing). Thus, the Epistle readings during Eastertide need to be heard and preached in relation to the reading from the week before and after.

Ordinary Time

The Revised Common Lectionary functions quite differently in Ordinary Time than it does during the liturgical cycle extending from Advent to Pentecost. Since the season is not thematically focused, neither are the lections. Semicontinuous readings, as a modified *lectio continua* approach to choosing biblical texts for weekly worship, are the standard for the Sundays after Pentecost.

The Revised Common Lectionary inherited this semicontinuous approach from *Lectionary for Mass*'s choices for Epistle and Gospel lections. The *Lectionary for Mass*, however, was not consistent in this approach. It continued to use the readings from the First Testament in a typologically supportive role for the Gospel reading for each Sunday.

The *New Common Lectionary*, in a theologically sound move, abandoned this practice of subordinating First Testament texts to New Testament ones and extended the semicontinuous approach to the First Testament lessons. The Revised Common Lectionary, however, offers both approaches as a compromise. Worship leaders can choose either the typological set of readings for the season or the semicontinuous set. Churches need to hear the First Testament texts on their own terms for at least part of the Christian year. Thus only the semicontinuous readings will be considered in this resource. This choice means that the width dimension all but disappears during the Sundays after Pentecost. On occasion, the semicontinuous readings are aligned in such a way that a significant thematic relation emerges between the lections assigned to a particular Sunday, but these are the exceptions that make the rule. Usually the only width connection is that the Psalter reading responds to the First Testament lection. Thus, in our search for cumulative tendencies in the Revised Common Lectionary lessons for Ordinary Time, our attention needs to be given only to the height and depth dimensions.

GOSPEL READINGS

We begin with the Gospel readings by exploring three cumulative tendencies. First, as already noted, each year of the three-year lectionary cycle has at its center one of the Synoptic Gospels (Year A: Matthew; Year B: Mark; Year C: Luke). During the Sundays after Epiphany (see above) the readings from the Gospels begin working through the opening ministry of Jesus in a semicontinuous fashion. On the Sunday after Trinity Sunday, the Revised Common Lectionary returns to this pattern and begins reading semicontinuously through the Gospel for the year at the point where the semicontinuous reading stopped on the Sunday before Transfiguration of the Lord. With the eschatological themes emphasized at the end of Ordinary Time as the Reign of Christ and Advent draw near, the semicontinuous Gospel readings end each year with a text taken from the eschatological discourse (Mt. 24—25; Mk. 13; Lk. 21), returning to the point at which the year began on Advent 1. (See above.)

A second pattern of the Revised Common Lectionary that is important to recognize is that the semicontinuous reading strategy during Ordinary Time is subordinate to the use of Gospel texts during the liturgical time. In other words, to utilize as much of the Gospel as possible, pericopae read during the liturgical seasons are not reread during Ordinary Time, even though this practice would aid the congregation in gaining a true sense of the whole of the Gospel's narrative. For example, while reading through the Synoptic narratives in Ordinary Time prepares readers to understand the stories of the cross and the resurrection at the end of the story in different ways, the Revised Common Lectionary does not return to those stories during Ordinary Time, since they have been read earlier in the year during Holy Week.

The third cumulative pattern that shapes the use of Gospel texts during Ordinary Time is the tendency toward harmonization among the three Synoptics. In other words, during Ordinary Time, the Revised Common Lectionary avoids a pericope when its parallel in another Gospel is chosen for a different year. The impetus behind this tendency need not be understood as either a theological or historical claim about the unity of the Gospel narratives. Instead, as with the previous tendency, this pattern simply results from the goal to include as much of the Gospel material as possible in three years.

EPISTLE READINGS

Throughout the Sundays after Pentecost, the Revised Common Lectionary has us read through various epistolary materials. Unlike the Gospel and First Testament lections for Ordinary Time, there is no clear pattern that seems to determine these choices across the three years. The primary aspect of the depth dimension to be noted is the principle of not repeating materials during Ordinary Time. A second is that in Years A and C, the season begins with extended reading from one of Paul's major "theological" works, Romans and Galatians, respectively. (In Year B the opening of the season is dedicated to continuing the readings from 2 Corinthians, which began during the Season after Epiphany earlier in the year.) Finally, as with all the readings, at the end of Ordinary Time eschatological emphases determine choices. Thus, in Years A and C, the liturgical year ends with 1 and 2 Thessalonians.

Likewise during each year there are only a few places where clear patterns that connect the choices of letters grouped together can be determined. In Year A all of the Epistles are undisputed Pauline letters. In Year B, James and part of Hebrews are placed side by side as general Epistles. And in Year C, 1 and 2 Timothy are together.

FIRST TESTAMENT READINGS

As noted above, although the Revised Common Lectionary offers two alternatives for the First Testament lections for each Sunday in Ordinary Time—a First Testament passage typologically related to the Gospel and a text that is part of a semicontinuous reading series—we will only consider the semicontinuous options. To continue to use the First Testament in a supportive role during Ordinary Time gives the impression that the First Testament is sub-canonical and robs preachers and hearers of the opportunity to listen to these texts on their own terms.

The height dimension of the First Testament readings during Ordinary Time extends over the whole of the three-year cycle, because the Revised Common Lectionary moves through ancient Israel's canonical story as a whole in a semicontinuous pattern across the three years. Year A draws its readings from narratives that lead to the constitution of the people of Israel as a nation—primarily from Genesis and Exodus, with a few readings from Deuteronomy, Joshua, and Judges. In Year B, the readings for the first half of Ordinary Time deal with the early years of Israel by focusing on Samuel, David, and Solomon as found in the narratives of 1 and 2 Samuel and 1 Kings. The introduction of Solomon is used to move into the wisdom literature and "The Writings" (*Kethuvim*) of the First Testament in the second half of the season. Finally, in Year C the readings come from later periods in the history of Israel and Judah as the texts focus on the prophets. The schema for the year is chronological: Elijah and Elisha, eighth-century prophets, Jeremiah, and post-exilic prophets.

Remembering the Woods while Examining the Trees

This broad overview of the cumulative liturgical tendencies of the Revised Common Lectionary serves to help us better utilize those tendencies homiletically season by season. In the material that follows, we will consider cumulative preaching strategies for each season of the three-year lectionary cycle. As preachers consider potential strategies for each season, it will be helpful to glance back to the corresponding section of the above overview to stay oriented toward the full potential for proclamation and theological development that the Revised Common Lectionary offers a congregation.

Cumulative
Preaching
Strategies for
Year A

ADVENT

Year A

(See pp. 8–9 for an overview of the three-dimensional character of the Revised Common Lectionary's approach to Advent.)

Lectionary Readings

	FIRST TESTAMENT	PSALTER	EPISTLE	GOSPEL
Advent 1	Isa. 2:1–5 In days to come the LORD's house will be established	122 Let us go to the house of the LORD	Rom. 13:11–14 It is time to wake from sleep	Mt. 24:36–44 Jesus' eschato- logical discourse: keep awake
Advent 2	Isa. 11:1–10 Root of Jesse will judge by righteousness	72:1–7,18–19 Give to the king your justice	Rom. 15:4–13 Root of Jesse for the Gentiles	Mt. 3:1–12 Preaching of John the Baptist
Advent 3	Isa. 35:1–10 When God comes, a highway will be made in the desert	146:5–10 The help of the LORD OR Lk. 1:47–55 The Magnificat	Jas. 5:7–10 Be patient waiting for the Lord	Mt. 11:2–11 Jesus tells John's disciples he is the one for whom they are waiting
Advent 4	Isa. 7:10–16 God promises a sign: Immanuel born of a young woman	80:1–7,17–19 Let your face shine upon us that we may be saved	Rom. 1:1–7 Letter opening: gospel promised beforehand	Mt. 1:18–25 Angel tells Joseph of Jesus' birth: fulfills proph- ecy of Emmanuel born of a virgin

Cumulative Preaching Strategies

Advent is the liturgical season in which the church expectantly awaits God to come (*vent*) to (*ad*) us. While the season prepares us for the celebration of the Incarnation, the advent of God-in-Christ toward which the season looks includes more than the past coming of Christ (Christmas). It also involves the present (the claim that God comes to us in our current lives) and the future (the eschatological claim that God is always before us). Liturgical preaching that works cumulatively through this season needs to recognize that the season is structured in reverse chronological order by moving from the eschatological claims about the coming of the Son of Man through John the Baptist's foreshadowing of the ministry of "the one who is to come," to the coming of the Christ child.

The lections for the season suggest a number of such potential cumulative preaching strategies:

STRATEGY 1—Since the liturgical year is rooted in the plot of the Christ Event, an obvious strategy for preaching through every season will be *focusing on the Gospel readings.* Indeed, the gospel themes for Advent date back at least five hundred years in worship practice and are the same each year of the Revised Common Lectionary cycle, regardless of which Synoptic Gospel anchors the year. Preaching these texts allows the congregation to experience variations found in each Gospel on themes found in all three. The themes deal specifically with different chronological expectations concerning the coming of Christ:

Advent 1: Jesus describes the coming of the Son of Man in the eschatological discourse

Advent 2 & 3: John the Baptist as a precursor to Jesus' ministry

Advent 4: Joseph and Mary's preparation for the birth of Jesus

During Year A, Matthew is the Synoptic Gospel that anchors the lectionary. The beginning of the liturgical year is a good time to buy a new commentary or two on Matthew, since preachers will return to this biblical text repeatedly throughout the year. Especially helpful at the beginning of the year is to read the introductory material on Matthew in a couple of commentaries to remind ourselves of the major themes and narrative emphases/structures in the Gospel. This will help preachers keep in mind Matthew's cumulative presentation of the Christ Event while focusing on individual Matthean pericopae. (See also the introductory notes for preaching the semicontinuous reading of Matthew during Ordinary Time on pp. 87–89.)

STRATEGY 2—Similar to the situation described above concerning the Gospel readings, the Epistle readings for the first two Sundays of Advent (Rom. 13:11–14 and 15:4–13) were the Epistle readings for the first two Sundays of Advent in the pre-Vatican II lectionary (established in 1570 and used until 1969). These two texts come from the paranetic section of Romans, in which Paul offers his closing moral exhortation. Thus one strategy for preaching cumulatively during Advent is to emphasize the preparatory nature of the season in terms of *exhortation.* Choices of texts would be as follows:

Advent 1: Romans 13:11–14, Paul's exhortation to wake from sleep, lay aside works of darkness, and put on the armor of light, for salvation is near.

OR: Matthew 24:36–44, the end of Jesus' eschatological discourse in which he instructs the disciples to be ready, for the Son of Man is coming at an unexpected hour.

Advent 2: Romans 15:4–13, drawn from the closing of Paul's moral exhortation to the Romans. The passage calls the ancient recipients, Jews and Gentiles, to live in harmony with one another.

OR: Matthew 3:1–12, the First Gospel's version of the ministry and witness of John the Baptist. In a cumulative focus on exhortation, the part of the text that would receive the greatest homiletical emphasis would be John's call for repentance in preparation for the coming of the one who is stronger than he.

Advent 3: James 5:7–10, the epistle's exhortation to wait for the coming of the Lord with the patience that a farmer exhibits, waiting for the coming crops.

Advent 4: Matthew 1:18–25, the story of the angel appearing to Joseph in a dream to reveal the nature of the child whom Mary will bear. While the emphasis in this scene is clearly on christology—the child is to be named Jesus for he will save his people from their sins, and he will fulfill the prophecy of the child named Emmanuel, God is with us, born of a virgin. In this strategy the preacher will ask the congregation to identify with Joseph, as one receiving instruction from God's messenger and responding obediently.

STRATEGY 3—As the first strategy focuses on the Gospel lections and the second comes from an emphasis found in the Epistle readings, a third option would be to preach on the *First Testament lections* (all of which are from Isaiah) through the whole season. If preachers have been emphasizing the First Testament lections from Ordinary Time in Year C leading up to Advent Year A, focusing on Isaiah would allow them to reinforce the introduction they gave to the eighth-century prophets and to the character of ancient prophecy in general. Moreover, this option especially makes sense since not only are all of the Advent First Testament readings drawn from Isaiah, but also Christmastide and the Sundays after Epiphany make great use of Isaiah. Thus by preaching through the Isaiah passages, preachers can make connections with both the season before and the seasons immediately following Advent.

While the Advent lections from Isaiah are primarily chosen to support the New Testament readings, preaching on them in their original historical and literary contexts can serve well to elucidate Advent themes. Indeed, each sermon could almost begin with a structure that states, "The early church interpreted this text in reference to Christ in such-and-such manner. While such an interpretation makes sense in the context of the first Christians shaping their preaching about Christ in ways that showed continuity with the ancient scriptures of Israel, it is also important to hear these texts in their own right..." This approach is the other side of the coin of strategy 6 below, dealing with New Testament hermeneutics.

Likewise, one can preach through the Isaiah passages and utilize the strategy that follows in strategy 4 or 5.

STRATEGY 4—This approach to cumulative preaching in Advent would be to deal with *eschatology* all four Sundays. Mainline Protestants tend to avoid eschatology because we do not want to sound like bedfellows with those on TV and in print who interpret biblical apocalyptic material in nonsensical ways. But this odd, "literal" (what a misnomer!) reading of such texts is exactly why preachers whose training has been informed by biblical criticism should preach about the eschatological emphases in scripture. Preachers need to unpack ancient eschatological expressions of living in the "already/not yet" as descriptions of religious experience in all times and places in contrast to linear, temporal interpretations of eschatology.

As the liturgical year opens with eschatology, so also it ends with eschatology. Thus the last few Sundays in Ordinary Time have already raised the themes that take central focus in Advent. To preach on eschatological questions now builds on the eschatological themes found in the post-exilic prophets, 2 Thessalonians, and Luke's temple teachings examined in year C.

Moreover, many of the texts of Advent invite the preacher to look at eschatological theology through different perspectives. Thus the depth of this important but neglected biblical theme and its dominant language and imagery (e.g., the day of the Lord, coming/nearness of the reign of God, waiting and expectation, reversal of current circumstances to a more peaceful and just world) can be unpacked throughout the season (even in combination with the end of Ordinary Time) without the preachers seeming as if they are preaching the same sermon repeatedly. Consider the different Advent texts that offer eschatological perspectives:

Advent 1: Isaiah 2:1–5, an oracle that envisions a future in which Jerusalem is the central politico-religious site, not just for Judah, but for the world. While the geographic focus is on Jerusalem, the thematic emphasis is not on nationalism but on an end to all war and God's establishment of peace.

OR: Romans 13:11–14, an expression that at the core of Paul's ethic is a view that we are to act as people who are awake. Especially important for today's Christians who uncritically and unconsciously hold to a soteriology of realized eschatology is Paul's claim that *for believers* salvation is still to come, i.e., it "is even nearer."

OR: Matthew 24:36–44, the end of Jesus' eschatological discourse in which the point of an apocalyptic worldview is summed up in the exhortation to live as one who is awake and ready for the Son of Man to appear at any unexpected hour.

Advent 2: Isaiah 11:1–10, an oracle predicting that from the current weak state of the leadership over Judah (i.e., the *stump* from David's family tree) shall come a mighty branch. What is at stake here is not political power for its own sake, but a government rooted in wisdom and justice so that oppression is ended and peace is instituted.

OR: Matthew 3:1–12, which includes the summary of John's (and Jesus') preaching: "Repent, for the [reign] of heaven has come near." Themes of repentance, baptism, and christology make this a rich eschatological text for Advent.

Advent 3: Isaiah 35:1–10, an oracle from the exilic period in which a hoped-for homecoming is lifted up in terms of salvation and healing. Moreover, the vision employs the dramatic image of a highway of return going through a land that had been a treacherous desert but now blossoms in a beautiful and luscious manner.

OR: Luke 1:47–55, the Magnificat, Mary's prophetic speech that eschatologically describes the effects of the coming of her child, Jesus. So confident is Mary in God's promises that she describes these effects (a salvific reversal of the status quo) in the past tense.

OR: James 5:7–10, a call for patience in waiting for the coming of the Lord. The underlying need for patience is evident when God is not experienced as near at all.

OR: Matthew 11:2–11, where John asks Jesus if he is "the one who is to come." What an odd (and presumably intentional) use of the future tense to ask a question of someone in the present!

Advent 4: Isaiah 7:10–16, part of the narrative description of the LORD's sign of the birth of Emmanuel for King Ahaz—the Revised Common Lectionary has inappropriately omitted verse 17 to subordinate the passage to the Matthean text for the day. The point is that God will be with and protect Judah, if Ahaz will trust God and not make an alliance with Syria and the Northern Kingdom. The claim that the coming of God's presence will provide comfort and safety can be interpreted in significant ways just before Christmas.

STRATEGY 5—Thanks to popular Christmas carols, the secular adaptation of Christmas, and uncritical seasonal preaching, too often Christmas is viewed as a sweet, sentimental celebration that demands little of us. But the story of the nativity and the doctrine of incarnation, as with any expression of the in-breaking of God in creation, has radical *sociopolitical implications.* A preacher would do well to emphasize these implications during Advent.

Advent 1: Isaiah 2:1–5 (echoed in some ways by Ps. 122; and echoed in terms of inner-communal relationships by Rom. 13:11–14) raises up the hope that God will bring peace.

Advent 2: Isaiah 11:1–10 and Psalm 72 express hope for a government that will rule in justice and protect the oppressed in society.

Advent 3: Isaiah 35:1–10, Psalm 146:5–10, and Matthew 11:2–11 all use language of healing to image the reversal of the status quo that occurs as a sign of God's providence. Likewise, Mary's ecstatic speech in Luke 1:47–55 summarizes Luke's views of such a soteriological reversal, which worshipers have heard in numerous readings from the Third Gospel throughout Year C.

Advent 4: Isaiah 7:10–16 deals with international relationships from a theological perspective (especially when interpreted in the context of 7:1–9).

STRATEGY 6—Much of contemporary misunderstanding (and dismissal of the real content) of biblical prophecy originates in the way prophetic texts have been interpreted as predicting events in the Christ Event. Preachers who attempt to correct this dynamic are often viewed as threatening to a traditional faith perspective. One strategy to cumulative preaching in Advent would be to focus on *New Testament hermeneutics.* In other words, a preacher can highlight some of the varied uses of the First Testament in the New Testament in ways that contextualize those uses within the needs of the first-century church but also release today's Christians from being bound by those same hermeneutics. (This is related to strategy 3 above, which attempts to appreciate the New Testament's use of the Isaiah texts but then read them in their original historical and literary contexts.)

Advent 1: In Matthew 24:36–44, Jesus compares the coming days with the days of Noah.

Advent 2: In Romans 15:4–13, Paul states an explicit hermeneutic in verse 4—that ancient scriptures were written for contemporary "instruction." As the apostle goes on to call for harmony between Jews and Gentiles, he puts his hermeneutic to use in verses 9–12 by quoting a number of First Testament texts (Ps. 18:49; Deut. 32:43; Ps. 117:1; and Isa. 11:10, which is part of the First Testament lection for the day).

OR: In Matthew 3:1–12, a number of First Testament items play a role in the presentation of John the Baptist. First, verse 3 explicitly describes John as fulfilling Isaiah 40:3. Second, verse 4 characterizes John in terms recalling Elijah. (See 2 Kings 1:8;

Zech. 13:4.) In his preaching, John reinterprets what it means to be a descendant of Abraham (v. 9).

Advent 3: Luke 1:47–55 presents Mary as speaking prophetically in a posture and with language that recalls Hannah's song concerning Samuel's birth in 1 Samuel 2:1–10. Phrases throughout the Magnificat echo First Testament language as well, and verse 55 contains a specific reference to the promise to Abraham and his descendants (see, for example, Gen. 17:6–8).

OR: In Matthew 11:2–11, Jesus presents himself as "the one who is to come" in language that is drawn from Isaiah 35:5–6 (part of the First Testament lection for the day).

Advent 4: In Romans 1:1–7, Paul again states an explicit hermeneutic, but one that is different from the one he offered in the lection for Advent 2. In this passage he describes the "gospel of God" as "promised beforehand through [God's] prophets in the holy scriptures." This view underlies much of New Testament hermeneutics and is worthy of being unpacked.

OR: In Matthew 1:18–25, the author uses one of his standard prophecy fulfillment citations (of which there are numerous examples in the opening chapters of the Gospel) to state that the birth of Jesus is a fulfillment of Isaiah 7:14. Asking the congregation to compare Matthew's use of the prophecy with the First Testament lection for the day will lead them to recognize the difference in language (virgin versus young woman) and give the preacher the opportunity to step a little into the first-century church's use of the Septuagint.

CHRISTMAS

Year A

(See pp. 10–11 for an overview of the three-dimensional character of the Revised Common Lectionary's approach to Christmas.)

Lectionary Readings

	FIRST TESTAMENT	PSALTER	EPISTLE	GOSPEL
Christmas Eve/Day Proper 1 (abc)[1]	Isa. 9:2–7 A child has been born for us	96 Sing a new song: the LORD is king	Titus 2:11–14 The grace of God has appeared	Lk. 2:1–14 (15–20) Birth story
Christmas Eve/Day Proper 2 (abc)	Isa. 62:6–12 See, your salvation comes…	97 The LORD is king! Let the earth rejoice	Titus 3:4–7 When the goodness and loving kindness of God our Savior appeared…	Lk. 2:(1–7) 8–20 Birth story
Christmas Eve/Day Proper 3 (abc)	Isa. 52:7–10 The return of the LORD to Zion	98 Make a joyful noise to the LORD	Heb. 1:1–4 (5–12) God has spoken to us through a Son, through whom God created the worlds	Jn. 1:1–14 John's Prologue—Incarnation of the Word
Christmas 1	Isa. 63:7–9 The presence of the LORD saved	148 (abc) Praise the LORD who has raised up a horn for God's people	Heb. 2:10–18 Christ suffered as we suffer	Mt. 2:13–23 Flight to Egypt; slaughter of innocents
Christmas 2 (abc)	Jer. 31:7–14 God will save a remnant	147:12–20 Praise God for divine providence	Eph. 1:3–14 God chose us in Christ before the foundation of the world	Jn. 1:(1–9) 10–18 John's Prologue—Incarnation of the Word
Epiphany (abc)	Isa. 60:1–6 Nations shall come to your light: camels, gold, frankincense	72:1–7, 10–14 Give the king your justice, O God	Eph. 3:1–12 Paul, a prisoner of Christ for Gentiles	Mt. 2:1–12 Magi

Cumulative Preaching Strategies

Proposing a variety of concrete, cumulative preaching strategies for the season of Christmas is difficult because the season takes a couple of different forms depending on which days of the week Christmas and Epiphany fall and what congregational practice is. For congregations that celebrate Epiphany on January 6, regardless of what day of the week it falls on, there will always be at least one Sunday after Christmas and sometimes there will be two (a little more than half the time). However, in congregations that celebrate Epiphany Sunday on the Sunday before January 6 when Epiphany falls on a day other than Sunday, there will never be a Second Sunday after Christmas. If Christmas falls on a Sunday or Monday (with Epiphany falling on a Friday or Saturday), there will be no Sunday "after Christmas" at all—only Christmas Eve or Christmas Day followed a week later by Epiphany Sunday. Thus approximately four of every six years will have one Sunday between Christmas and Epiphany Sunday with the other two having none. Narrowing our focus to only Year A of the three-year lectionary cycle, four of the next six times Year A cycles around will have one Sunday after Christmas (2010, 2013, 2016, 2019) and two years will have no Sunday between Christmas and Epiphany Sunday (2016, 2022).[2]

The brevity of the season and the dominance of the Gospel lections limit our strategies. In the proposals below, there are suggestions for each possibility—no Sunday after Christmas, one Sunday, and two Sundays. Each proposal builds on the one that precedes it. Note also that the dominance of the liturgical themes of the nativity and Incarnation and the ways the First Testament texts were chosen to be subordinate to those New Testament themes has led me not to offer proposals for preaching from the First Testament or Psalter lections for this short, focused season.

Christmas and Epiphany Sunday only:

STRATEGY 1—On Christmas and Epiphany, preachers will usually want to focus their sermons on the *Gospel readings,* since the accounts of Jesus' birth in Luke and Matthew anchor the liturgical remembering of the Christ Event. Placing Luke's version next to Matthew's is a great way to highlight the theological and narrative differences between the two accounts and undo the harmonizing misinterpretation of the texts that has occurred through centuries of using nativity scenes that place the shepherds and the magi side by side. Note some of the differences:

LUKE (Christmas)	MATTHEW (Epiphany)
Joseph and Mary forced to go to Bethlehem by the emperor's census	Joseph and Mary presumably live in Bethlehem
Setting is a stable	Setting is a house
Angel(s) reveal the birth	Star reveals the birth
Shepherds receive the revelation	Magi receive the revelation
Shepherds proclaim what they have seen	Magi depart in secret

But pointing out the differences between the two versions should also lead a preacher to claim a root similarity: God does not reveal the birth of the Christ child to those in power (Augustus in Luke or Herod in Matthew), but to outsiders (shepherds who are economically marginalized in Luke and Gentile astrologers [i.e., magicians] in Matthew). Thus both present a soteriological understanding of the Incarnation that has sociopolitical implications that could be unpacked in two related but distinct sermons.

STRATEGY 2— Another option is to follow a Christmas sermon on Luke 2:1–14 (15–20) with an Epiphany sermon on the *Epistle lection* (Eph. 3:1–12). The Ephesians text actually speaks more directly to the liturgical theme of revelation to the Gentiles than does the traditional Matthean lesson. Similar to strategy 1 above, the preacher could highlight the outsider character of the recipients of the revelation of the God of Israel: poor shepherds in Luke on Christmas and Gentiles in Ephesians on Epiphany.

One Sunday after Christmas:

STRATEGY 3—If the season has one Sunday in between Christmas and the congregation's celebration of Epiphany, the preacher may still want to focus on the *Gospel lections.* For Year A, the Gospel reading for Christmas 1 (Mt. 2:13–23) is the story of the flight to Egypt and the slaughter of the innocents, which immediately follows the Gospel lesson for Epiphany (Mt. 2:1–12). This chronological reordering does not offer great service to cumulative preaching but is not a terrific hurdle either. (Compare the First Sunday of Christmas' emphasis on Jesus' childhood preceding Epiphany with the use of Acts during the Season of Easter, before Ascension and Pentecost have occurred liturgically, and thus before the readings that set everything else in Acts in motion have been offered in worship.) In preaching on the flight to Egypt and the slaughter of the innocents on the Sunday before Epiphany, the preacher will simply need to offer some teaching about the structure of liturgical time. Some preachers may want to avoid Matthew 2:13–23 immediately after Christmas, because to move from celebration to this text and back to celebration is difficult to manage liturgically. However, this movement mimics reality, does it not? For many, Christmas is a time of pain, suffering, and depression. Moreover, if the preacher is noting the social implications of the Incarnation (as noted above in strategy 1; cf. strategy 5 for Advent Year A), then naming the "Herods" of life and of the world that hinder the work of the gospel is especially appropriate. So while many children are innocently murdered, Herod is ultimately unable to stop God's work in Christ.

STRATEGY 4—Another approach is to preach on the *Hebrews 2* passage on the Sunday sandwiched between Christmas and Epiphany. This text speaks in the realm of incarnational theology but pans out the wide-angle lens to help us see beyond the specifics of Jesus' childhood to the incarnational nature of Jesus' ministry culminating in the crucifixion.

STRATEGY 5—The earlier Common Lectionary recommended that if the second alternate set of lections for Christmas (Christmas Proper 3) were not used on Christmas Eve or Day, they should be used later during the Christmas season due to the importance of John's prologue for the New Testament understanding of incarnation.[3] A similar option is to **substitute the readings for Christmas 2** (which include Jn. 1:[1–9], 10–18) for Christmas 1 in years and worshiping traditions in which there is only one Sunday after Christmas. John 1:1–18 serves well to follow the Christmas focus on the nativity by inviting us to step back and reflect on the meaning of incarnation in a broader way. Likewise, the text's language of light overcoming darkness sets up the move toward the emphasis on revelation on Epiphany and during the Season after Epiphany.

Two Sundays after Christmas:

STRATEGY 6—For congregations that celebrate Epiphany on January 6 and not on the Sunday before, the lectionary provides more possibilities for cumulative preaching. The preacher may still want to focus on the *Gospel lessons* for the entire season. The themes mentioned in strategies above all still work together. The only difference is that now the two Matthew lections (2:13–23 for Christmas 1 and 1:1–12 for Epiphany) are separated by John's prologue (1:1–18), and thus a little extra work will be required of the preacher to keep the connection between them strong in the congregation's liturgical experience.

STRATEGY 7—A final option would be to *bookend* this short season with the Gospel readings from Luke 2:1–14 (15–20) on Christmas and Matthew 2:1–12 on Epiphany and to preach on the Epistle texts on the Sundays in between. Or one could focus on Luke on Christmas and preach the other three sermons on the Epistles. Both of the Epistle texts between Christmas and Epiphany (Heb. 2:10–18 for Christmas 1 and Eph. 1:3–14 for Christmas 2) expand the narrative portrayals of the birth and revelation of the Christ child to offer a view of the soteriological implications of the Incarnation. Moreover, preaching on Ephesians for Christmas 2 and Epiphany offers continuity of theology.

SUNDAYS after EPIPHANY

Year A

(See pp. 11–13 for an overview of the three-dimensional character of the Revised Common Lectionary's approach to Epiphany.)

Lectionary Readings

	FIRST TESTAMENT	PSALTER	EPISTLE	GOSPEL
Epiphany (abc)	Isa. 60:1–6 Nations shall come to your light: camels, gold, frankincense	72:1–7,10–14 Give the king your justice, O God	Eph. 3:1–12 Paul, a prisoner of Christ for Gentiles	Mt. 2:1–12 Magi
Epiphany 1 Baptism of the Lord	Isa. 42:1–9 First Servant Song: My servant, my chosen, in whom my soul delights; I have sent out my spirit on him to bring justice	29 (abc) Voice of the LORD is over the waters	Acts 10:34–43 Peter's sermon to Cornelius: Jesus anointed by the Holy Spirit	Mt. 3:13–17 Baptism of Jesus
Epiphany 2	Isa. 49:1–7 Second Servant Song: called me before I was born; in whom I will be glorified	40:1–11 I waited for the LORD and God heard my cry	1 Cor. 1:1–9 Opening of the letter—greeting and thanksgiving	Jn. 1:29–42 John the Baptist witnesses to Jesus' baptism and sends his disciples to follow Jesus
Epiphany 3	Isa. 9:1–4 A light for Galilee of the nations	27:1, 4–9 The LORD is my light and salvation	1 Cor. 1:10–18 Do not be divided	Mt. 4:12–23 Beginning of Jesus' ministry, citation of Isa. 9, call of the first disciples
Epiphany 4	Mic. 6:1–8 What does the LORD require but to do justice, love kindness, walk humbly	15 Who will abide in your tent: those who walk blamelessly	1 Cor. 1:18–31 Foolishness of the cross	Mt. 5:1–12 Beginning of Sermon on the Mount: Beatitudes
Epiphany 5	Isa. 58:1–9a (9b–12) Is not this the fast that I choose: to loose the bonds of injustice…	112:1–9 (10) Happy are those who delight in God's commandments	1 Cor. 2:1–12 (13–16) God's wisdom	Mt. 5:13–20 Sermon on Mount: I came to fulfill the law

Epiphany 6 Proper 1	Deut. 30:15–20 I set before you life and death	119:1–8 Happy are those whose way is blameless	1 Cor. 3:1–9 I planted, Apollos watered, but God gave the growth	Mt. 5:21–37 Sermon on Mount: Antitheses
Epiphany 7 Proper 2	Lev. 19:1–2, 9–18 Various commandments	119:33-40 Teach me the way of your statutes	1 Cor. 3:10–11, 16–23 You are God's temple	Mt. 5:38–48 Sermon on Mount: Antitheses cont'd
Epiphany 8 Proper 3	Isa. 49:8–16a The Lord has comforted God's people	131 I have calmed and quieted my soul	1 Cor. 4:1–5 Trustworthy stewards	Mt. 6:24–34 Sermon on the Mount: Lilies of the field
Epiphany Last Transfigur- ation	Ex. 24:12–18 Moses enters the cloud of the Lord upon the mountain	2 You are my son, today I have begotten you Or 99 (ac) Lord is King—worship at holy mountain	2 Pet. 1:16–21 We heard the voice of God glorify Jesus on the mountain	Mt. 17:1–9 Transfiguration

Cumulative Preaching Strategies

As we consider a variety of cumulative preaching strategies for the Season after Epiphany, we need to keep two challenging considerations in mind. First is the fact that the season's length varies year to year depending first on the date of Easter, which can fall anywhere from March 22 to April 25, and second on which day of the week Epiphany falls—the later in the week that January 6th falls, the earlier in January the Baptism of the Lord occurs. In other words, including Baptism of the Lord and Transfiguration Sunday, the season can last from four to nine Sundays after Epiphany, although the minimum and maximum are quite rare and most years fall between five and eight Sundays.

The second consideration involves the tension between the bookends of the season and the Sundays in between. On the Solemnities of the Lord at both ends of the season (Baptism on the first Sunday after Epiphany and Transfiguration on the last Sunday after Epiphany) the liturgical themes will focus the sermon. During the two to seven weeks in between, however, the Epistle and Gospel lections take on the form of semicontinuous readings found during the Sundays after Pentecost, while the First Testament and Psalter lections continue to be chosen to support the Gospel.

With these two complications in mind, let us consider possible cumulative strategies for preaching through the Sundays after Epiphany.

STRATEGY 1   Since the ecumenical lectionary has its roots in the *Lectionary for Mass,* which considers the Sundays between Baptism of the Lord and Ash Wednesday to be Ordinary Time, during the Season after Epiphany the Revised Common Lectionary has us begin reading through the Gospel of Matthew in a semicontinuous fashion that will be picked up again after Pentecost. (See the introductory notes for preaching the semicontinuous reading of Matthew during Ordinary Time on pp. 87–89.) This reading through Matthew begins after Baptism of the Lord and Epiphany 2, which always utilizes a reading from John. So one obvious cumulative preaching strategy for this season is to focus one's sermons on the *Gospel lessons.* This strategy makes good sense for two reasons. (A) Although the majority (though not all) of Gospel lections since Year A began have been drawn from Matthew, the semicontinuous readings from Matthew beginning on the Third Sunday after Epiphany offer the first extended glance at Matthew. This is a good opportunity for preachers to present, as part of their sermons, an introduction to Matthew's sociohistorical background, narrative, and theology. (B) Since the majority of the Gospel readings come from early in Matthew, preaching on these lections will provide a coherent view of Matthew's picture of the beginning of Jesus' ministry. The readings offer a helpful narrative chronology for the congregation:

Epiphany 1: Baptism (Matthew 3:13–17)

Epiphany 2: John's testimony concerning the baptism and sending the first disciples to Jesus (John 1:29–42)

Epiphany 3: Summary of preaching and call of first disciples (Matthew 4:12–23)

Epiphany 4 through the next to last Sunday after Epiphany: Jesus' first specific example of preaching as found in the Sermon on the Mount (from Matthew 5—6)

One problem with giving extended attention to the Sermon on the Mount is that the Revised Common Lectionary divides the discourse poorly. For example, the six antitheses of 5:21–48 illustrate Matthew's hermeneutic described in 5:17–20, but the Revised Common Lectionary joins the hermeneutical declaration with the verses preceding it in the discourse (vv. 13–16) on Epiphany 5 instead of the verses that follow. Moreover, it divides the antitheses into two groups of four and two on Epiphany 6 and 7. Then skipping the first half of chapter 6, which is traditionally read on Ash Wednesday, the Revised Common Lectionary has us read about possessions for the last pre-Transfiguration Gospel lection.

Depending on the number of Sundays during the season in any given year, the lectionary preacher may wish to alter the boundaries of some of the readings, omit some readings, and add others from this section of Matthew to honor the implicit strengths of the Revised Common Lectionary's focus on the Sermon on the Mount. Since the discourse as a whole focuses on Christian ethics, shifting the choices drawn from the Sermon on the Mount would not destroy the width dimension since the First Testament and Psalter readings focus on the themes of God's law in broad ways.

STRATEGY 2—Another straightforward strategy for cumulative preaching on the Sundays between Baptism of the Lord and Transfiguration is to focus on the semicontinuous readings from *1 Corinthians,* again a reflection of the *Lectionary for Mass*'s view of this season as Ordinary Time. The Revised Common Lectionary's selection of readings do an excellent job of allowing the preacher to walk slowly through the opening of the letter, painting a full picture of the schismatic situation in the Corinthian house churches.

This cumulative approach has two downsides, both of which should be taken into consideration but neither of which should be prohibitive. The first is that these semicontinuous readings have no explicit connection with Epiphany themes or the other three lections for each Sunday. However, in Paul's discussion of preaching Christ crucified with a demonstration of the Spirit and of power, there is certainly a relation to the season's focus on God's self-revelation in Christ that can be appropriately emphasized. (See strategy 3 below.) Moreover, a liturgical balance can be created in which the language of much of the worship service grows out of the thematic core of the other lections, while the sermon draws on Paul's writing.

The second problem is that the semicontinuous reading of 1 Corinthians is limited to the seasons of Epiphany across the three-year cycle. Thus, the preacher and the congregation will not return to 1 Corinthians until January of the following year. While the opening chapters do a good job of *introducing* us to the divisions in the church that Paul is addressing, it is only an introduction. Later in the letter more troubling aspects of the schism come to light, and the depth of Paul's theology is brought to bear on the situation in a way that is only foreshadowed in these opening chapters. This means that even while preaching on the opening passages of 1 Corinthians, preachers need to keep their eye on and point the congregation's eyes toward the bigger ecclesial and theological picture of the letter. Certainly this can and should be done as part of the sermons themselves by referring to, citing, and quoting from later parts of the letter. But outside of worship, individuals and groups within the congregation should be invited to read through and study the whole of 1 Corinthians while the pastor preaches through the opening chapters—historically, sociologically, and theologically contextualizing what they are reading.

It may be helpful to name some of the parts of the bigger picture of the letter at this point. (See the comments on preaching Pauline letters in a cumulative fashion on pp. 81–83.) But these brief comments are a poor substitute for reading the introduction to a critical commentary on the epistle. First Corinthians is actually not Paul's first letter to the church at Corinth, but only the first canonical letter to the Corinthians. (See 1 Cor. 5:9.) The two canonical letters to the Corinthians and the passing references to other letters make it clear that Paul and the church have an extended conversation via correspondence and messengers. In this particular letter we call 1 Corinthians, Paul is responding to a range of questions and issues that have come to him in writing and through oral information. The topics of discussion includes sexual behavior (marriage, celibacy, and divorce), taking fellow Christians to court, eating meat offered as a sacrifice to idols, the Lord's supper, spiritual gifts and leadership in the church, the conduct of men and women in the church, and the resurrection of the body. Paul deals with these issues not as a systematic theologian but as an involved pastor offering practical theological critique and guidance. Underneath these issues seems to be a conflict between the "weak" and the "strong" in the house churches of Corinth that is not easy to reconstruct two thousand years later. Suffice it to say in these brief comments that the conflict is multilayered and involves socioeconomic divisions in the community, different levels of maturity in the faith, differing views of spirituality, and disagreement over eschatology.

STRATEGY 3—The remaining strategies are thematic in nature. First among these is the central Epiphany theme of ***revelation.*** In today's world, when churchgoers hear the word *revelation* they most likely think of the last book of the canon. They have not been asked often enough to think about the traditional theological claim that God is unknowable by our own efforts and that God has revealed whatever we know of God. To spend a season helping the church remember some of the ways we claim God has gone about revealing aspects of God's character—for example, revealing God's self in the person and ministry of Jesus Christ or God's will through those proclaiming the faith—would be a significant contribution to the congregation's thinking through issues of Christian epistemology. This theme is prevalent in the lections for the season, thus inviting the preaching to explore the issue of revelation from many different perspectives.

> **Epiphany 1:** Matthew 3:13–17, the heavenly voice (along with the cloud and the descent of the Spirit) reveals Jesus as God's Son.
>
> **OR:** Psalm 29, the voice of the LORD reveals itself in the thunderstorm.
>
> **OR:** Acts 10:34–43, Peter's sermonic summary of Jesus' ministry, death, and resurrection describes Jesus' message as God's message.
>
> **Epiphany 2:** Isaiah 49:1–7, the second "servant song" in which God reveals God's salvation for all by establishing Israel as a light to the nations.
>
> **OR:** Psalm 40:1–11, the psalmist refuses to conceal God's faithfulness and proclaims God's good news of deliverance.
>
> **OR:** 1 Corinthians 1:1–9, as Paul reminds the recipients that revelation is future as well as past when he says they are not lacking in any spiritual gift as they await the revelation of Jesus Christ.
>
> **OR:** John 1:29–42, John the Baptist's testimony to the revelation of the Lamb of God for which his ministry prepared and which he has received.
>
> **Epiphany 3:** Isaiah 9:1–4, salvation is described in metaphors of revelation—"The people who walked in darkness/have seen a great light."
>
> **OR:** Psalm 27:1, 4–9, as with the Isaiah text, salvation and revelation are paired by describing God as "my light and my

salvation," but is made all the more poignant with the plea, "Do not hide your face from me."

OR: Matthew 4:12–23, the narrator uses Isaiah's language of revelation and salvation to describe Jesus' ministry as the light dawning in darkness.

Epiphany 4: 1 Corinthians 1:18–31, Paul makes clear that revelation does not come as we might expect when he declares that the saving message of the cross is foolishness to those who are perishing.

Epiphany 5: Isaiah 58:1–9a (9b–12), the people are fasting in order to provoke the silent God to reveal God's self, but the prophet makes clear that God has already revealed the kind of fast that is acceptable to God.

OR: 1 Corinthians 2:1–12 (13–16), Paul emphasizes that the core of the mystery of God that is revealed in the gospel is the crucified Christ.

OR: Matthew 5:13–20, Jesus describes his followers as those who illumine the world.

Epiphany 6 (Proper 1): 1 Corinthians 3:1–9, Paul describes his initial proclamation as milk offered to infants, reminding them that revelation does not come all at once.

Epiphany 7 (Proper 2): Leviticus 19:1–2, 9–18, the call to holiness depends upon God's revealed holy character.

Epiphany 8 (Proper 3): 1 Corinthians 4:1–5, Paul describes apostolic ministry as stewardship of God's mysteries.

OR: Matthew 6:24–34, as Jesus calls his hearers to abandon slavery to money, he reminds them that God's providence reveals itself in the birds of the sky and the lilies of the field.

Last Sunday after Epiphany (Transfiguration): In Matthew 17:1–9, the heavenly voice (along with the cloud and the transfigured appearance itself) reveals Jesus' glory as God's Son.

OR: Exodus 24:12–18, a dramatic description of the glory of the Lord revealed on the mountain.

OR: Psalm 99, recalls God's speaking to Moses, Aaron, and Samuel in the pillar of the cloud.

OR: 2 Peter 1:16–21, grounds the apostolic prophetic message in the revelation of Jesus as God's Son in the transfiguration.

STRATEGY 4—We find a number of thematic connections across the height dimension of the Season after Epiphany during Year A that do not fill out the whole season. Depending on the length of the season in any given year and the preacher's willingness to move some texts around, these thematic links may serve a cumulative approach for portions of the season. The most prominent of these themes stretches from Epiphany 4 to Epiphany 8 and deals with *God's commandments/law*. This theme grows out of the semicontinuous readings from the Sermon on the Mount but encompasses the supporting First Testament and Psalter lections. These texts invite preachers to replace the popular misunderstanding of "righteousness" in terms of personal piety with the biblical understanding of communal justice.

Epiphany 4: Matthew 5:1–12, while the Beatitudes in Matthew do not have as strong a social justice tone as their parallels in Luke 6:20–26, they do involve some key ethical themes.

OR: Micah 6:1–8, a trial scene in which God accuses Israel for not responding to God's salvific acts with justice, kindness, and humility.

OR: Psalm 15, a psalm of ascent that describes the ethical character of those who are acceptable to enter God's presence in the temple.

Epiphany 5: Matthew 5:13–20, Jesus commands his listeners to let their good works be the light of the world and then pronounces that he has not come to abolish the law and the prophets but to fulfill them.

OR: Isaiah 58:1–9a (9b–12), the LORD commands the prophet to denounce the people's false piety exhibited in a fast and calls instead for a metaphorical fast that takes the form of works of justice and charity.

OR: Psalm 112:1–9 (10), a wisdom psalm blessing those who love God's law and practice righteousness.

Epiphany 6: Matthew 5:21–37, the first four antitheses (concerning murder/anger, adultery/lust, divorce/adultery, false swearing/

swearing) illustrating the hermeneutic expressed in verses 17–20 and specifying Matthew's understanding of the way the early church should view, interpret, and live out ancient scriptural commandments.

OR: Deuteronomy 30:15–20, a classic text in which Moses lays out God's torah, God's way, as the path to life and other ways as the path to death.

OR: Psalm 119:1–8, opening stanza of a very long acrostic psalm celebrating God's law (as is next week's Psalter lection).

Epiphany 7: Matthew 5:38–48, the last two antitheses (eye for an eye/turn the other cheek, love your neighbor/love your enemy) illustrating the hermeneutic expressed in verses 17–20 and specifying Matthew's understanding of the way the early church should view, interpret, and live out ancient scriptural commandments.

OR: Leviticus 19:1–2, 9–18, a call to holiness, unpacked by numerous ethical commands including, "You shall love your neighbor as yourself."

OR: Psalm 119:33–40, fifth stanza of a very long acrostic psalm celebrating God's law.

Epiphany 8: Matthew 6:24–34, although not presented as interpreting ancient torah (as with the last three Gospel lections), this passage deals with the command to trust in God over wealth.

STRATEGY 5—Another theme that can be identified on some but not all of the Sundays after Epiphany deals with the claim that God is not only the God of Israel but the God of the nations, i.e., God of the *Gentiles.* This is an important theme for the Season after Epiphany, given that the church has traditionally interpreted Matthew's story of the visit of the magi, which marks the turning point from Christmastide to the Sundays after Epiphany, as the first revelation of Christ to the Gentiles. Preaching about the inclusion of the Gentiles from various biblical perspectives allows the church to reflect on theological issues concerning God's love offered to all, as well as ecclesiological issues concerning inclusivity and hospitality. The lections that follow the Day of Epiphany approach this theme in a variety of ways.

Epiphany 1: Acts 10:34–43, Peter's sermon to the household of Cornelius, the first Gentile converts, in which the apostle declares, "God shows no partiality."

OR: Isaiah 42:1–9, the first "Servant Song," in which the prophet presents Israel as the servant who will bring justice to the nations and who is a light to the nations.

Epiphany 2: Isaiah 49:1–7, the second "Servant Song," in which the prophet again images Israel as a light to the nations but also recognizes that Israel is abhorred by the nations.

Epiphany 4: 1 Corinthians 1:18–31, while Paul contrasts Jews (as those who demand signs) and Greeks (as those demanding wisdom), he claims that the message of Christ crucified is for all those called by God, both Greeks and Jews.

STRATEGY 6—Some of the themes that take up only a portion of the season and thus offer shorter opportunities for cumulative preaching are actually *paired readings* on two successive Sundays.

Epiphany 1 and 2: There are two potential pairs. First, the readings from Isaiah 42:1–9 and 49:1–7 represent what are traditionally referred to as the first and second "Servant Songs." It is good to preach these texts in a season when the focus is not on Jesus as the personification of the Suffering Servant so that congregations can hear the texts on their own terms.

Second, the Gospel lections from Matthew 3:13–17 and John 1:29–42 both relate accounts of Jesus' baptism. Looking at the two versions side by side helps congregations kick the habit of harmonizing the Gospels and appreciate the theological differences between the different narratives of the Christ Event. Few Gospel pericopae do this better than the baptism narratives in the four Gospels.

Epiphany 2 and 3: The Gospel lessons are closely related to each other. The lections are John 1:29–42 and Matthew 4:12–23, respectively. Both of these passages narrate Jesus calling the first disciples. As with the descriptions of Jesus' baptism, these call scenes vary greatly, inviting a compare and contrast approach to preaching the pair.

Epiphany 3 and 4. The Psalter readings (Ps. 27:1, 4–9 and Ps. 15) make a nice pair because they are both ascent psalms—in other words, psalms sung by pilgrims as they draw near to Jerusalem. In these texts, those praying are concerned with fulfilling the requirements to enter into God's presence in the temple. As mentioned earlier, the Revised Common Lectionary uses the Psalter readings as responses to the First Testament lections instead of readings in their own right. Preachers, therefore, have little opportunity to preach them in a cumulative fashion. When such an opportunity comes along, it should be taken seriously, even if it is only for two Sundays.

Epiphany 4 and 5: The prophetic readings from Micah 6:1–8 and Isaiah 58:1–9a (9b–12) form a pair in that both present the Lord as accusing the people of sinning against God, rejecting their ritual expressions of devotion, and calling them to acts of justice.

Epiphany 6 and 7: Two separate stanzas are read from Psalm 119 on these two Sundays (vv. 1–8 and 33–40 respectively). Psalm 119 is the longest psalm in the Bible and thus could not be preached in a sermon. Preaching on two stanzas over the course of two Sundays, however, could serve as an adequate glimpse into the whole of this complex poem.

LENT and HOLY WEEK

Year A

(See pp. 13–17 for an overview of the three-dimensional character of the Revised Common Lectionary's approach to Lent.)

Lectionary Readings

	FIRST TESTAMENT	PSALTER	EPISTLE	GOSPEL
ASH WEDNESDAY				
Ash Wed. (abc)	Joel 2:1–2, 12–17 Blow the trumpet—call to repentance	51:1–17 Penitential prayer, confessing sin and asking forgiveness	2 Cor. 5:20b—6:10 Ambassadors of Christ commended in every way	Mt. 6:1–6, 16–21 Practice your righteousness
SUNDAYS IN LENT				
Lent 1	Gen. 2:15–17; 3:1–7 Adam and Eve eating of the tree in the garden	32 Happy are those whose transgression is forgiven	Rom. 5:12–19 Death came through one man's trespass (Adam); grace through one man's righteousness (Christ)	Mt. 4:1–11 Jesus' Temptation
Lent 2	Gen. 12:1–4a God promises to make a nation from Abram	121 I lift up my eyes to the hills—from where will my help come?	Rom. 4:1–5, 13–17 Abraham was justified by faith	Jn. 3:1–17 Nicodemus visits Jesus in the night and is told he must be born from above
Lent 3	Ex. 17:1–7 God gives water from the rock to Moses and the Israelites at Massah and Meribah	95 Call to worship—do not harden hearts as at Meribah and Massah	Rom. 5:1–11 While we still were sinners, Christ died for us	Jn. 4:5–42 Jesus and the Samaritan woman at the well
Lent 4	1 Sam. 16:1–13 Samuel anoints David to be the future king	23 The LORD is my shepherd	Eph. 5:8–14 Live as children of light; everything exposed by the light becomes visible	Jn. 9:1–41 Jesus heals the blind man, who is then expelled from the synagogue
Lent 5	Ezek. 37:1–14 God brings to life the valley of dry bones	130 My soul waits on the LORD	Rom. 8:6–11 The One who raised Christ from the dead will give life to your mortal bodies also	Jn. 11:1–45 Jesus raises Lazarus from the dead

50

HOLY WEEK				
Palm		118:1–2,19–29 (abc) Hallel Psalm: Festal procession with branches		Mt. 21:1–11 Triumphant Entry
Passion	Isa. 50:4–9a (abc) Suffering Servant	31:9–16 (abc) Lament in the face of bodily suffering	Phil. 2:5–11 (abc) Christ Hymn	Mt. 26:14—27:66 Last Supper to Burial
Holy Mon. (abc)	Isa. 42:1–9 Suffering Servant	36:5–11 God's steadfast love	Heb. 9:11–15 Christ's blood of the new covenant	Jn. 12:1–11 Mary anoints Jesus; leaders seek his & Lazarus' death
Holy Tue. (abc)	Isa. 49:1–7 Suffering Servant	71:1–14 Prayer for deliverance from enemies	1 Cor. 1:18–31 Foolishness of the message of Christ crucified	Jn. 12:20–36 Jesus withdraws from public ministry & announces the hour of his glorification has arrived
Holy Wed. (abc)	Isa. 50:4–9a Suffering Servant	70 Prayer for deliverance from enemies	Heb. 12:1–3 Jesus, the pioneer & perfecter of faith through endurance of the cross	Jn. 13:21–32 Jesus predicts Judas' betrayal
Holy Th. (abc)	Ex. 12:1–4 (5–10) 11–14 First Passover	116:1–2, 12–19 Thanksgiving— cup of salvation	1 Cor. 11:23–26 Institution of Lord's Supper	Jn. 13:1–17, 31b–35 Jesus' New Commandment– to love one another and the footwashing
Good Fri. (abc)	Isa. 52:13—53:12 Suffering Servant	22 Lament: My God, my God…	Heb. 10:16–25 Blood of Jesus	Jn. 18:1—19:42 Arrest to Burial
Holy Sat. (abc)	Job 14:1–14 Lament concerning human mortality OR Lam. 3:1–9, 19–24 Suffering God's wrath	31:1–4,15–16 Petition for refuge	1 Pet. 4:1–8 Prepare to suffer in the flesh as Christ did	Mt. 27:57–66 Jesus' burial OR Jn. 19:38–42 Jesus' burial

Cumulative Preaching Strategies

When developing cumulative preaching strategies for Lent, one must take into account a few factors. First, the season begins on Ash Wednesday, for which the Revised Common Lectionary offers the same readings every year. Ash Wednesday creates a strong depth dimension, defining the liturgical season in the same manner every year by focusing on themes of mortality, confession, repentance, and Christian disciplines. Beyond this general emphasis, the lessons for Ash Wednesday, however, do not lead into the lections that follow throughout the rest of the season. Therefore the lections for Ash Wednesday should not be strongly considered when developing a cumulative preaching strategy for Lent.

Second, the liturgical focus of the First Sunday in Lent every year is the temptation of Jesus in the wilderness, based on the Synoptic Gospel of the year. This lection is offered as a rationale for the forty-day length of the season as well as to reinforce the Lenten practices of fasting and prayer. Again, this lectionary pattern serves the depth dimension of the three-year liturgical cycle more than the height dimension. Thus the connection between Lent 1 and the following Sundays in Lent, especially in terms of the Gospel readings, may be weak.

Third, the season concludes with Holy Week, which begins on Palm/Passion Sunday and continues through Holy Saturday. In some sense, Holy Week (leading to the Easter Vigil on Saturday night or to Easter Sunday) represents a season in and of itself (this is especially true of the Easter Triduum—Holy Thursday, Good Friday, Easter). However, most Protestant congregations worship only on Holy Thursday and/or Good Friday between Palm/Passion Sunday and Easter Sunday.

In sum, preachers should think of Ash Wednesday (and possibly Lent 1) and Holy Week as bookends to the season that work cumulatively in terms of their annual recurrence, and focus primarily on Lent 1–5 (or Lent 2–5) in developing a cumulative preaching strategy that deals with the height dimension. What follows, therefore, are separate potential strategies for the Sundays in Lent and for Holy Week.

For the Sundays in Lent A

The first three strategies proposed below deal with the lections as ordered by the lectionary itself, while the ones that follow those two offer thematic options.

STRATEGY 1—Apart from the First Sunday in Lent, the Gospel readings for Year A during this season come from the *Gospel of John.* A preacher will do well to work through these readings in order. Not only will the four Sundays in a row allow the preacher to unpack some distinctive elements of Johannine theology, each of the lengthy passages focuses on Jesus' interactions with an individual. Sermons in the form of character studies—that is, interpretation of the way these characters reveal key elements of Johannine christology and soteriology—are quite appropriate for the Lenten season.

Since it is during Lent and Easter every year that John shows up to supplement the Synoptic Gospel that anchors the lectionary calendar, Year A is a good time to purchase a new commentary or two on John. Preachers will return to this biblical text each Lent, Holy Week, and Easter, as well as for a number of weeks during Ordinary Time Year B. Especially helpful at this point is to read the introductory material on John in a couple of commentaries to remind ourselves of the major themes, narrative emphases, and structures in the Gospel. Conveying to a congregation John's unique qualities over against the Synoptics is essential, but not easy. Reviewing the big picture of the Fourth Gospel will help preachers keep in mind John's cumulative presentation of the Christ Event while focusing on individual Johannine pericopae here and there across the three-year cycle.

STRATEGY 2—For the most part, the Gospel lections thematically dominate the liturgical year from Advent through Pentecost. The series of *First Testament lessons* during Lent, however, is one of the exceptions to this rule. As noted in the Introduction, during this season the First Testament readings are structured in accordance with a salvation history schema that stands alone and is not subordinate to the Gospel readings (although there are connections between the First Testament readings and the other lections here and there through Lent). The salvation history schema for Year A is as follows:

Lent 1—Origins (Gen. 2:15–17; 3:1–7, eating from the forbidden tree)

Lent 2—Abraham (Gen. 12:1–4a, God promises to make a nation from Abram)

Lent 3—Exodus (Ex. 17:1–7, God makes water flow from a rock)

Lent 4—Nation (1 Sam. 16:1–13, Samuel anoints David)

Lent 5—Eschatological hope (Ezek. 37:1–14, God raises the valley of dry bones)

By widening one's view beyond the individual lection to include the broad movements in Israel's history represented by the Lenten First Testament lections as a group, the preacher can place the salvific work of Christ celebrated during Holy Week in the context of God's salvific work throughout Hebraic history.

STRATEGY 3—Even though the Revised Common Lectionary designates a psalm or portion of a psalm for every Sunday of the three-year lectionary cycle, preachers give the Psalter short shrift. Indeed, the lectionary use of the Psalms is not directed toward homiletical goals. They are chosen as responses to the First Testament reading. But it would be a shame if the Psalms receive no attention in the pulpit. Lent is an ideal time to correct this deficiency. With Lent's emphasis on the discipline of prayer, a congregation will be well served by a series of sermons focusing on *praying the psalms* offered by the Revised Common Lectionary for the season. In Year A, the psalms chosen share a common theme of God's providence and salvation. In contrast to the Revised Common Lectionary's practice of often assigning only a portion of a psalm, the Psalter readings for each Sunday in Lent include the whole psalm.

STRATEGY 4—Since Lent leads into the remembrance and celebration of Christ's crucifixion and resurrection, it is not surprising that the lections for the season have strong soteriological tones. The lections for the season offer the preacher and congregation an opportunity to explore a wide variety of metaphors, images, and interpretations of *God's salvific work.* One way of doing this would be to preach exclusively on the Epistle readings, since they especially focus on this theme. The strong presence of Romans would set up a cumulative approach to preaching through the semicontinuous lessons assigned from Romans for the beginning of Ordinary Time, Year A. One need not be limited to the Epistle lections, however. As can be seen in the following list, this is a prevalent theme in Lent:

Lent 1: Psalm 32 is a penitential psalm, like Psalm 51 assigned to Ash Wednesday. Using a standard wisdom rhetorical motif of blessing, the psalmist describes the joy of God forgiving one's transgressions.

OR: Romans 5:12–19 is a passage in which Paul argues that as death came into the world through one person, specifically Adam (cf. the use of Gen. 2:15–17; 3:1–7 for the First Testament lesson), so has the free gift of Jesus Christ conquered death and overcome the trespass of our sins.

Lent 2: Psalm 121 is a psalm of ascent, probably sung as pilgrims made their way to Jerusalem ("the hills" in v. 1) for a festival at the temple. The question, "From where will my help come?" receives the answer: "from the LORD." God is our rescuer.

OR: Romans 4:1–5, 13–17 is Paul's discussion of the justification of the ungodly, of faith reckoned as righteousness. The apostle's theological claim is rooted in an interpretation of God's covenant with Abraham (cf. the First Testament lection for the day).

OR: John 3:1–17 presents a dialogue between Jesus and Nicodemus in which Jesus speaks of the need to be born again/ from above and of God saving the world by giving to it God's only child.

Lent 3: Exodus 17:1–7 tells of God producing water from a rock for the thirsty Israelites in the desert. This text offers both rescue from a physical threat and a sign of divine immanence as types of salvation.

OR: Psalm 95, which is a psalm sung by pilgrims on their way to Jerusalem, praises God as the rock of our salvation and calls the people to worship.

OR: Romans 5:1–11 tells of God's love revealed in Christ's willingness to die for us while we are yet sinners.

OR: John 4:5–42 presents Jesus as offering himself to the Samaritan woman at the well as the living water that leads to eternal life. He also proclaims a future in which Jew and Samaritan will worship together.

Lent 4: Psalm 23 expresses confidence in God's salvific providence using the image of a shepherd caring for his sheep.

OR: Ephesians 5:8–14 is an hortatory passage that calls readers to live as children of the light. This exhortation is based on the claim that "in the Lord" the readers have already moved out of the darkness of their former pagan lives and into the light of Christian existence.

OR: John 9:1–41 portrays Jesus as healing a blind man after the disciples ask whose sin, the man's or his parents' sin, caused his blindness. The lengthy story unfolds in a way that at the end the blind man sees and is faithful while the religious leaders who have opposed Jesus are condemned as blind and sinful.

Lent 5: Ezekiel 37:1–14 offers exilic Judah a vision of a valley of dry bones given new life as a metaphor for the salvation God wills for the people.

OR: Psalm 130 is one of the seven penitential psalms and is a prayer of one awaiting God's forgiveness. The prayer moves from an expression of guilt and the need for pardon to one of confidence in God's goodness.

OR: Romans 8:6–11 is Paul's juxtaposition of having one's mind set on the flesh, which leads to death, and having the mind set on the Spirit, which is life and peace.

OR: John 11:1–45 narrates the raising of Lazarus and presents Jesus as declaring himself to be the resurrection and the life.

STRATEGY 5—Traditionally, Lent is a season of preparation for those who will be initiated into the church through baptism (and confirmation) on Easter. Therefore, it is no surprise that the lections for the season are filled with *imagery related to baptism.* While this imagery is not central in many of the pericopae, homiletical use of it can enhance a congregation's experience of rituals of baptism and confirmation that are coming on Easter and help them remember their baptism and renew their baptismal covenant. Preachers must be careful, however, that—as they relate these images to reflections on baptism during Lent—they not go down the path of eisegesis.

Ash Wednesday: Psalm 51 is a penitential psalm in which petitioners request that God wash them of their iniquity.

Lent 1: Psalm 32 is also a penitential psalm. The prayer talks about mighty waters (v. 6). This image, however, refers not to the cleansing power of water but is a metaphor for the destructive forces from which the psalmist seeks rescue.

OR: Matthew 4:1–11 is the scene of Jesus' temptation. However, this scene is properly interpreted as proceeding directly from the baptism scene that precedes it. Notice that in the baptism scene, God declares Jesus to be God's child and in the temptation story, Satan challenges Jesus on the basis of this baptismal identity.

OR: While the lection from Romans 5:12–19 does not contain a reference to baptism, the opening of chapter 6, which flows from chapter 5, does. Specifically, Paul describes baptism as a participation in Christ's death and a sign of eschatological participation in Christ's resurrection. The preacher may wish to consider a sermon on the broader passage.

Lent 2: John 3:1–17 presents Jesus describing what it means to be born again/from above to Nicodemus. Jesus says that one must be born of water and the Spirit (v. 5). This soteriological image is explicitly connected to baptism.

Lent 3: While Exodus 17:1–7 does not deal with issues related to initiation, the image of God bringing forth water from a rock associates water and salvation, and has been used liturgically to celebrate the waters of baptism.

OR: In John 4:5–42, the dialogue between Jesus and the Samaritan woman at the well is filled with water metaphors that evoke connections with baptism. Specifically, the image of Jesus as the living water suggests the idea of baptism into God's eternal life.

Lent 4: While 1 Samuel 16:1–13 does not include images of water, preaching the story of Samuel anointing David with oil during the season of Lent can certainly lead to reflections on God's act of choosing us in baptism and of practices of anointing related to baptism in some traditions.

OR: As with the First Testament lection, Psalm 23 refers to the act of anointing.

OR: John 9:1–41 tells of Jesus healing a blind man. In this miracle story, Jesus' ritual of healing involves washing.

Lent 5: None of the readings for this Sunday offer imagery as explicitly related to baptism as do those mentioned above for Lent 1–4. Instead, they deal with resurrection in an eschatological manner that foreshadows the Easter celebration—the resurrection of the valley of dry bones (Ezek. 37:1–14), the Spirit of God who raised Jesus from the dead will raise us also (Rom. 8:6–11), and Jesus as the resurrection and the life who raises Lazarus from the dead (Jn. 11:1–45). The symbolic connection between emerging from the baptismal waters and resurrection from the dead is an appropriate connection to draw homiletically on this day.

STRATEGY 6—Another potential preaching strategy appropriate to Lenten emphases is to explore the use of *the theme of faith* in various texts through the season. Given that Lent evolved out of a time of extensive catechism and thus emphasizes growing in the faith, this is an extremely appropriate cumulative approach for the season.

Lent 1: Matthew 4:1–11 presents Jesus as being faithful and obedient to his baptismal identity in the midst of Satan's testing.

OR: Romans 5:12–19 juxtaposes the disobedience of Adam and Eve (see the Genesis lection) and the faithfulness of Jesus Christ, through whom we are saved.

Lent 2: In Romans 4:1–5, 13–17, Paul contrasts faith and works, to clarify that we are saved by faith (specifically the faithfulness of Jesus Christ) and not by our deeds.

OR: In John 3:1–17, Jesus tells Nicodemus that those who have faith in the Son of Man may have eternal life.

Lent 3: Romans 5:1–11 continues, from the previous week's Epistle lection, the discussion of justification by faith.

OR: John 4:5–42, the story of Jesus and the woman at the well, ends with Samaritans first believing in Jesus because of the witness of the woman and subsequently because of Jesus' own words.

Lent 4: John 9:1–41, as with the Gospel lesson for Lent 3, ends with declarations of belief. In juxtaposition to the previous Gospel lection, which raises the relation between hearing and faith, this extended healing story and dramatic dialogue metaphorically connects seeing with faith.

Lent 5: Ezekiel 37:1–14 offers a vision of God's ability to bring new life into the midst of desolate situations more than it raises issues about faith. Nevertheless, the exchange between God and the prophet in verse 3 offers a glimpse of a faithful attitude toward God's power. When God asks the prophet if the bones can live, the prophet responds, "O Lord GOD, you know."

OR: John 11:1–45 offers the more explicit reference to faith for this Sunday. When Jesus arrives and finds Lazarus dead, he and Martha have an exchange in which Jesus not only emphasizes his identity as the resurrection but also invites Martha to believe in him and thus participate in resurrection.

For Holy Week, Year A

Many Protestant congregations do not have Holy Week services on the weekdays of Holy Week, or only have services on Holy/Maundy Thursday and/or Good Friday. Moreover, congregations that do have services throughout the week may well not have a service on Holy Saturday due to celebrating the Easter Vigil on Saturday night. Because of these varying practices it is difficult, and likely not helpful, to offer preaching strategies to be used for the entire week. Nevertheless, noting some of the broad cumulative patterns exhibited during the week will help preachers adapt them to whatever liturgical practices their congregations follow.

STRATEGY 1—The first pattern concerns *the juxtaposition of John and Matthew's versions of the Jerusalem narratives.* Beginning with Palm/Passion Sunday, all of the lectionary readings for Holy Week are the same for all three years of the lectionary cycle, with the exception of the Gospel lections for Palm/Passion Sunday. The Gospel readings for the Liturgy of the Palms and the Liturgy of the Passion come from the Synoptic Gospel for the year. The Gospel texts for the rest of Holy Week come from John. Thus, in Year A, preachers who have been preaching through the Gospel of John for the Sundays in Lent will be able to return to the lengthy Jerusalem narrative from Matthew on Palm/Passion Sunday before preaching on portions of the passion narrative in John through the week. This allows the congregation to experience two different perspectives on Jesus' suffering and death.

STRATEGY 2—The *Suffering Servant oracles* from Isaiah dominate the First Testament lections. While preachers must avoid eisegetical errors of the past in which the church read these oracles as predictions about Christ, they can nevertheless be used to discuss the complex and confusing relation of vicarious suffering and redemption that is reiterated throughout much of the Judeo-Christian tradition and which is central to the Christ Event.

STRATEGY 3—In spite of the fact that the *Epistle readings* are not drawn from the same author or school and are subordinate to the Gospel lections for the week, they have some cohesion. They all interpret the death of Jesus from different theological perspectives and by using a range of metaphors. Although the liturgical emphasis for the week is on the story of Jesus' passion, preaching through various interpretations of his death has much homiletical potential.

EASTER

Year A

(See pp. 17–21 for an overview of the three-dimensional character of the Revised Common Lectionary's approach to Easter.)

Lectionary Readings

	FIRST TESTAMENT	PSALTER	EPISTLE	GOSPEL
Easter Day	Acts 10:34–43 (abc) Peter's sermon to Cornelius…"but God raised him on the third day"	118:1–2, 14–24 (abc) Rejoicing in God's providence: "I shall not die, but I shall live,… / but he did not give me over to death"	Col. 3:1–4 If you have been raised with Christ, seek the things that are above	Jn. 20:1–18 (abc) Empty Tomb OR Mt. 28:1–10 Empty Tomb
Easter Evening (abc)	Isa. 25:6–9 The salvation of the Lord will wipe away tears	114 Creation trembles at God's power exhibited in the exodus	1 Cor. 5:6b–8 Clean out the old yeast	Lk. 24:13–49 Jesus on the road to Emmaus & appearing to the disciples
Easter 2	Acts 2:14a, 22–32 Peter's Pentecost sermon: God raised Jesus up; we are witnesses	16 You do not give me up to Sheol	1 Pet. 1:3–9 God has given us a new birth through the resurrection of Jesus Christ from the dead	Jn. 20:19–31 (abc) Giving of the Spirit; Thomas
Easter 3	Acts 2:14a, 36–41 Response to Peter's Pentecost sermon	116:1–4, 12–19 I love the LORD, because the LORD has heard my voice	1 Pet. 1:17–23 Live in reverent fear during the time of your exile	Lk. 24:13–35 Jesus on the road to Emmaus
Easter 4 Good Shepherd	Acts 2:42–47 Pentecost converts devote themselves to the teaching of the apostles	23 (abc) The LORD is my shepherd	1 Pet. 2:19–25 You have returned to the shepherd and guardian of your souls	Jn. 10:1–10 I am the gate for the sheep
Easter 5	Acts 7:55–60 Stoning of Stephen before Saul	31:1–5, 15–16 In you, O LORD, I seek refuge	1 Pet. 2:2–10 Once you were not a people, but now you are God's people	Jn. 14:1–14 Farewell discourse: I am the way, truth, life

Easter 6	Acts 17:22–31 Paul's Areopagus speech	66:8–20 Truly God has listened	1 Pet. 3:13–22 If you suffer for doing what is right, you are blessed	Jn. 14:15–21 Farewell discourse: Those who love me keep my commandments
Ascension (abc)	Acts 1:1–11 Opening of Acts—Ascension	47 The Lord is king	Eph. 1:15–23 God seated Christ at the right hand in the heavenly places	Lk. 24:44–53 Ending of Luke—Ascension
Easter 7	Acts 1:6–14 Ascension and gathering of disciples afterward	68:1–10, 32–35 Praise to God, the protector	1 Pet. 4:12–14; 5:6–11 Maintain constant love for one another	Jn. 17:1–11 Jesus' prayer for the disciples
Pentecost	Acts 2:1–21 (abc) Giving of Holy Spirit and opening of Peter's Pentecost sermon	104:24–34, 35b (abc) O Lord, the earth is full of your creatures—when you send forth your spirit	1 Cor. 12:3b-13 Varieties of gifts of the Spirit	Jn. 20:19-23 Resurrected Jesus gives the Holy Spirit OR Jn. 7:37–39 Jesus speaks about the spirit, which will come when he is glorified

Cumulative Preaching Strategies

As noted in the overview of the Revised Common Lectionary's approach to Easter (found in the Introduction), multiple, competing cumulative patterns are at play in the choices of lections for this season that complicate developing cumulative preaching strategies. These patterns are further complicated by the fact that three holy days—Easter, Ascension, and Pentecost—occur within the season and give it its unique character. Indeed, Easter and Pentecost (or, in some sense, Easter on the one hand and Ascension/Pentecost on the other hand) serve as bookends to the season. These different dynamics lead to cumulative preaching strategies that can be combined or divided up in different ways to work through the season.

Easter Sunday

STRATEGY 1—On Easter Sunday, preachers will almost surely preach (and usually should preach) on the Gospel lection. Colossians 3:1–4 describes new life in Christ rooted in the resurrection and is fitting material for homiletical consideration on this holy day. In Acts

10:34–43, Peter preaches the resurrection to a Gentile household—also a fitting text for the day. But Easter Sunday is the day people come to church to hear the story they know by heart, the story of *the empty tomb.*

However, lectionary preachers who follow this traditional route must still choose between Matthew 28:1–10 and John 20:1–18. Choosing the Matthean passage allows the preacher to connect the Easter sermon to the extended reading from Matthew on Passion/ Palm Sunday. Choosing John 20, on the other hand, allows preachers to connect with Johannine themes that they may have explored while preaching the Gospel lections during the Sundays in Lent or Holy Week, or that they will explore on Easter 2 and 4–7.

Easter Sunday, Ascension, Pentecost

STRATEGY 2—The *three holy days* during Eastertide provide much of the continuity of the season by drawing a conclusion to the liturgical half of the year. Although the celebrations are spaced according to Lukan narrative chronology (forty days from Easter Sunday to Ascension and ten more days to Pentecost), they express different dimensions of the same theological reality and form a cumulative whole. That is, they call the church to remember that its very being rests upon the paradox of Christ's exaltation (transcendence) and the divine spiritual presence (immanence). Regardless of which texts preachers focus their sermons on for the rest of the season, preaching on the empty tomb in the Gospel lection and on the ascension and gift of the Spirit in Acts can and should give cohesion to the season as a whole. For churches that do not gather to celebrate Ascension on Thursday, Ascension can (i.e., should) be celebrated on Easter 7. This shift creates a sense of the season having bookends: Easter Sunday at the start and Ascension/Pentecost at the end.

Gospel Lections in Eastertide

As noted in the Introduction, Eastertide offers three thematic movements focused by the *Gospel lections.* These movements can serve to focus the preacher's attention.

STRATEGY 3—The first three Sundays—Easter Sunday through Easter 3—deal with *resurrection appearances.* Each of these, especially if one chooses to preach from the Matthean text on Easter Sunday, offers a different perspective on and interpretation of the resurrection. On Easter Sunday, the focus is the initial news of the empty tomb and Jesus' first appearance; on Easter 2, the Johannine text tells of Jesus giving the Spirit to his disciples (John's version of the Pentecost story) and of Jesus revealing himself to Thomas; and on Easter 3 the story of Jesus appearing to the disciples on the road to Emmaus and in the breaking of the bread undergirds a resurrection emphasis to be held in the continuing sacramental practice of the church.

Easter 4 divides the season in half. It is *Good Shepherd Sunday*, and the Gospel reading is always drawn from the mixture of shepherding metaphors found in John 10. In Year A, the reading is naturally taken from the opening of the chapter. (Note also the shepherd language in Ps. 23 and 1 Pet. 2.)

Each year, the Gospel lessons for Easter 5–7 proceed from the *Johannine farewell discourse* (John 13—17). As noted earlier, while it may, at first glance, seem odd to preach from texts in which Jesus prepares his disciples for his departure during Eastertide, two things are important to recognize. First, when John has Jesus speak of his departure or glorification, he is speaking of the whole of his crucifixion, resurrection, and exaltation. Thus in these passages from the farewell discourse, Jesus interprets not only his pending death, but also his being raised from the dead. Second, the theme of preparing for Jesus' departure fits the latter part of Eastertide in terms of preparing for Ascension and the coming of the Spirit.

Semicontinuous Readings

STRATEGY 4—As noted in the overview, during Eastertide the Revised Common Lectionary substitutes readings from *Acts of the Apostles* for the First Testament lections. A glance at the Acts readings for Year A will likely raise some level of frustration in preachers. Certainly choices that connected together better could have been made. Nevertheless, this series of texts has homiletical potential. Broadly speaking, by examining narrative moments in the life of the early church that flowed out of the gift of the Spirit, a congregation prepares for the celebration of Pentecost that closes liturgical time before Ordinary Time begins. This is especially true of the readings for Easter 2–4. On Easter 2 we read a portion of Peter's Pentecost sermon (2:14a, 22–32); on Easter 3, the immediate response to that sermon (2:14a, 36–41); and on Easter 4, a summary of the long-term response to that sermon—the establishing of a post-Pentecostal community devoted to the gospel (2:42–47).

What follows on Easter 5 and 6 are key moments in the spread of the gospel in the Acts narrative. On Easter 5 we read of the first Christian martyr, Stephen (7:55–60). Stephen's inspiring example of faith is also the occasion, in Luke's narrative, where the gospel begins to spread beyond Judea because of the persecution that followed (in fulfillment of Acts 1:8). On Easter 6 we read Paul's philosophical sermon to Gentiles in Athens (17:22–31). This is the same Paul who on the previous Sunday was presented as a persecutor of Stephen. In the Acts reading from Easter Sunday, the congregation would have already heard a portion of the first sermon preached to Gentiles (in the narrative world of Acts). Now, we hear an attempt at making the gospel intelligible to Greek thought.

Not only do these lections from Acts skip around in the narrative in a manner that is not as helpful as it might be, homiletically speaking, they also truncate pericopae in inappropriate ways. The problems invite preachers to fill in the gaps and tell some of the story of Acts in broad strokes to set up a more focused look at the lection for the day. Moreover, a little tissue connecting the material between lections will go a long way to introducing congregations to the plot of a much-neglected book of the New Testament.

STRATEGY 5—If Acts is a much-neglected narrative of the New Testament, *1 Peter* is a far too often overlooked epistle. Eastertide, when 1 Peter is presented in a semicontinuous series of readings, is a quite fitting season to correct this mistake.

It is unclear who wrote this letter that has been attributed to the apostle Peter. But it was likely written in the late first century to churches that were facing persecution in the region of the Roman Empire that is modern-day Turkey. In contrast to an empire-wide pogrom, the kind of persecution directed toward these churches seems to have been a significant level of social ostracism caused in part by the fact that those Gentiles who converted to Christianity no longer participated in popular Greco-Roman religious activities. Such ostracism would have resulted in significant economic, emotional, and perhaps at times physical suffering.

First Peter is written to offer comfort and hope to Christians by reminding them that any suffering that they must endure is worth the reward they have received. This reward is characterized by the author as being in Christ and is consistently contrasted with the kind of lives the readers led before their conversion.

This is clearly an Easter message. Even though the church in North America today is not persecuted for its faith, there is the potential for a meaningful analogy between the circumstances the letter addresses and that of today's church. Reminding our hearers, who have perhaps been Christians all of their lives, of the newness and meaningfulness that Christ's resurrection offers them in the midst of exile in a post-Christendom world is a timely and worthy exercise. To be a Christian, in other words to live a life defined by resurrection, is to be countercultural and thus to not "fit" in society.

Pastors who choose to preach through the 1 Peter lessons in a cumulative fashion that fits with the above suggestion will need to pay careful attention to consider the broader context of each lection because the Revised Common Lectionary does a poor job of setting the boundaries of all the Epistle readings for Eastertide. If preachers want to be true to 1 Peter's message, they will have to adjust the beginnings and endings of the passages read and interpreted for the congregation.

Thematic Approaches

Because Eastertide is thematically divided in half by the manner in which the Gospel lections focus the season (see strategies 3–5 above), it is difficult to find thematic emphases that stretch across the whole season. Nevertheless, two dominant themes in Year A deserve mention.

STRATEGY 6—The first theme is, obviously, *resurrection.* It saturates the readings for the first few Sundays of the season and then dissipates. Nevertheless, it still arises here and there in the later Sundays in subtle ways. The pattern for the whole season is as follows:

Easter 1: Both of the gospel choices (Mt. 28:1–10 and Jn. 20:1–18) narrate the story of the women finding the empty tomb, but they are quite different versions of the story.

OR: Peter's sermon in Acts 10:34–43, like all of the sermons in Acts, is anchored to a witness to the resurrection. The consistent pattern of the Easter proclamation in Acts is (1) you killed Jesus; (2) God raised him; (3) we [the apostles] are witnesses to the resurrection.

OR: Psalm 118:1–2, 14–24 is a portion of a song of thanksgiving, in which an individual faithfully proclaims, "I shall not die, but I shall live" (v. 17).

Easter 2: The reading from John 20:19–31 presents the resurrected Jesus appearing to the majority of the disciples on Easter evening and to Thomas a week later. Thomas' discourse highlights the Johannine understanding of a post-apostolic faith in the resurrection.

OR: Peter's Pentecost sermon in Acts 2:14a, 22–32 is anchored to the witness of the resurrection. This proclamation follows the same pattern noted for Acts 10 on Easter Sunday.

OR: As the semicontinuous reading from 1 Peter begins with 1:3–9, the author proclaims to the persecuted churches he is comforting that new birth comes to us through Christ's resurrection.

OR: Psalm 16 is a prayer for God's protection, which expresses confidence that God does not give us up to Sheol (i.e., the dwelling place of the dead) but instead shows us the path of life (vv. 10–11).

Easter 3: Luke 24's version of Easter evening (vv. 13–35) tells of the resurrected Jesus' appearance to the disciples on the way to Emmaus and revelation in the breaking of the bread in one of the disciple's house.

OR: The reading from 1 Peter 1:17–23 speaks of salvation through Christ and the trustworthiness of the God who raised Christ from the dead.

OR: Following the previous week's reading from Peter's Pentecost sermon in Acts 2:14a, 22–32, this week's lesson comes from a later portion of the sermon (vv. 36–41) that closes with a reference to Jesus' exaltation.

OR: In Psalm 116:1–4, 12–19, the psalmist offers thanksgiving for divine rescue from death.

Easter 4: Psalm 23 has long been associated with funerals because of the traditional translation of verse 4 including "the valley of the shadow of death." While most contemporary translations today do not retain this language, clearly the psalm implies that life-threatening situations abound and affirms that God restores life (v. 3).

Easter 5: The lesson from Acts 7:55–60 tells of Stephen's martyrdom. Just as he is being stoned to death, Stephen has a vision of the exalted Son of Man standing at the right hand of God.

Easter 6: 1 Peter 3:13–22 refers not only to Christ's resurrection but also to his proclamation of the good news of salvation to the "spirits in prison" from the days of Noah. For congregations who affirm their faith with the use of creeds in worship and who profess a faith in Christ who was crucified, dead, and buried, descended into hell, and raised from the dead on the third day all in one breath (or who see a footnote with the line about descent into hell omitted), this can be an important text to read and have interpreted in worship along with 4:6. The strange claim that Christ descended into hell needs to be understood in its ancient, literary context.

OR: In Acts 17:22–31, Paul's sermon in Athens (as is true of Peter's sermons from Acts 2 and 10 that were read earlier in the season) witnesses to the resurrection as central to Christian faith and devotion.

Ascension: Acts 1:1–11 opens the book of Acts with the story of the ascension and a summary of Jesus' resurrection appearances narrated at the end of Luke. The reference makes it clear that all that follows in Acts flows forth from the resurrection.

OR: In Luke 24:44–53, the account of the ascension at the end of the Third Gospel (which differs somewhat from Luke's version of the ascension at the beginning of Acts) presents Jesus himself as proclaiming the resurrection as a fulfillment of scripture.

OR: Ephesians 1:15–23 speaks of the resurrection and the exaltation/ascension of Christ as a unity of divine action, through which God gave dominion over the world to Christ.

Easter 7: The lection from John 17:1–11 is Jesus' prayer for his disciples, which draws to a close the farewell discourse. In the prayer, Jesus states that the time for his glorification has come so that eternal life might be given to all.

Pentecost John 20:19–23 (which is also a portion of the lection for Easter 2, and thus why John 7:37–39 is offered as an alternative lection for Pentecost) is the story of the resurrected Jesus appearing to the disciples on Easter evening, breathing upon them, and giving them the Holy Spirit.

STRATEGY 7—As the first theme grows out of the beginning of the season, so the second theme leans toward the end of the season. This theme is the *Holy Spirit.* Theology of the Spirit (pneumatology) varies greatly from denomination to denomination, from congregation to congregation, and indeed from Christian to Christian. Taking time in the pulpit to look at different New Testament views of the Holy Spirit can be a helpful and engaging exercise for hearers trying to make sense of diverse language concerning the Spirit.

Easter 1: In Acts 10:34–43, as Peter proclaims the power of Jesus leading up to his resurrection, he describes Jesus as having been anointed with the power of the Spirit.

Easter 2: John 20:19–31 recounts the Johannine version of the resurrected Jesus breathing the Holy Spirit upon the disciples and connecting possession of the Spirit with the forgiveness of sins.

Easter 3: In Acts 2:14a, 36–41, the crowd asks Peter what they should do in response to God making Jesus Lord and Christ. Peter's answer is that they should be baptized, and in so doing they will receive the Holy Spirit.

Easter 5: Acts 7:55–60 describes Stephen, who is about to be martyred for the Christian interpretation of salvation history he has just proclaimed, as "filled with the Holy Spirit." For Luke, such language of possession of the Spirit is a sign of being a prophet.

Easter 6: In John 14:15–21, part of the farewell discourse, Jesus promises the disciples that they will not be orphaned by his departure. God will give them another advocate, the Spirit of truth, which represents Jesus coming to the disciples himself.

Ascension: In Acts 1:1–11, even as Jesus is leaving, he instructs the disciples to remain in Jerusalem to receive the promise from God, which is the Holy Spirit.

Easter 7: The lection from Acts for this day (1:6–14) overlaps with but also extends the Acts lection for Ascension (1:1–11). Thus it repeats the promise of the coming of the Holy Spirit.

OR: In the concluding words read from 1 Peter for Eastertide (4:12–14; 5:6–11), the writer summarizes the main emphasis of the epistle in terms of the Holy Spirit: "If you are reviled for the name of Christ, you are blessed, because the spirit of glory, which is the Spirit of God, is resting on you" (4:14).

Pentecost: This thematic focus climaxes, of course, in Acts 2:1–21, Luke's story of the gift of the Spirit to the church.

OR: In both Gospel lection choices for Pentecost, the Holy Spirit is a main focus. In John 20:19–23, the resurrected Jesus breathes the Spirit on the disciples (a repetition of the reading for Easter 2). In John 7:37–39 Jesus speaks of satisfying thirst, which the narrator interprets as a foreshadowing of the gift of the Spirit to follow Jesus' glorification.

OR: 1 Corinthians 12:3b–13 is Paul's response to a church divided over attempts to rank in importance different gifts of the Spirit. The apostle speaks of need for a diversity of gifts for building up the community as the body of Christ. (He goes on in chapter 13 to speak of love as the greatest gift, and the gift that all possess.)

OR: The portion of Psalm 104 read on Pentecost (vv. 24–34, 35b) speaks of God creating and renewing creation through God's Spirit.

ORDINARY TIME (Sundays after Pentecost)

Year A

(See pp. 21–23 for an overview of the three-dimensional character of the Revised Common Lectionary's approach to the Season after Pentecost.)

Lectionary Readings

	FIRST TESTAMENT	PSALTER	EPISTLE	GOSPEL
Trinity Sun.	Gen. 1:1—2:4a Creation…let us make humanity in our image	8 Praise God for the place of humans in glorious creation	2 Cor. 13:11–13 Grace of Christ, love of God, communion of Holy Spirit be with all of you	Mt. 28:16–20 Great commission: baptize in name of Father, Son, Holy Spirit
Proper 4 5/29–6/4	Gen. 6:9–22; 7:24; 8:14–19 Noah	46 God is our refuge…we will not fear…though the waters roar	Rom. 1:16–17; 3:22b–28 (29–31) To the Jew first and also to the Greek	Mt. 7:21–29 End of Sermon on the Mount
Proper 5 6/5–6/11	Gen. 12:1–9 Call of Abram	33:1–12 Sing a new song…Happy is the nation whose God is the Lord	Rom. 4:13–25 Abraham justified through righteousness of faith	Mt. 9:9 13, 18 26 Came for sinners, not righteous; healing of girl & woman
Proper 6 6/12–6/18	Gen. 18:1–15, (21:1–7) God promises a son to aged Abraham & Sarah	116:1–2, 12–19 Thanksgiving for help in distress	Rom. 5:1–8 Boast in our sufferings	Mt. 9:35—10:8-(9–23) Missionary discourse: choosing & sending out of the Twelve
Proper 7 6/19—6/25	Gen. 21:8–21 Casting out Hagar & Ishmael	86:1–10, 16–17 Prayer for help against life-threatening circumstances	Rom. 6:1b–11 Should we continue in sin in order that grace may abound?	Mt. 10:24–39 Missionary discourse: discipleship in the midst of strife
Proper 8 6/26–7/2	Gen. 22:1–14 Near sacrifice of Isaac	13 Prayer for help	Rom. 6:12 23 Should we sin because we are not under law but under grace?	Mt. 10:40–42 Missionary discourse: whoever welcomes you welcomes me…
Proper 9 7/3–7/9	Gen. 24:34–38, 42–49, 58–67 Rebekah chosen as Isaac's wife	45:10–17 Prayer for a royal wedding OR **Song of Solomon 2:8–13** Love poem speaking of beauty	Rom. 7:15–25a I do not do the good I want, but the evil I do not want is what I do	Mt. 11:16 19, 25–30 Various sayings: come to me all who…

Proper 10 7/10–7/16	**Gen. 25:19–34** Esau & Jacob's sibling rivalry	**119:105–112** Your word is a lamp to my feet…the wicked have laid a snare for me	**Rom. 8:1–11** There is no condemnation for those who are in Christ Jesus	**Mt. 13:1–9, 18–23** Parables discourse: parable of the sower & interpretation
Proper 11 7/17–7/23	**Gen. 28:10–19a** Jacob's vision at Bethel	**139:1–12, 23–24** Prayer for help from the omnipresent God	**Rom. 8:12–25** If by the Spirit you put to death the deeds of the body, you will live	**Mt. 13:24—30, 36–43** Parables discourse: parable of the wheat and the tares
Proper 12 7/24–7/30	**Gen. 29:15–28** Jacob marries Leah & Rachel	**105:1–11, 45b** Praise to the God of history…chil- dren of Jacob **OR 128** Your wife will be like a fruitful vine	**Rom. 8:26–39** Nothing can separate us from the love of God	**Mt. 13:31–33, 44–52** Parables dis- course: parables of mustard seed, treasure, pearl, catch of fish
Proper 13 7/31–8/6	**Gen. 32:22–31** Jacob wrestling God at Peniel	**17:1–7, 15** Prayer for help from persecution	**Rom. 9:1–5** Paul's concern for Israel	**Mt. 14:13–21** Feeding the five thousand
Proper 14 8/7–8/13	**Gen. 37:1–4, 12–28** Joseph is sold into Egypt	**105:1–6, 16–22, 45b** Praise to the God of history…sent Joseph ahead to Egypt	**Rom. 10:5–15** If you confess with your lips that Jesus is Lord, you will be saved	**Mt. 14:22–33** Jesus walking on water
Proper 15 8/14–8/20	**Gen. 45:1–15** Joseph receives his brothers in Egypt	**133** How good it is when kindred live together	**Rom. 11:1–2a, 29–32** God has not rejected Israel	**Mt. 15:(10–20) 21–28** What comes out of the mouth defiles…Canaan- ite woman
Proper 16 8/21–8/27	**Ex. 1:8—2:10** Saving baby Moses	**124** The Lord is on our side—saved from waters	**Rom. 12:1–8** One body, many members	**Mt. 16:13–20** Peter's confes- sion at Caesarea Philippi
Proper 17 8/28–9/3	**Ex. 3:1–15** Moses & the burning bush	**105:1–6, 23–26, 45c** Praise to God of history…sent Moses and Aaron	**Rom. 12:9–21** Let love be genuine	**Mt. 16:21–28** Take up your cross and follow me…
Proper 18 9/4–9/10	**Ex. 12:1–14** First Passover	**149** Praise for God's salvation of Israel and punishment of enemies	**Rom. 13:8–14** Love one another	**Mt. 18:15–20** Community dis- course: if another member of the church sins against you…
Proper 19 9/11–9/17	**Ex. 14:19–31** Crossing the Red Sea	**114** Hymn of praise for the exodus	**Rom. 14:1–12** Welcome those who are weak in faith	**Mt. 18:21–35** Community dis- course: parable of unforgiving slave

Proper 20 9/18–9/24	Ex. 16:2–15 Manna & quails	105:1–6, 37–45 Praise to the God of history… quails, food from heaven, water from rock	Phil. 1:21–30 Living is Christ and dying is gain	Mt. 20:1–16 Community discourse: parable of the vineyard workers' wages
Proper 21 9/25–10/1	Ex. 17:1–7 Water from the rock at Massah and Meribah	78:1–4, 12–16 Recounting the glorious deed of the LORD: God split rocks open in the wilderness	Phil. 2:1–13 Christ hymn	Mt. 21:23–32 Temple conflicts: By what authority…?
Proper 22 10/2–10/8	Ex. 20:1–4, 7–9, 12–20 Decalogue	19 The torah of the LORD is perfect, reviving the soul	Phil. 3:4b–14 Surpassing value of knowing Christ Jesus	Mt. 21:33–46 Temple conflicts: parable of the vineyard owner
Proper 23 10/9–10/15	Ex. 32:1–14 Golden calf	106:1–6, 19–23 Song of praise for God's goodness in spite of Israel's sin	Phil. 4:1–9 Rejoice in the Lord always	Mt. 22:1–14 Temple conflicts: parable of the wedding banquet
Proper 24 10/16–10/22	Ex. 33:12–23 Moses asks to see God's glory	99 Praise for God's glorious reign	1 Thess. 1:1–10 Letter opening	Mt. 22:15–22 Temple conflicts: Is it lawful to pay taxes to emperor?
Proper 25 10/23–10/29	Deut. 34:1–12 Death of Moses	90:1–6, 13–17 Psalm attributed to Moses	1 Thess. 2:1–8 We had courage in our God to declare to you the gospel	Mt. 22:34–46 Temple conflicts: greatest commandment; David's son
Proper 26 10/30–11/5	Josh. 3:7–17 The Ark passes through the Jordan	107:1–7, 33–37 Prayer of thanksgiving	1 Thess. 2:9–13 You remember our labor and toil	Mt. 23:1–12 Temple conflicts: do what scribes teach, not what they do.
Proper 27 11/6–11/12	Josh. 24:1–3a, 14–25 Choose this day whom you will serve	78:1–7 Recounting the glorious deed of the LORD: established a decree in Jacob	1 Thess. 4:13–18 God will bring with God those who have died	Mt. 25:1–13 Eschatological discourse: parable of ten bridesmaids
Proper 28 11/13–11/19	Judg. 4:1–7 Deborah	123 Prayer for mercy	1 Thess. 5:1–11 Re: times and seasons, you do not need to have anything written to you	Mt. 25:14–30 Eschatological discourse: parable of Talents
Proper 29 Reign of Christ 11/20–11/26	Ezek. 34:11–16, 20–24 I will judge between sheep and sheep	100 Call to praise and worship	Eph. 1:15–23 Opening thanksgiving: exaltation of Christ over all dominions	Mt. 25:31–46 Eschatological discourse: parable of king judging between sheep and goats

Cumulative Preaching Strategies

After Pentecost, the function of the readings of the Revised Common Lectionary changes significantly, and so must also one's cumulative preaching strategies. The lections chosen for liturgical time are determined by seasonal themes related to the remembrance and celebration of various aspects of the Christ Event. Thus the four readings assigned to a particular Sunday are chosen to relate to or interact with one another in such a way as to shape the church's experience of the liturgical occasion. In other words, the scripture lessons are subordinate to the liturgical theme, and a preacher's interpretation of a particular lection within the set of readings is influenced by that liturgical context.

In Ordinary Time, with the exception of a few Solemnities here and there (see below), no liturgical themes are at work. Neither the season nor individual Sundays are thematically determined. Instead, the scripture readings shape the season and the individual Sundays. Indeed, apart from the Psalter reading serving as a response to the First Testament, the lections for each Sunday are not related at all.[4] The three-dimensional lectionary of the liturgical season gives way to a two-dimension lectionary during Ordinary Time. Put differently, a predominant width dimension gives way to a strong height (connection from week to week) and depth (relation of each of the three years).

This means that there will be no reason at all to look for thematically oriented cumulative preaching strategies for the Sundays after Pentecost. Because the series of First Testament, Epistle, and Gospel lessons are each structured in a semicontinuous fashion, preachers should look for ways to preach in ways that allow congregations to experience significant segments of the canon. In other words, the flow of the lections themselves will provide a cumulative quality to sermons throughout Ordinary Time as long as preachers do not hop from one kind of lection to another Sunday after Sunday. They must have the patience to stay with a particular series (i.e., the Gospel, First Testament, or Epistle series) long enough to allow the connections across time to influence the congregation's experience of the biblical writing being explored.

Before we consider specific strategies for dealing with the semicontinuous flow of the different series of lections, it will be helpful to name a few overarching issues related to the Season after Pentecost.

First, preachers should remember that the Season after Epiphany also utilized semicontinuous readings for the New Testament texts. The Epistle readings for all three years work through 1 Corinthians and take a small detour through the opening of 2 Corinthians in Year B. The Gospel lessons work through opening scenes from Jesus' Galilean ministry. Preachers need to recall what strategy they used for the Sundays after Epiphany and consider whether and to what extent that strategy should influence the approach to preaching through the Season after Pentecost, or, at least, the beginning of the Season after Pentecost. For example, preachers who focused on the Matthean lections and worked through portions of the Sermon on the Mount may or may not want to return to a focus on Matthew at this point, following the use of John in Lent and Easter. Or those who preached on the opening chapters of 1 Corinthians may or may not want to continue working with Pauline letters.

Second, although Ordinary Time is not shaped by liturgical themes related to the Christ Event, a few thematic celebrations occur during the season. The lections for these solemnities break from the semicontinuous pattern of the readings for all other Sundays.

Trinity Sunday follows on the heels of Pentecost and opens the season. Since the doctrine of the Trinity represents a post-biblical theological development, the readings for this Sunday are usually related to the doctrine in a tentative or formulaic fashion. During Year A, there are two connections between the lections for this celebration and the Sundays that follow. (1) The First Testament lection taken from the creation story in Genesis 1 serves both the thematic focus on the Trinity and the semicontinuous approach of reading through Genesis and Exodus throughout the season. (2) The Gospel lection is Matthew 28:16–20. Although this passage represents the final verses of the First Gospel and, therefore, does not follow the semicontinuous pattern of the readings from Matthew that begin in Matthew 7, it does relate thematically and theologically to the Gospel lections that will be read throughout the season.

While it is not recognized by the Revised Common Lectionary, many North American mainline congregations and denominations celebrate **World Communion Sunday** on the first Sunday of October. For some preachers, this will cause no problem because they will still follow the lectionary. For others who use thematically oriented scripture lessons chosen for the day, World

Communion Sunday will force a break in a cumulative strategy based on the semicontinuous readings of the Revised Common Lectionary.

All Saints' Day falls in the middle of the Season after Pentecost on November 1. Since many churches celebrate this day on the first Sunday of November and since November 1 occasionally falls on a Sunday for churches that celebrate it on the first day of November, this day may force the preacher to take a break in the pattern of preaching through semicontinuous readings.

The **Reign of Christ** (also referred to as Christ the King) closes the season and indeed the whole liturgical year. This day has a strong eschatological tone, which leads well into Advent and for which the lections late in Ordinary Time begin to prepare. Nevertheless, with the exception of the Gospel lections, the readings for Reign of Christ are not in literary continuity with the readings for the Sundays leading up to it.

Third, because Easter is a movable feast (it can occur as early as March 22 or as late as April 25), the opening of the season will vary greatly year to year. Easter must occur very early for all of the readings assigned to Ordinary Time to be available, but this is rare. It is more likely that a set of readings or two assigned to the Sundays after Trinity Sunday will be dropped at the beginning of the season.

Fourth, the "semi" in the semicontinuous readings presents significant challenges to preachers and congregations during the Season after Pentecost. The semicontinuous approach to reading through sections of the canon in worship is a modification of the *lectio continua* approach to choosing biblical texts for worship. *Lectio continua* (or "continual reading") works through a biblical writing verse by verse, passage by passage. The semicontinuous approach, on the other hand, works through a biblical work in its literary order by reading key and representative passages from the work, but not by examining the entire writing. Preachers will often find themselves frustrated at the significant gaps between the semicontinuous readings assigned by the Revised Common Lectionary. Therefore, preaching during Ordinary Time can be greatly enhanced by inviting congregations to read and study the materials that fall between the lections in group Bible studies and/or private devotion. More to the homiletical point, preachers must fill in something of these gaps in their sermons. Indeed, they should think of their sermons as having a dual focus in relation to the biblical text. First, as with all Sundays, sermons should focus on the individual lection of choice. This, of course, should be the primary focus. Second, however, sermons should also deal in some sense with the entire section of the biblical writing that extends from the previous week's reading through the current week's lesson. Thus the preacher is invited to offer a message that takes a wide-angle glance at the broad sweep of a section of a biblical work but that ultimately zooms in on a particular moment within that narrative.

Finally, while the First Testament, Epistle, and Gospel lections for the Season after Pentecost work through different portions of the canon in a semicontinuous fashion, pastors who desire to preach cumulatively are not forced to choose one route (e.g., the Gospel lections) and stay with that route through the whole season. Since the season comprises approximately half of a calendar year, many pastors will think this is too long to stay with a single strategy. Certainly preachers *can* stay with one such route for the whole season and enter into a portion of the canon with more depth than is allowed when they jump around in the canon. The lections in a series vary enough over time that preaching the series need not become stale or repetitive. Nevertheless, the series have natural breaks (e.g., the shift from one epistle to another or from one narrative section of a gospel to the next) that allow preachers to move from one series to another and utilize more than one cumulative strategy. However, the shifts that occur in, say, the First Testament series of readings will not necessarily coincide with the shifts in the Epistle or Gospel lections. One way to manage the gaps between ending one strategy and starting the next is to preach from the Psalter readings during the gap. We read from the Psalms more than from any other writing in the Bible, but preach on it less than most. An occasional sermon on the Psalter, especially on texts that vary thematically and rhetorically, will help a congregation better understand the Psalter as its canonical hymnal and prayer book.

With these general comments in hand, let us turn to specific cumulative strategies inherent in the semicontinuous structure of the readings through the Season after Pentecost. For each series of lections (i.e., First Testament, Epistle, and Gospel), we will begin with an overview of how the readings work as a whole throughout the season and then we will consider smaller units that lend themselves to a cumulative approach.

First Testament Lections

In Year A, the First Testament lessons for Ordinary Time come primarily from Genesis and Exodus, with a few readings taken from Deuteronomy, Joshua, and Judges at the end of the season. These readings move from the beginning of the world to the point just before a monarchy is initiated in Israel. In other words, the lections focus on the creation of humanity, the establishment of Israel as a people, the enslavement and liberation of Israel, and the constitution of Israel as a nation in the form of a confederacy of tribes.

Since twenty-two of the twenty-seven First Testament lections stretching from Trinity Sunday to the Reign of Christ come from Genesis (thirteen lections) and Exodus (nine lections), it is important that preachers have a sound overview of the two books in mind if these texts are going to be preached. Preachers need to work with solid commentaries on these two books to preach them well and to keep before the preachers' eyes the broad sweep of story and theology these works represent. Nevertheless, a couple of framing comments may be helpful at this point.

Both are part of the Pentateuch (Genesis—Deuteronomy), whose history of composition stretches over centuries, moving from oral tales to a finally edited collection of writings in the fifth century B.C.E. The complex debate concerning source theories need not detain us here, but it is important to recognize that the driving force in pulling everything together into long, theological, historical narrative (Genesis—2 Kings) was the development of Judah's faith and religious practices during the exile.

The Genesis narrative flows through four primary movements. It is helpful to see how the First Testament lections represent these movements during Year A:

Chapters 1—11, the beginnings of humanity (Trinity–Proper 4)

Chapters 12—25, the Abraham cycle (Propers 5–9)

Chapters 25—36, the Jacob cycle (Propers 10–13)

Chapters 37—50, the Joseph cycle (Propers 14–15).

Two things should be immediately evident from this list. First, the Revised Common Lectionary gives more attention to the Abraham cycle than to any off the other narrative sections. However, if Trinity Sunday occurs late, a reading or two from this cycle may be lost.

Second, there are huge omissions of material. Even though the Abraham cycle is assigned five lections, one cannot help be aware how poorly five passages can represent some eight and a half chapters of biblical narrative. But, alas, this is the nature of semicontinuous readings, and Genesis gets much more sustained attention than most First Testament writings.

As with Genesis, it is helpful to consider the structure of the Exodus narrative and see how the Revised Common Lectionary's choices relate to this structure. Exodus can be divided into three main narrative sections:

Chapters 1—15, the liberation of Israel from Egypt (Propers 16–19)

Chapters 15—18, the journey to Sinai (Propers 20–21)

Chapters 19—40, the covenant at Sinai (Propers 22–24)

Again, when seeing the lections laid out in this manner, one cannot help but experience some level of frustration from how much biblical material must be omitted to try to cover the First Testament canon in three cycles of Ordinary Time, which equals approximately one and a half years. Still, the Revised Common Lectionary probably offers a better sense of the flow of the Exodus narrative than it is able to do with Genesis.

When we turn to discuss different cumulative strategies for preaching through the First Testament series of readings, we are really asking a question about observing structures in the flow of the narratives that invite grouping lections together in different ways. We have a number of such potential structures from which to choose. These structures also suggest possibilities for dividing the six-month long series into phases so that congregations can shift focus to other series of readings if desired.

STRATEGY 1—Preachers would do well to work through the *whole series of First Testament readings* with a congregation, for the narratives from which they proceed are the stories upon which so much of the biblical worldview rests. Psalms, prophetic oracles, gospel narratives, and Pauline arguments that quote, refer to, or echo these texts will have more meaning for a congregation after these texts have been explored in sermons. Central to the First Testament writings explored during Year A are the interrelated themes of *promise, covenant,* and *blessing*. Preachers who work through these texts will get the opportunity to touch on the salvation history that moves through the covenants God established with—and the blessing God bestows upon—Noah (Proper 4), Abraham (Propers 5–6), Isaac (Propers 8–10), Jacob (Propers 10–13), Joseph (Propers 14–15), Moses (Proper 22–23), and Joshua (Proper 27).

STRATEGY 2—The second strategy is to preach the two books that get the majority of attention. Enough representative texts are offered by the lectionary that a preacher can explore the major themes and storylines of *Genesis* and/or *Exodus.* The unity of the narrative of the two books invites preaching through them both, while the canonical division allows the preacher to focus on just one or the other. Preaching through either of these invites a study of the "book of the Bible" homiletical approach.

STRATEGY 3—Another approach is to offer a series of *character studies* on these texts. This strategy works well for Genesis, which shifts main characters often (Abraham and Sarah, Propers 5–8; Isaac and Rebekah, Propers 6, 8–9; Jacob and Rachel, Propers 10–13; and Joseph, Propers 14–15), and for the quick glance at Joshua and Judges (Joshua, Propers 25–27 and Deborah, Propers 28). The lengthy time spent in Exodus (Propers 16–24), however, will feel redundant if the preacher focuses on a character study of Moses the whole time. When the Revised Common Lectionary shifts its focus from one protagonist to another, preachers can shift to another series of texts if they wish.

STRATEGY 4—Another possible cumulative strategy is to focus on the various *time periods* through which the narrative readings walk in a presentation of God active in history. The periods explored over the course of the season are as follows:

Forebears of humanity: Trinity Sunday–Proper 4;

Forebears of Israel: Propers 5–15

Israel freed from slavery: Propers 16–19

Israel in the wilderness: Propers 20–25

Israel in the promised land: Propers 26–28

STRATEGY 5—A final strategy that should be mentioned does offer different ways to divide the texts across the season. Instead, it deals with a specific socio-theological concern, that is, the patriarchy of the biblical texts. Indeed, the patriarchy of the texts and of the time period explored in Year A is evident in the list of those with whom God establishes covenants (see strategy 1), which includes only men. However, *women* play an important role in these narratives as well. While God's blessing for Israel is passed from father to son, it is passed through women: Sarah (Propers 5–7), Rebekah (Propers 9–10), Rachel (Proper 12). Moreover, Hagar receives a promise for her son Ishmael (Proper 7), Shiphrah and Puah refuse to be complicit in Pharaoh's attempt to kill newborn Israelite boys while a mother and daughter conspire to save Moses (Proper 16), and Deborah leads the confederation of tribes as a judge and prophet (Proper 28). As earlier noted in the Introduction, one of the critiques of the New Common Lectionary was that women were poorly represented in the lections chosen especially from the First Testament. As can be seen from the list above, the Revised Common Lectionary made some efforts to correct this problem. When the ancient texts and the contemporary church have so often silenced women's voices (and indeed lives), it is important for preachers to pause over the women in these texts as important to our tradition and faith.

Epistle Lections

In Year A, the New Testament lessons for Ordinary Time come from Romans, Philippians, and 1 Thessalonians. While Paul naturally dominates the Epistle readings every year (and indeed across all the different liturgical seasons), only in Year A are the readings for the Season after Pentecost drawn solely from undisputed Pauline letters. These lections offer the preacher and congregation a significant opportunity to explore Pauline theology as well as the situations facing early Pauline house churches.

There are a few general things to keep in mind and indeed to offer to the congregation if one chooses a cumulative preaching strategy that involves these Pauline letters. First, these epistles are letters in the true sense of the word. In other words, they are occasional in nature, written for a specific reason to address specific circumstances. The church later decided that the letters contained pastoral/theological discourse significant enough to be saved and distributed to other congregations, but Paul originally wrote them with very specific recipients in mind. Even in the letter to the church at Rome—a community that Paul did not establish and had never visited—the apostle names numerous people with whom he had a personal connection. The church often ignores this occasional nature of the letters because of its recognition of them as scripture.

The Revised Common Lectionary reinforces this ignorance by primarily choosing lections that exhibit theological dimensions of the letters instead of passages that focus on pastoral/communal issues. This is not inappropriate in that in worship (in contrast to a Bible study in a setting of educational ministry) the church seeks from the Bible a word of good news to proclaim. Thus preaching is public theology that informs the congregation's Christian worldview. However, viewing the reading of Pauline letters as a process of overhearing half of an ongoing pastoral conversation between apostle and ancient congregation enhances our theological reading of the texts, and indeed allows us to see with better focus the potential for drawing homiletical analogies between the Pauline context and our own.

Second, preachers need to teach congregations that letters were understood and functioned somewhat differently in antiquity than today. While it is important to recognize the occasional nature of the Pauline letters, it is also important that they served an official purpose in the life of the early church. The letters were epistles in the sense that they were not personal correspondence between friends or relatives, but were public addresses to a community of faith. The letters were composed to be read orally to the community as a whole. Thus although Paul did not write or dictate the letters for the sake of being distributed widely (much less to be preserved as Holy Scripture), they were public in the sense of being addressed to the whole community. (This is likely true to some extent even of the letter to Philemon.) In the ancient mind, writers were thought to be present in the letters they sent, and thus they carried something of the sender's persona, social status, and authority. Thus the letters to the Philippians and Thessalonians carried the weight of the founder of the church, and Romans carried the weight of Paul's reputation as a missionary.

Third, in preaching passages from Pauline letters, not only should preachers (and congregations) be clear about the circumstances that necessitated the writing of the letter and of the relationship between Paul and the recipients, they must also ascertain how individual lections function within the structure of the letter. As is true of letters today, ancient letters were composed using set structural forms. Pauline letters have five parts: (a) the greeting, which names the sender and the recipient; (b) a prayer of thanksgiving for the recipients; (c) the body of the letter, in which Paul addresses the main pastoral and theological main issue(s); (d) ethical exhortation, which can flow out of the material in the body of the letter and/or grow out of formulaic ethical instruction found in the ancient Mediterranean world; and (e) closing greetings and blessing. By understanding the function of a passage within the structure of the letter, the preacher will be better able to evaluate the rhetorical strategy behind Paul's language and to shape the function of a sermon based on that text. As mentioned earlier, when preaching from semicontinuous readings, preachers will often need to fill in gaps to help congregations contextualize a pericope. This is especially important in terms of understanding how passages from epistles function in relation to the standard parts of ancient letters.

Finally, it is important to remember that the Revised Common Lectionary often sets the boundaries for Epistle lections inappropriately. It divides texts in the middle of logical developments and thus arguments are skewed. Preachers who are following a cumulative strategy of preaching through a New Testament letter should be willing, at times, to designate different beginnings and endings to lessons.

Given these broad insights into preaching from Pauline letters, what particular preaching strategies are available during Ordinary Time of Year A?

STRATEGY 6—The first possible cumulative preaching strategy is to focus on the *whole series of Epistle readings* throughout the whole season. This approach will allow preachers to explore Romans, Philippians, and 1 Thessalonians individually (see strategies 7–9 below) as well as thinking through broader issues of Paul's ministry and theology. Indeed, the length of the season invites the preacher and congregation to look beyond the trees to see the woods.

STRATEGY 7—Preachers who do not want to spend the whole of Ordinary Time on Paul may, however, find it worthwhile to spend part of the season on one or two of the three letters offered by the Revised Common Lectionary. The letter to the *Romans* is the first option, and it occupies approximately the first half of the Season after Pentecost (sixteen Propers). This is the longest stretch of readings assigned by the lectionary to any epistle of the New Testament. The letter gets this amount of attention for the same reason that it is the first epistle in the New Testament canon—it is the longest of Paul's letters.

However, it also receives extended attention for its theology. Romans has often been viewed as a systematic expression of Paul's theology. This assessment is incorrect, or at least exaggerated. Like all of Paul's correspondence, Romans is an occasional letter with the argument found in the body shaped toward a specific church and for a specific purpose. The epistle functions as a sort of letter of self-reference: Paul, who neither established the church in Rome nor had ever visited the church there, was hoping to go to the congregation to spend some time with them and have them sponsor his missionary work on into Spain. He does not present the Christian gospel in a vacuum, therefore. Instead, he specifically formulates his theological claims in a way to secure the church's support. Nevertheless, Paul's description in Romans of the human condition and of God justifying humanity though the faithfulness of Jesus Christ has had immeasurable influence on the shaping of Christian, and especially Protestant, theology. In a day of biblical and theological illiteracy throughout much of the church, working through Paul's theological argument in Romans is time well spent in the pulpit.

Indeed, this theological argument dominates the Revised Common Lectionary's choices for lections from Romans. The opening greeting and prayer of thanksgiving are found in 1:1–15. In this section, Paul introduces the occasion for writing (1:10–15), but no lection is chosen from this section. In the closing greetings and blessing (15:14—16:27), Paul revisits the purpose for writing in more detail, but again no lection is drawn from this section. A few lections are taken from the ethical exhortation 12:1—15:13 (Propers 16–19). But twelve lections (Propers 4–15) are taken from Paul's central theological argument (1:16—11:36).

This pattern of choices has a number of implications for preaching through the semicontinuous series from Romans in a cumulative fashion. First, preachers must fill in the situational gaps omitted by the Revised Common Lectionary. Paul did not shape the theological claims in this epistle in abstraction, and they should not be preached as if he did. To read the passages from Romans in their historical context offers preacher and congregation nuances that otherwise are lost on uninformed interpreters.

Second, the division of the lectionary choices between the body and the ethical instruction offers preachers a way of dividing the series of lections into two sections, if they do not wish to preach the whole series. The better choice of the two would be to preach the *body*, for the ethical discourse is especially disembodied if it is read in isolation.

Third, while the greatest portion of lections proceeds from the body, there are nevertheless serious omissions. The material is simply too long and too dense to be read in its entirety, even in twelve weeks; and, of course, some weeks may be lost at the beginning of the season depending on when Trinity Sunday occurs. Because the theological argument is complex, preachers will have a difficult time filling in these gaps. But they must find a way, or the movement of Paul's argument as a whole will be lost on the congregation, for it is the flow of Paul's thought (moving from human sin to divine rectification in various ways) that is especially powerful. Inviting laity to read through Romans and leading a Bible study on Romans concurrent with preaching this semicontinuous series are two ways preachers can narrow the gaps for a congregation outside the pulpit. Yet even with such complimentary processes preachers will need to find ways to connect the readings week to week in the pulpit.

STRATEGY 8—Another cumulative option from the Epistles during Year A is to preach from *Philippians* (Propers 20–23). While Philippians does not have the same level of extensive, complex theological argument found in Romans, it does offer some powerful glimpses at Paul's understanding of the gospel (and the lectionary chooses these passages during this series). Part of this power resides in the very personal, pastoral tone of this letter.

In some sense these glimpses are easier to preach because the gaps between the choices for lections is not as problematic. There are gaps, to be sure, and the preacher must deal with them. But they are less troublesome than the gaps in Romans for a couple of reasons. First, the Revised Common Lectionary chooses lessons that present at least some elements of the occasion behind the letter—specifically, the choices reveal that Paul wrote from prison where he was facing possible execution, that the community was being confronted with rival missionaries, and that there was some level of division within the community itself. Two essential missing elements are that Paul writes (a) to thank the church for the care package they sent to him in prison and (b) to send back to the church Epaphroditus, who delivered the care package but became seriously ill while he was with Paul. Yet these two elements are easily imaged for a congregation.

A second reason that the gaps are more easily filled than they were in Romans is that Philippians is so much shorter than Romans. Thus while we find only four readings from four chapters, it is much easier for the preacher to paint a picture of the full literary product than it is with Romans' sixteen chapters.

STRATEGY 9—Finally, a preacher can choose to preach on the semicontinuous readings taken from *1 Thessalonians* (Propers 24–28). It may seem odd to end the series of Epistle readings in Ordinary Time with Paul's earliest letter (written ca. 50 C.E.); but the rationale is liturgical, not chronological. As the liturgical year draws to a close, climaxing with the Reign of Christ and then starting over again with Advent, eschatological themes take center stage. And 1 Thessalonians is thoroughly apocalyptic in content.

Paul writes the young church he founded in Thessalonica for pastoral reasons. On the one hand, Paul has received news from Timothy that the church is concerned that Paul has not been able to return to them. He immediately sends them a letter by way of Timothy so that he might be present with them through this intermediary.

On the other hand, Paul addresses some distress that arose in the church concerning what happens to those who die before the *parousia*. The apostle assures the Thessalonians that those who have died in the faith will join those living in the faith on the day the Lord returns. It is this issue that makes 1 Thessalonians a perfect choice for the end of the Season after Pentecost.

Today, mainline congregations hear little eschatology in worship, although every page in the New Testament has eschatological elements. At best, some traditional liturgical phrases contain eschatological remnants. But the pulpit rarely lifts up eschatological visions. This is likely due to the insecurity of mainline preachers (and congregations), who are unsure of what to do with eschatological language in the pulpit (hermeneutically speaking) except for the fact that they are very sure that they do not want to sound like apocalyptic TV-preachers who speak of Jesus "literally" surfing in on the clouds. It is outside the scope of this book to attempt to prescribe a specific hermeneutic for dealing with eschatological texts. But it is at the core of a lectionary-based, cumulative homiletic to claim that it is extremely important that preachers not ignore the intersection of eschatological themes in the liturgical movement of the church year and in the biblical text. That said, because of its strong pastoral tone, 1 Thessalonians is an ideal opportunity for congregations to explore the meaning of traditional eschatology for a contemporary Christian worldview.

Moreover, working through the semicontinuous readings from 1 Thessalonians will allow preachers to teach a little about the structure of New Testament letters. This was impossible with the readings from Romans and Philippians, since the readings were only taken from the body and the ethical instruction. But the first lection from 1 Thessalonians includes the greeting and prayer of thanksgiving (Proper 24), and is followed by lections from the body (Propers 25–26) and the section of ethical exhortation (Propers 27–28). Only the concluding greeting and blessing is not represented.

Gospel Lections

Matthew is the Gospel that anchors Year A of the lectionary. As one considers using Matthew to develop a cumulative preaching strategy for the Sundays after Pentecost, however, it is important to remember that Matthew has been absent for a while. Matthew anchored the lectionary readings from Advent through the Sundays after Epiphany. Indeed, during the Season after Epiphany, the lectionary began working through Matthew in a semicontinuous fashion, focusing primarily on the Sermon on the Mount. But during Lent and Easter, the Gospel of John takes center stage. The First Gospel peeks out again during these seasons only for Palm/Passion Sunday and perhaps for the Easter Vigil or Easter Sunday. Thus when Matthew appears on Trinity Sunday and the Sundays that follow, preachers will need to reintroduce the congregation to the Gospel, as opposed to assuming that they have remained close friends.

Preachers should have a couple of recent, critical commentaries on Matthew to use as conversation partners while working through

Year A as a whole, but especially through Ordinary Time. Given the amount of time spent in Matthew, preachers will need the level of detail offered in commentary introductions to the Gospel and comments on the various pericopae that relate to a sense of the whole narrative. Still, a few items of introduction can be named here in passing to give a sense of how Matthew can be presented over time for the sake of a deeper, cumulative hearing on the part of the congregation.

Although we know nothing of the author or the location in which the Gospel was written, it seems fairly likely that Matthew was written in the 80s of the first century c.e., ten or so years after the destruction of the Jerusalem Temple. This would have been in a time when the church was competing with the synagogue over who was the proper heir to the Jewish cult and how the Jewish scriptures were to be interpreted for a new day. This dynamic of conflict accounts for why Matthew has such strong elements that reflect a Jewish-Christian orientation as well as some of the most strident anti-Jewish elements found in the New Testament at the same time.

Scholars commonly hold that Matthew used Mark and "Q" (a hypothetical sayings source) as his two main sources for adapting/writing the story of Jesus for his community in its specific circumstances. This view can be helpful to a cumulative preaching strategy on Matthew. For example, whereas Mark was probably written around 70 c.e. in response to a christological crisis related to the fall of the temple, Matthew does not appear to be responding to such a specific issue. Instead, the First Gospel represents an attempt to present a fuller (albeit at times less provocative) picture of Jesus to ground and direct the ongoing life of the church. To offer a narrative example, Matthew extends Mark's narrative backward and forward by adding the birth narrative to answer questions of Jesus' origin and including Jesus meeting the disciples in Galilee after the resurrection.

More than adding narrative details, however, Matthew adds sayings material. So whereas Mark primarily focuses on developing a theological plot without a great deal of Jesus' teaching, Matthew spends a lot of time on presenting Jesus' teaching for the edification of the church. Matthew collects much of Jesus' teaching into five thematic discourses (see below). Much of this teaching material comes from "Q" and is found in Luke as well, but with changes in wording and literary context. Thus, for a cumulative approach, preachers can show patterns of distinct elements in Matthew's versions of the sayings material over against Luke's use of the same traditions.

Given these broad insights into preaching from Matthew, what particular strategies are available during Ordinary Time of Year A?

STRATEGY 10—The first obvious cumulative approach is to preach on *all of the Gospel lections* throughout the Season after Pentecost. This strategy has the potential of building on the congregation's familiarity with Matthew through its use during the liturgical seasons.

The Revised Common Lectionary in Ordinary Time uses Matthew primarily by choosing teaching materials as lections. Of course, key narrative elements are read on Sundays in Advent, Epiphany, Palm Sunday, and Easter. Otherwise, only a few narrative passages appear here and there during Ordinary Time.

Year A, then, allows preachers to engage Jesus the teacher (or better, Matthew's presentation of Jesus as teacher) in great detail. Matthew divides Jesus' teaching into primarily five major thematic discourses. The first is the ethical discourse best known as the Sermon on the Mount. The Revised Common Lectionary drew texts from this discourse during the Season after Epiphany (Epiphany 4–8). Proper 4 during Ordinary Time draws one last text from that sermon, thus inviting the link between the Gospel lections from several months in the past with those of Ordinary Time (that is, if Proper 4 does not fall on dates prior to Trinity Sunday).

Preaching through the Gospel lections for the whole of Ordinary Time will primarily be a process of working through each of the other four discourses, with a passage or so read in between. While this will work for an overall cumulative strategy, focusing on the readings taken from an individual discourse (and perhaps a reading or two leading up to or following up on the discourse) is an appropriate strategy for working through portions of the season cumulatively.

STRATEGY 11—The second of Matthew's discourses is the *missionary discourse* (10:1–42). Jesus chooses the twelve apostles and sends them out with the instructions for ministry in this sermon. The Revised Common Lectionary directs our attention to the discourse for three weeks (Propers 6–8). The opening reading (9:35—10:8 [9–23]) establishes the context and theme of discourse. Jesus sends the twelve out to the lost sheep of the house of Israel only. This mission, therefore, should be held in tension with Matthew's understanding of the post-resurrection mission prescribed in the great commission (28:16–20, see Trinity Sunday). During Jesus' ministry, the apostles are sent only to Jews, but after his death and resurrection they are sent to make disciples of "all nations."

In spite of the narrative-chronological construct Matthew used to justify the inclusion of Gentiles after the resurrection, it is likely that Matthew composed this discourse to guide his church in the way it reached out to the world. Given a post-Pentecost season that begins with the great commission on Trinity Sunday (because of the Trinitarian language that appears in the baptismal formula, 28:19), a preacher will do well to spend a few Sundays reflecting on how the church engages (i.e., ministers to) the world in light of the missionary discourse.

STRATEGY 12—Matthew's third discourse is actually taken from Mark 4, although Matthew modifies it and expands it in significant ways. It is the *parables discourse* (13:1–53), and the Revised Common Lectionary directs the church to read three passages from it (Propers 10–12). Although the lectionary omits verses 10–17, it is important for preachers to review this section and contrast it with Mark 4:10–12. Through such a comparison, preachers will discover that Matthew envisions parables functioning quite differently than Mark.

Likewise, preachers will do well to consider these parables in the wider context of Matthew. These are parables of the reign of God (or in most translations of Matthew, "the kingdom of heaven"). Matthew presents the proclamation of the arrival of the reign of God as central to Jesus' ministry (4:17). However, the gospels never present Jesus as defining the kingdom of heaven/God, but only as describing it metaphorically. Exploring this concept with the help of a concordance and a critical Bible dictionary will serve preaching on the Synoptic Gospels in general, and Matthew specifically, far beyond just these three Sundays.

Another issue of wider Matthean context relates to the prevalence of parables throughout Matthew. Following this series on the parables discourse, parables appear in the Gospel lections for Propers 19–20, 22–23, and 27–Reign of Christ. Finding a reference work on Synoptic parables with which to converse will be time and money well spent for the preacher.

STRATEGY 13—Propers 18 19 come from Matthew's fourth discourse (18:1–35), the *community discourse.* This discourse deals with behavior and relationships within the church. Indeed, the discourse is anachronistic in that Matthew presents Jesus as speaking of "the church" when there is no church yet. This discourse offers preachers a significant opportunity to demonstrate the way gospel writers construed the story of Jesus not for historical-journalistic purposes but for theological-pastoral purposes.

To present the discourse in this way, it can be helpful to contrast with other discourses that have already been considered. Whereas the ethical discourse deals with individual behavior in the world and the missionary discourse deals with the church's behavior toward the world to which it is ministering, the community discourse deals with behavior within the community—behavior between members of the community of faith. Matthew seems to be addressing a community that has experienced some kind of internal strife. It is not difficult to find analogies to such conflict in today's congregations, denominations, and ecumenical relations that are worth considering in the pulpit.

STRATEGY 14—Before presenting lections drawn from the fifth discourse, the Revised Common Lectionary pauses over *conflicts in the temple* between Jesus and the religious authorities (Mt. 21:23—23:39; Propers 21–26). Preachers must be careful not to transform Matthew's ancient competition with the synagogue into contemporary anti-Semitism. Naming post-temple competition with Rabbinic Judaism as the primary reason for Matthew's anti-Jewish tone will help avoid this, but preachers should also consider creating sermons in which the congregation is invited to identify *with* the religious authorities Jesus is addressing instead of identifying with Jesus over against the religious leaders. Such a connection will invite a different (and more honest) hearing of the pericopae than possible when we take a stance of superiority or supersessionism toward the Jews in the text.

Even though the focus of the plot at this point in Matthew is the conflict between Jesus and the religious authorities, the Gospel addresses a range of issues in the controversy scenes—authority, christology, inclusion in the reign of God, paying taxes, the greatest commandment, and hypocrisy in religious leadership. Preaching through these texts, therefore, will not be experienced as the same sermon repeated several times.

STRATEGY 15—When the liturgical cycle rolls toward its close and Advent appears on the horizon, the Revised Common Lectionary turns to readings from the fifth and final discourse in Matthew, the *eschatological discourse* (Mt. 24:1—25:46, Propers 27–Reign of Christ). The first reading from Matthew for the Christian Year on Advent 1 was the description of the parousia in Matthew 24:36–44, so with these closing lections we have returned to the End at which we started. The three Gospel lections here at the end of Year A proceed from Matthew 25 and are all parables. As noted early in strategy 9, in today's mainline church, eschatology seems to be a lost concept. In contrast to the 1 Thessalonians discourse, the use of parables in Matthew may seem a less threatening presentation of eschatology to the contemporary hearer. While eschatology should not be interpreted in a literal fashion, neither should is be discarded or ignored. Viewing God as in our future and thinking of life as oriented toward that future holds much promise for broken lives in a broken world.

Cumulative
Preaching
Strategies for
Year B

ADVENT

Year B

(See pp. 8–9 for an overview of the three-dimensional character of the Revised Common Lectionary's approach to Advent.)

Lectionary Readings

	FIRST TESTAMENT	PSALTER	EPISTLE	GOSPEL
Advent 1	Isa. 64:1–9 Lament: God, who works for those who wait	80:1–7, 17–19 Prayer for restoration	1 Cor. 1:3–9 Opening greeting: wait for the revealing of our Lord	Mk. 13:24–37 Eschatological discourse: Keep awake
Advent 2	Isa. 40:1–11 Comfort my people…In the wilderness prepare the way of the Lᴏʀᴅ	85:1–2, 8–13 God's restoration is at hand…	2 Pet. 3:8–15a Awaiting the day of the Lord	Mk. 1:1–8 Beginning of the gospel: introduction to and preaching of John the Baptist
Advent 3	Isa. 61:1–4, 8–11 The Spirit of the Lᴏʀᴅ is upon me to bring good news…	126 The Lord restored the fortunes of Zion OR Lk 1:47–55 (abc) The Magnificat	1 Thess. 5:16–24 Rejoice always	Jn. 1:6–8, 19–28 John the Baptist claims the role of precursor: the one who follows will baptize with the Holy Spirit
Advent 4	2 Sam. 7:1–11, 16 God establishes the Davidic line/ covenant	Lk. 1:47–55 The Magnificat OR 89:1–4, 19–26 Praise for Davidic covenant	Rom. 16:25–27 Closing blessing: the mystery that was kept secret for many ages is now disclosed	Lk. 1:26–38 Annunciation

Cumulative Preaching Strategies

Advent is the liturgical season in which the church expectantly awaits for God to come (vent) to (ad) us. While the season prepares us for the celebration of the Incarnation, the advent of God-in-Christ toward which the season looks includes more than the past coming of Christ (Christmas). It also involves the claims that God comes to us in our current lives (the present) and that God is always before us (the future). Liturgical preaching that works cumulatively through this season needs to recognize that the season is structured in reverse chronological order by moving from the eschatological claims about the yet-to-occur coming of the Son of Man through John the Baptist's foreshadowing of the adult ministry of "the one who is to come," to the coming of the Christ child.

There are not as many obvious cumulative preaching strategies for Advent suggested by the lections for Year B as there were for Year A, but preachers have some significant options:

STRATEGY 1—Since the liturgical year is rooted in the plot of the Christ Event, an obvious strategy for preaching through every season will be focusing on the *Gospel readings.* Indeed, the Gospel themes for Advent date back at least five hundred years in worship practice and are the same each year of Revised Common Lectionary cycle, regardless of which Synoptic Gospel anchors the year. Preaching these texts allows the congregation to experience variations found in each Gospel on themes found in all three. The themes deal specifically with different chronological expectations concerning the coming of Christ:

Advent 1—Jesus describes the coming of the Son of Man in the eschatological discourse

Advent 2 & 3—John the Baptist as a precursor to Jesus' ministry

Advent 4—Joseph & Mary's preparation for the birth of Jesus

During Year B, Mark is the Synoptic Gospel that anchors the lectionary calendar. The beginning of the liturgical year is a good time to buy a new commentary or two on Mark, since preachers will return to this biblical text repeatedly throughout the year. Especially helpful at the beginning of the year is to read the introductory material on Mark in a couple of commentaries to remind ourselves of the major themes and narrative emphases/structures in the Gospel. This will help preachers keep in mind Mark's cumulative presentation of the Christ Event while focusing on individual Markan pericopae. (See also the introductory notes for preaching the semicontinuous reading of Mark during Ordinary Time on pp. 147–49.)

Having said that, however, it is important to note that only two of the four Sundays of Advent are drawn from the Second Gospel. Mark has no birth narrative, and thus the fourth Sunday's Gospel lection must come from Luke. Moreover, because Mark is the shortest of the Synoptic Gospels, John (which does not have a year assigned to it) takes the place of Mark here and there in addition to Lent and Easter.

STRATEGY 2—A second approach to cumulative preaching in Advent that is possible every year is to focus on *eschatology* all four Sundays. Mainline Protestants tend to avoid eschatology because we do not want to sound like bedfellows with those on TV and in print who interpret biblical apocalyptic material in nonsensical ways. But this odd, "literal" reading of such texts is exactly why preachers whose training has been informed by biblical criticism should preach about the eschatological emphases in scripture. Preachers need to unpack ancient eschatological expressions of living in the "already/not yet" as descriptions of religious experience in all times and places in contrast to linear, temporal interpretations of eschatology.

As the liturgical year opens with eschatology, so also it ends with eschatology. The last few Sundays in Ordinary Time of Year A have already raised questions for the congregation with the readings drawn from Matthew's eschatological discourse and Paul's First Letter to the Thessalonians. To preach on eschatological themes of the gospel at this point will build on those readings.

Moreover, many of the texts of Advent invite the preacher to look at eschatological theology through different perspectives. Thus the depth of this important but neglected biblical theme and its dominant language and imagery (e.g., the day of the Lord, coming/nearness of the reign of God, waiting and expectation, reversal of current circumstance to a more peaceful and just world) can be unpacked throughout the season (even in combination with the end of Ordinary Time) without the preacher sounding like she or he is preaching the same sermon over and over. Consider the different Advent texts that offer eschatological perspectives:

> **Advent 1:** Mark 13:24–37 is a passage from Jesus' eschatological discourse, which he speaks as he leaves the temple. As noted above, a different Synoptic version of Jesus' prophecy concerning the parousia occurring with great cosmic signs serves as the Gospel lection for Advent 1 of each year. The call to stay awake found in these passages is a common New Testament eschatological motif.
>
> **OR:** Isaiah 64:1–9, a prayer that God might make God's presence known and restore the people of Judah after the exile. Whereas the Markan text speaks of cosmic signs, the Isaiah passage speaks of natural signs; and while Mark speaks of keeping awake, Third Isaiah speaks of waiting for God.

OR: 1 Corinthians 1:3–9, Paul's opening blessing for the church at Corinth. Similar to the First Testament lection's emphasis on waiting for God, Paul speaks of waiting for the revelation of Jesus Christ. Here the emphasis is on God's will to prepare the Corinthians for that day by giving them every necessary spiritual gift and strengthening them.

Advent 2: Isaiah 40:1–11, a multi-voiced call to prepare for God's coming to lead the exiles back to Judah. The dominant metaphor of preparation is to clear a roadway for God's coming where roads do not usually exist. The end of the passage emphasizes the effects of God's coming.

OR: 2 Peter 3:8–15a, a passage in which the author defends a belief in the parousia based on a distinction between human and divine time. The purpose of the defense is to call people to remain faithful as they wait for the day of God (see the theme of waiting in Advent 1).

OR: Mark 1:1–8, the beginning of Mark's Gospel, in which John the Baptist's ministry is introduced as a precursor to Jesus' ministry. In this passage John describes Jesus' ministry as an eschatological event in the sense that Jesus' power and baptism with the Holy Spirit represent a radically new manifestation of God.

Advent 3: 1 Thessalonians 5:16–24, a portion of the letter's conclusion in which Paul blesses the readers. Blessings are by their very nature future oriented, and in this one Paul explicitly prays that God will prepare the readers for the coming of Christ.

OR: Luke 1:47–55, the Magnificat. This text is an alternative to the Psalter reading for Advent 3 if it is not used in place of the psalm for Advent 4. Mary's poetic speech uses the present tense to display prophetic confidence in God's future acts of salvation in Christ.

OR: Isaiah 61:1–4, 8–11, a claim of God's eschatological purpose for the prophet. Because this passage is well known as the text cited by Jesus in Luke 4 to describe his Messianic ministry, one of the benefits of preaching this text on Advent 3 is to enable congregants to hear and relate to the passage on its own terms.

This text offers an eschatological view of God radically changing the world through the work of God's faithful servants. One who chooses to preach on this text will likely need to alter the delineation of the passage.

OR: John 1:6–8, 19–28, a lesson similar to last week's Gospel reading from Mark. Here John the Baptist explicitly states that he is not the messiah and describes the coming of Jesus in dramatic eschatological terms.

Advent 4: Luke 1:47–55, see the description under Advent 3.

OR: Luke 1:26–38, the Annunciation. Again the coming of Jesus (which for us is in the past) is represented as an eschatological event that radically changes the future. Notice the strong use of the future tense throughout the passage. Especially significant for using this text on Advent 4 are verses 32–33, which describe the coming reign of Christ as eternal.

STRATEGY 3—Thanks to popular Christmas carols, the secular adaptation of Christmas, and uncritical seasonal preaching, too often Christmas is viewed as a sweet, sentimental celebration that demands little of us. But the story of the nativity and the doctrine of Incarnation, as with any expression of the in-breaking of God in creation, has significant sociopolitical implications. During Year B, the theme of the *restoration of God's people* from situations of oppression is especially prominent.

The Isaiah passages for Advent 1–3 all come from the context of the prophet offering a vision of the return of the exiles from Babylon and the restoration of the homeland of Judah. Likewise, the psalms respond with very similar expressions of hope for restoration. In a day when a number of theologians refer to the church's situation in a post-Christian culture as one of exile, these texts offer much to the preacher and the church who want to look beyond immediate circumstance to ultimate meaning and eternal hope.

The Magnificat, which can be used on Advent 3 or 4, speaks of restoring the divinely willed balance that oppression has distorted.

The dominant theme that connects 2 Samuel 7, Psalm 89, and Luke 1 for Advent 4 is the throne of David. Specifically, the christological language of Luke 1:32–33 speaks of Jesus restoring the throne of David. To preach this text one must recognize that this is not an expression of early followers of Jesus misunderstanding his messiahship in terms of militarism, especially since Luke puts these words in the mouth of Gabriel. Instead, this eschatological claim must be heard in the context of Jews and Christians being suppressed communities under Roman rule.

STRATEGY 4—Interestingly, the *Holy Spirit* is prominent in the Advent readings for Year B. Since the high liturgical seasons end each year with an emphasis on the Holy Spirit with Pentecost, it would be intriguing to begin the year by reflecting on the Holy Spirit as something other than just an expression of God's post-resurrection presence. Advent's emphasis on the coming of God-in-Christ is paradoxical. Pardon the awkward wording of the following statement, but it expresses the paradoxical nature of the claim: the tension of waiting for the One who is already here to come is expressed in the already/not yet nature of eschatology and the imminent/transcendent nature of God. Drawing out the role of the Holy Spirit in the lections for this season may highlight these theological paradoxes in interesting ways.

> **Advent 1:** 1 Corinthians 1:3–9 does not explicitly mention the Holy Spirit but instead mentions spiritual gifts God gives us as we wait for the revealing of our Lord Jesus Christ. With quick use of a concordance, one will see how significant the Holy Spirit is in this epistle and be able to place the language of spiritual gifts in its proper context.

> **Advent 2:** Mark 1:1–8 contrasts John, who baptizes with water, with Jesus, who baptizes with the Holy Spirit.

> **Advent 3:** Isaiah 6:1–4, 8–11 opens with the prophetic claim that "the spirit of the Lord is upon me." The spirit anoints the prophet to proclaim a message of comfort and reversal in expectation that God will come to restore justice, equity, and mercy.

> **OR:** 1 Thessalonians 5:16–24 is a call to rejoice always in spite of whatever circumstances the people are enduring as they wait for the coming of Christ. One sentence unpacking this call is the line, "Do not quench the Spirit."

> **Advent 4:** Luke 1:26–38 presents Gabriel announcing to Mary that she will give birth to Jesus, the Son of God. When she asks how

this can happen, Gabriel explains that the Holy Spirit, the power of the Most High, will come upon her.

CHRISTMAS

Year B

(See pp. 10–11 for an overview of the three-dimensional character of the Revised Common Lectionary's approach to Christmas.)

Lectionary Readings

	FIRST TESTAMENT	PSALTER	EPISTLE	GOSPEL
Christmas Eve/Day Proper 1 (abc)[1]	Isa. 9:2–7 A child has been born for us	96 Sing a new song: the LORD is king	Titus 2:11–14 The grace of God has appeared	Lk. 2:1–14 (15–20) Birth story
Christmas Eve/Day Proper 2 (abc)	Isa. 62:6–12 See, your salvation comes...	97 The LORD is king! Let the earth rejoice	Titus 3:4–7 When the good-ness and loving kindness of God our Savior appeared...	Lk. 2:(1–7) 8–20 Birth story
Christmas Eve/Day Proper 3 (abc)	Isa. 52:7–10 The return of the LORD to Zion	98 Make a joyful noise to the LORD	Heb. 1:1–4 (5–12) God has spoken to us through a Son, through whom God cre-ated the worlds	Jn. 1:1–14 John's Prologue— Incarnation of the Word
Christmas 1	Isa. 61:10—62:3 Restoration of Zion	148 (abc) Praise the LORD who has raised up a horn for God's people	Gal. 4:4–7 When the full-ness of time had come, God sent his Son	Lk. 2:22–40 Presentation of Jesus in the temple: Simeon & Anna
Christmas 2 (abc)	Jer. 31:7–14 God will save a remnant	147:12–20 Praise God for divine provi-dence	Eph. 1:3–14 God chose us in Christ before the foundation of the world	Jn. 1:(1–9) 10–18 John's Pro-logue—the Word
Epiphany (abc)	Isa. 60:1–6 Nations shall come to your light: camels, gold, frankincense	72:1–7, 10–14 Give the king your justice, O God	Eph. 3:1–12 Paul, a prisoner of Christ for Gentiles	Mt. 2:1–12 Magi

Cumulative Preaching Strategies

Proposing a variety of concrete, cumulative preaching strategies for the season of Christmas is difficult because the season takes a couple of different forms depending on which days of the week Christmas and Epiphany fall and what congregational practice is. For congregations that celebrate Epiphany on January 6, regardless of what day of the week it falls on, there will always be at least one Sunday after Christmas and sometimes there will be two (a little more than half the time). However, in congregations that celebrate Epiphany Sunday on the Sunday before January 6 when Epiphany falls on a day other than Sunday, there will never be a Second Sunday after Christmas. If Christmas falls on a Sunday or Monday (with Epiphany falling on a Friday or Saturday), there will be no Sunday "after Christmas" at all—only Christmas Eve or Christmas Day followed a week later by Epiphany Sunday. Thus approximately four of every six years will have one Sunday between Christmas and Epiphany Sunday, with the other two having none.

The brevity of the season and the dominance of the Gospel lections limit our strategies. In the proposals below, there are suggestions for each possibility—no Sunday after Christmas, one Sunday, and two Sundays. Each proposal builds on the one that precedes it. Note also that the dominance of the liturgical themes of the nativity and Incarnation and the ways the First Testament texts were chosen to be subordinate to those New Testament themes has led me not to offer proposals for preaching from the First Testament or Psalter lections for this short, focused season.

Christmas and Epiphany Sunday only:

STRATEGY 1—On Christmas and Epiphany, preachers will usually want to focus their sermons on the Gospel readings, since the accounts of Jesus' birth in Luke and Matthew anchor the liturgical remembering of the Christ Event. Placing Luke's version next to Matthew's is a great way to highlight the theological and narrative differences between the two accounts and undo the harmonizing misinterpretation of the texts that has occurred through centuries of using nativity scenes that place the shepherds and the magi side by side. Note some of the differences:

LUKE (Christmas)	MATTHEW (Epiphany)
Joseph and Mary forced to go to Bethlehem by the emperor's census	Joseph and Mary presumably live in Bethlehem
Setting is a stable	Setting is a house
Angel(s) reveal the birth	Star reveals the birth

Shepherds receive the revelation	Magi receive the revelation
Shepherds proclaim what they have seen	Magi depart in secret

But pointing out the differences between the two versions should also lead a preacher to claim a root similarity: God does not reveal the birth of the Christ child to those in power (Augustus in Luke or Herod in Matthew), but to outsiders (shepherds who are economically marginalized in Luke and Gentile astrologers [i.e., magicians] in Matthew). Thus both present a soteriological understanding of the Incarnation that has sociopolitical implications that could be unpacked in two related but distinct sermons.

STRATEGY 2—Another option is to follow a Christmas sermon on Luke 2:1–14 (15–20) with an Epiphany sermon on the Epistle lection (Eph. 3:1–12). The Ephesians text actually speaks more directly to the liturgical theme of revelation to the Gentiles than does the traditional Matthean lesson. Similar to strategy 1 above, the preacher could highlight the outsider character of the recipients of the revelation of the God of Israel: poor shepherds in Luke on Christmas and Gentiles in Ephesians on Epiphany.

One Sunday after Christmas:

STRATEGY 3—If the season has one Sunday in between Christmas and the congregation's celebration of Epiphany, the preacher may still want to focus on the *Gospel lections.* For Year B, the Gospel reading for Christmas 1 is the story that immediately follows the reading for Christmas. After having heard the angels and shepherds witness to the salvation that has arrived in Christ on Christmas Eve/Day, on Christmas 1 we can listen to Simeon and Anna offer similar witness. Moreover, if you preach on the Magnificat (Mary's prophetic speech) during Advent, preaching on the Nunc Dimittis (Simeon's prophetic speech) connects the two seasons.

STRATEGY 4—Another option for Christmas 1 is to preach on the Galatians 4 passage. In his letters, Paul usually emphasizes the cross and resurrection. In this passage, however, he draws an inseparable theological link between our being adopted as God's children with Jesus being born of a woman.

STRATEGY 5—The earlier Common Lectionary recommended that if the second alternate set of lections for Christmas (Christmas Proper 3) were not used on Christmas Eve or Day, they should be used later during the Christmas season due to the importance of John's prologue for the New Testament understanding of incarnation.[2] A similar option is to substitute the readings for Christmas 2 (which include Jn. 1:[1–9] 10–18) for Christmas 1 in years and worshiping traditions where there is only one Sunday after Christmas. John 1:1–18 serves well to follow the Christmas focus on the nativity by inviting us to step back and reflect on the meaning of the Incarnation in a broader way. Likewise, the text's language of light overcoming darkness sets up the move toward the emphasis on revelation on Epiphany and during the Season after Epiphany.

Two Sundays after Christmas:

STRATEGY 6—For congregations that celebrate Epiphany on January 6 and not on the Sunday before, the lectionary provides more possibilities for cumulative preaching. The preacher may still want to focus on the *Gospel lections* for the entire season. The themes mentioned in strategies above all still work together. On Christmas Eve/Day and Christmas 1, the focus is on the birth and presentation of Jesus. On Christmas 2, the focus is on John's understanding of the Incarnation. On Epiphany, Matthew tells of the revelation of the Christ child to foreign magi.

STRATEGY 7—A final option would be to bookend this short season with the Gospel readings from Luke (Christmas) and Matthew (Epiphany) and to preach on the Epistle texts on the Sundays after Christmas, or to focus on Luke on Christmas and preach the other three sermons on the Epistles. Both of the Epistle texts between Christmas and Epiphany (Gal. 4:4–7 for Christmas 1 and Eph. 1:3–14 for Christmas 2) expand the narrative portrayals of the birth and revelation of the Christ child to offer a view of the soteriological implications of the Incarnation. Moreover, preaching on Ephesians for Christmas 2 and Epiphany offers continuity of theology.

SUNDAYS after EPIPHANY

Year B

(See pp. 11–13 for an overview of the three-dimensional character of the Revised Common Lectionary's approach to Epiphany.)

Lectionary Readings

	FIRST TESTAMENT	PSALTER	EPISTLE	GOSPEL
Epiphany (abc)	Isa. 60:1–6 Nations shall come to your light: camels, gold, frankincense	72:1–7, 10–14 Give the king your justice, O God	Eph. 3:1–12 Paul, a prisoner of Christ for Gentiles	Mt. 2:1–12 Magi
Epiphany 1 Baptism of the Lord	Gen. 1:1–5 Creation: Wind/ Spirit passing over the water	29 (abc) Voice of the LORD is over the waters	Acts 19:1–7 Replacing John's baptism with baptism in the name of Jesus	Mk. 1:4–11 Baptism of Jesus
Epiphany 2	1 Sam. 3:1–10 (11–20) God calls Samuel	139:1–6, 13–18 For it was you who formed my inward parts	1 Cor. 6:12–20 The body is the temple of the Holy Spirit	Jn. 1:43–51 Jesus calls Philip and Nathanael
Epiphany 3	Jon. 3:1–5, 10 Jonah proclaims judgment to Nineveh, who repent and receive forgiveness	62:5–12 Trustworthiness of God	1 Cor. 7:29–31 The present form of this world is passing away	Mk. 1:14–20 Jesus' proclama- tion (kingdom is at hand) & call of the fishermen
Epiphany 4	Deut. 18:15–20 God will raise up for you a prophet like me	111 Great are the works of the LORD	1 Cor. 8:1–13 Idol meat: knowledge puffs up, but love builds up	Mk. 1:21–28 Jesus' first exorcism
Epiphany 5	Isa. 40:21–31 Those who wait for the LORD shall renew their strength	147:1–11, 20c God's providence	1 Cor. 9:16–23 In my proclama- tion, I offer the gospel free of charge	Mk. 1:29–39 Healing of Simon's mother-in-law, summary of heal- ings, itinerant ministry
Epiphany 6 Proper 1	2 Kings 5:1–14 Elisha cleanses Naaman, the leper	30 I cried to you, and you healed me	1 Cor. 9:24–27 In a race the runners all com- pete, but only one receives the prize	Mk. 1:40–45 Cleansing the leper

Epiphany 7 Proper 2	Isa. 43:18–25 I am about to do a new thing	41 Be gracious to me; heal me, for I have sinned against you	2 Cor. 1:18–22 In Christ every one of God's promises is a "Yes"	Mk. 2:1–12 Jesus forgives the sins of the paralytic
Epiphany 8 Proper 3	Hos. 2:14–20 The Lord takes Israel as wife	103:1–13, 22 Bless the Lord, O my soul	2 Cor. 3:1–6 You are our letter of recommenda-tion	Mk. 2:13–22 Call of Levi; Jesus' disciples do not fast
Epiphany Last Transfigu-ration	2 Kings 2:1–12 Ascension of Elijah	50:1–6 The heavens declare God's righteousness	2 Cor. 4:3–6 Our gospel is veiled for those who are perishing	Mk. 9:2–9 Transfiguration

Cumulative Preaching Strategies

As we consider a variety of cumulative preaching strategies for the Season after Epiphany we need to keep two challenging considerations in mind. First, the season's length varies year to year depending first on the date of Easter, which can fall anywhere from March 22 to April 25, and second on which day of the week Epiphany falls—the later in the week that January 6 falls, the earlier in January the Baptism of the Lord occurs. In other words, including Baptism of the Lord and Transfiguration Sunday, the season can last from four to nine Sundays after Epiphany, although the minimum and maximum are quite rare and most years fall between five and eight Sundays.

The second consideration involves the tension between the opening and closing of the season and the Sundays in between. On the Solemnities of the Lord at both ends of the season (Baptism on the first Sunday after Epiphany and Transfiguration on the last Sunday after Epiphany) the liturgical themes will focus the sermon. During the two to seven weeks in between, however, the Epistle and Gospel lections take on the form of semicontinuous readings found during the Sundays after Pentecost, while the First Testament and Psalter lections continue to be chosen to support the Gospel.

STRATEGY 1—Since the ecumenical lectionary has its roots in the Lectionary for Mass, which considers the Sundays between Baptism of the Lord and Ash Wednesday to be Ordinary Time, the Revised Common Lectionary has us begin reading through Gospel of Mark in a semicontinuous fashion during the Season after Epiphany (with the exception of Epiphany 2, which each year has assigned to it a lesson taken from the early portion of John). This pattern will be resumed again after Pentecost. Therefore, one obvious cumulative preaching strategy for this season is to focus on the *Gospel lections.* This strategy makes good sense for two reasons: (A) Because Mark does not include an infancy narrative, we have not read much from the Second Gospel yet. Thus the semicontinuous readings from Mark beginning on the Third Sunday after Epiphany offer the first extended glance at Mark. This is a good opportunity for preachers to present, as part of their sermons, an introduction to Mark's sociohistorical background, narrative, and theology. (See also the introductory notes for preaching the semicontinuous reading of Mark during Ordinary Time on pp. 147–49.) (B) Since the Markan readings come from early in the narrative, preaching on these lections will provide a coherent view of Mark's picture of the beginning of Jesus' ministry. The readings offer a helpful narrative chronology to the congregation:

Epiphany 1: Baptism (Mark 1:4–11)

Epiphany 2: Jesus calls Philip and Nathanael (John 1:43–51)

Epiphany 3: Summary of preaching and call of the first disciples (Mark 1:14–20)

Epiphany 4 through the next to last Sunday after Epiphany: Moments in the opening of Jesus' ministry—mainly healing stories (from Mark 1—2)

Depending on the number of Sundays during the season in any given year, the lectionary preacher may wish to alter the boundaries of some of the readings, omit some readings, and add others from this section of Mark to honor the implicit strengths of the Revised Common Lectionary's focus on the healing stories.

For instance, one Markan element that the lections highlight well is the literary motif of the "Messianic Secret." It shows up when Jesus silences the demons because they know who he is (Epiphany 4 and 5), when Jesus instructs the man with a skin disease to tell no one about being cleansed (Epiphany 6), and when Jesus instructs the disciples who witnessed the transfiguration to tell no one what they had seen until after the resurrection. The Sundays after Epiphany are an appropriate season to explore this motif since this season begins and ends with the heavenly voice declaring Jesus to be God's Son.

No human character in Mark refers to Jesus as God's Son until the centurion witnesses the manner in which he dies (15:39). Thus Mark seems to be narrating a theology that claims that Jesus' true or full identity is not known in his miracles but in his crucifixion. Bringing out this narrative dynamic prepares a congregation well for Lent and particularly for the extended reading of Mark's Jerusalem narrative on Palm/Passion Sunday.

STRATEGY 2—Another straightforward strategy for cumulative preaching on the Sundays in between Baptism of the Lord and Transfiguration is to focus on the semicontinuous readings from *Paul's correspondence with the Corinthians*, again a reflection of the Lectionary for Mass's view of this season as Ordinary Time. The Revised Common Lectionary's selection of readings for Year B are, however, not as strongly connected week to week as those for Year A. Indeed, during the season a shift occurs from the middle of 1 Corinthians (Epiphany 2–6) to the opening of 2 Corinthians (Epiphany 7–Transfiguration). Of course, if the season is shorter this year, this shift may not be a problem.

Whereas the focus of the readings from 1 Corinthians in Year A was the general division in the Corinthians house churches, the focus of the readings in Year B is some of the specific issues facing the community. The focus of the readings from 2 Corinthians is Paul's conflict with the community. It is helpful to note that the semicontinuous readings of 2 Corinthians will pick up again in Ordinary Time after Pentecost. (See pp. 143–44 for a discussion of 2 Corinthians in that context.)

This cumulative approach has two downsides, both of which should be taken into consideration but neither of which should be prohibitive. The first is that these semicontinuous readings have no explicit connection with Epiphany themes or the other three lections for each Sunday. However, a liturgical balance can be created in which the language of much of the worship service grows out of the thematic core of the other lections, while the sermon draws on Paul's writing.

The second problem is that the semicontinuous reading of 1 Corinthians is limited to the seasons of Epiphany across the three-year cycle. Thus, while the congregation will return to 2 Corinthians after Pentecost, they will not return to 1 Corinthians until January of the following year. This means that each Epiphany, when preaching from

1 Corinthians, the congregation will need to be reintroduced to the significant social, theological, and ecclesiological struggles facing the church at Corinth. (See the introductory comments on 1 Corinthians in the discussion of the epistle readings for the Season after Epiphany, Year A, on pp. 42–43.) Certainly this can and should be done as part of the sermons themselves by referring to, citing, and quoting from early and later parts of the letter. But, while the pastor preaches through the middle chapters, individuals and groups within the congregation should be invited to read through and study the whole of 1 Corinthians outside of worship—historically, sociologically, and theologically contextualizing what they are reading.

STRATEGY 3—The remaining strategies are thematic in nature. First among these is the central Epiphany theme of *revelation.* In today's world, when churchgoers hear the word revelation, they most likely think of the last book of the canon. They have not been asked often enough to think about the traditional theological claim that God is unknowable by our own efforts and that God has revealed whatever we know of God. To spend a season, which flows forth from the celebration of the revelation of God-in-Christ to the magi, helping the church remember some of the ways we claim God has gone about revealing aspects of God's character—for example, revealing God's self in the person and ministry of Jesus Christ or God's will through those proclaiming the faith—would be a significant contribution to the congregation's thinking through issues of Christian epistemology. This theme is prevalent in the lections for the season, thus inviting the preaching to explore the issue of revelation from many different perspectives.

> **Epiphany 1 (Baptism of the Lord):** Mark 1:4–11, the heavenly voice (along with the cloud and the descent of the Spirit) reveals to Jesus that he is God's Son.
>
> **OR:** Psalm 29, the voice of the Lord reveals itself in the thunderstorm.
>
> **OR:** Acts 19:1–7, after being baptized in the name of Jesus, some disciples begin speaking in tongues and prophesying.
>
> **Epiphany 2:** John 1:43–51, Jesus is the fulfillment of scripture and promises that he will reveal heaven (i.e., God) to those who follow him.

OR: 1 Samuel 3:1–10 (11–20), the Lord speaks to Samuel for the first time.

Epiphany 3: Mark 1:14–20, Jesus proclaims the revelation of God's reign.

OR: Jonah 3:1–5, 10, Jonah proclaims God's judgment.

Epiphany 4: Mark 1:21–28, the demons reveal Jesus' identity as the Holy One of God, but Jesus silences them in order to control his self-revelation.

Epiphany 5: Mark 1:29–39, the demons again reveal Jesus' identity as the Holy One of God, but Jesus silences them.

OR: Isaiah 40:21–31, God makes God's self known in creation.

Epiphany 6: Mark 1:40–45, after healing the man with a skin disease, Jesus instructs the man to tell no one in order to control his self-revelation, but the man does not obey.

OR: 2 Kings 5:1–14, the healing of Naaman reveals that there is a prophet in Israel, implying God is in Israel.

Epiphany 7: Mark 2:1–12, Jesus heals a paralytic in order to reveal that he has the authority to forgive sins.

OR: Isaiah 43:18–25, God reveals a new beginning for Israel, a beginning rooted in forgiveness.

Epiphany 8: Psalm 103:1–13, 22, praises God for God's mercy and connects it with the revelation of God's ways to Moses.

Last Sunday after Epiphany (Transfiguration): Mark 9:2–9, the heavenly voice (along with the cloud and the transfigured appearance itself) reveals Jesus' glory as God's Son.

OR: Psalm 50:1–6, celebration of God's summoning voice.

OR: 2 Corinthians 4:3–6, contrasts the gospel being veiled to unbelievers and the proclamation of Christ as the light shining out in darkness.

STRATEGY 4—A second thematic approach, for part of the season, would be to focus on *healing.* Although this theme does not stretch over the course of the whole season, it is (as mentioned above) a major focus of the Markan readings.

Epiphany 4: Mark 1:21–28, Jesus heals a man who is possessed by an unclean spirit—a healing declared to be a "new teaching."

Epiphany 5: Mark 1:29–39, Jesus heals Simon's mother-in-law and many others, and then itinerates to proclaim and cast out demons in neighboring towns.

OR: Psalm 147:1–11, 20c, a song of praise that speaks of God's restoration of Israel in terms of healing the brokenhearted and binding up wounds.

Epiphany 6: 2 Kings 5:1–14, Naaman desires pomp and circumstance, but Elisha offers healing of his skin disease with simple washing.

OR: Mark 1:40–45, Jesus heals a man with skin disease, thus allowing him to reenter society.

OR: Psalm 30, celebrates God's healing power.

Epiphany 7: Mark 2:1–12, Jesus forgives and heals a paralytic.

OR: Psalm 41, a prayer asking for divine healing.

Epiphany 8: Mark 2:13–22, Jesus defends his practice of eating with tax collectors and sinners with the metaphor of those who are sick needing a physician, not those who are well.

OR: Psalm 103:1–13, 22, a song of praise from one who has experienced healing from God.

STRATEGY 5—A third theme worth exploring for part of the season is that of *calling*. What does it mean to be called to a life of faith, a life of discipleship, to the priesthood of all believers?

Epiphany 1: Mark 1:4–11, Mark's version of the story of Jesus' baptism functions as a call narrative in contrast to the way it functions in the other gospels. Mark has no infancy narrative declaring Jesus' status at birth and in this scene the voice speaks to Jesus alone, "adopting" Jesus as God's Son.

Epiphany 2: John 1:43–51, the calling of Philip and Nathanael. The Synoptics have no parallel to this story. Especially intriguing for preaching the theme of calling cumulatively is the role Philip plays in the calling of Nathanael.

OR: 1 Samuel 3:1–10 (11–20), the story of God speaking to Samuel on the floor of the Shiloh temple serves as Samuel's prophetic call.

Epiphany 3: Mark 1:14–20, Mark's version of the call of the first disciples presents the call as Jesus' first specific act of ministry.

OR: Jonah 3:1–5, 10, the whole of the Jonah narrative raises issues of responding to God's call. While this lection is not part of the narrative section portraying God's initial call, Jonah fleeing from that call and God pulling him back to that vocation do grow out of that section. Preachers can and should present that dynamic of call as the backdrop for this lesson.

Epiphany 4: Deuteronomy 18:15–20, a speech by Moses in which he prophesies that God will call ("raise up") Joshua to succeed him. Of special interest for this preaching strategy is Moses' description of the accountability that comes with accepting the call to be a prophet.

Epiphany 5: 1 Corinthians 9:16–23, while this passage plays a different role in the context of Paul's argument than simply unpacking an element of his sense of apostolic vocation, it does, nevertheless, do that as well. The apostle's description of his vocation as obligation instead of choice is a compelling sermonic topic.

OR: Mark 1:29–39, Jesus speaks of his sense of vocation when he withdraws from the crowds who surround him so that he can go proclaim his gospel to other towns and says, "For that is what I came out to do."

Epiphany 8: Mark 2:13–22, Jesus calls Levi the tax collector to follow him and then must defend his ministry of calling sinners into discipleship.

OR: Hosea 2:14–20, using the metaphor of marriage, the prophet speaks of calling Israel into a covenantal relationship characterized by righteousness, justice, steadfast love, mercy, and faithfulness.

Transfiguration: 2 Kings 2:1–12, although not Elisha's initial call (see 1 Kings 19:19–21), this scene does represent the passing of the mantle from one generation to the next (especially if reading through v. 14 where Elisha picks up and uses Elijah's prophetic mantle in the same way Elijah had).

LENT and HOLY WEEK

Year B

(See pp. 13–17 for an overview of the three-dimensional character of the Revised Common Lectionary's approach to Lent.)

Lectionary Readings

	FIRST TESTAMENT	PSALTER	EPISTLE	GOSPEL
ASH WEDNESDAY				
Ash Wed. (abc)	Joel 2:1–2, 12–17 Blow the trumpet—call to repentance	51:1–17 Penitential prayer, confessing sin and asking forgiveness	2 Cor. 5:20b—6:10 Ambassadors of Christ commended in every way	Mt. 6:1–6, 16–21 Practice your righteousness
SUNDAYS IN LENT				
Lent 1	Gen. 9:8–17 God's covenant (rainbow) with Noah	25:1–10 Do not let me be put to shame; forgive my transgressions	1 Pet. 3:18–22 Crucified Christ proclaimed to spirits in prison—baptism as an appeal to God for a good conscience	Mk. 1:9–15 Baptism & Temptation
Lent 2	Gen. 17:1–7, 15–16 God's covenant with Abram (Abraham) and Sarai (Sarah)	22:23–31 All the ends of the earth shall remember and turn to the LORD	Rom. 4:13–25 The promise came to Abraham through the righteousness of faith	Mk. 8:31–38 First passion prediction and call to self-denial/discipleship
Lent 3	Ex. 20:1–17 Decalogue	19 The law of the LORD is perfect	1 Cor. 1:18–25 The message about the cross is foolishness	Jn. 2:13–22 Cleansing the temple
Lent 4	Num. 21:4–9 Moses' bronze serpent	107:1–3, 17–22 Give thanks to the LORD for God is good	Eph. 2:1–10 By grace you have been saved through faith	Jn. 3:14–21 As Moses lifted up the serpent, so must the Son of Man be lifted up
Lent 5	Jer. 31:31–34 New covenant written on the heart	51:1–12 Penitential prayer, confessing sin and asking forgiveness OR 119:9–16 Young people keep their way pure by guarding it according to your word.	Heb. 5:5–10 High priest of Melchizedek: Jesus prayed with loud cries and tears	Jn. 12:20–33 The hour has come for the Son of Man to be glorified…My soul is troubled

HOLY WEEK				
Palm Passion	Isa. 50:4–9a (abc) Suffering Servant	118:1–2, 19–29 (abc) Hallel Psalm: Festal procession with branches 31:9–16 (abc) Lament in the face of bodily suffering	Phil. 2:5-11 (abc) Christ Hymn	Mk. 11:1–11 Triumphant entry OR Jn. 12:12–16 Triumphant entry Mk. 14:1–15:47 Last Supper–Burial
Holy Mon. (abc)	Isa. 42:1–9 Suffering Servant	36:5–11 God's steadfast love	Heb. 9:11–15 Christ's blood of the new covenant	Jn. 12:1–11 Mary anoints Jesus; leaders seek his & Lazarus' death
Holy Tue. (abc)	Isa. 49:1–7 Suffering Servant	71:1–14 Prayer for deliverance from enemies	1 Cor. 1:18–31 Foolishness of Christ crucified	Jn. 12:20–36 Jesus withdraws from public min- istry & announces the hour of his glorification has arrived
Holy Wed. (abc)	Isa. 50:4–9a Suffering Servant	70 Prayer for deliverance from enemies	Heb. 12:1–3 Jesus, pioneer & perfecter of faith thru endurance of cross	Jn. 13:21–32 Jesus predicts Judas' betrayal
Holy Th. (abc)	Ex. 12:1–4 (5–10) 11–14 First Passover	116:1–2, 12–19 Thanksgiving-cup of salvation	1 Cor. 11:23–26 Institution of Lord's supper	Jn. 13:1–17, 31b–35 New command- ment–footwashing
Good Fri. (abc)	Isa. 52:13—53:12 Suffering Servant	22 Lament: My God, my God...	Heb. 10:16–25 Blood of Jesus	Jn. 18:1—19:42 Arrest–Burial
Holy Sat.	Job 14:1–14 Lament concern- ing human mortality OR Lam. 3:1–9, 19–24 Suffering God's wrath	31:1–4, 15–16 Petition for refuge	1 Pet. 4:1–8 Prepare to suffer in the flesh as Christ did	Mt. 27:57–66 Jesus' burial OR Jn. 19:38–42 Jesus' burial

Cumulative Preaching Strategies

When developing cumulative preaching strategies for Lent, one must take into account a few factors. First, the season begins on Ash Wednesday, for which the Revised Common Lectionary offers the same readings every year. Ash Wednesday creates a strong depth dimension defining the liturgical season in the same manner every year by focusing on themes of mortality, confession, repentance, and Christian disciplines. Beyond this general emphasis, the lessons for Ash Wednesday, however, do not lead into the lections that follow throughout the rest of the season. Therefore the lections for Ash Wednesday should not be strongly considered when developing a cumulative preaching strategy for Lent.

Second, the liturgical focus of the First Sunday in Lent every year is the temptation of Jesus in the wilderness, based on the Synoptic Gospel of the year. This lection is offered as a rationale for the forty-day length of the season as well as to reinforce the Lenten practices of fasting and prayer. Again, this lectionary pattern serves the depth dimension of the three-year liturgical cycle more than the height dimension. Thus the connection between Lent 1 and the following Sundays in Lent, especially in terms of the Gospel readings, may be weak.

Third, the season concludes by Holy Week, which begins on Palm/Passion Sunday and continues through Holy Saturday. In some sense, Holy Week (leading to the Easter Vigil on Saturday night or to Easter Sunday) represents a season in and of itself (this is especially true of the Easter Triduum—Holy Thursday, Good Friday, Easter). However, most Protestant congregations worship only on Holy Thursday and/or Good Friday in between Palm/Passion Sunday and Easter Sunday.

In sum, preachers should think of Ash Wednesday (and possibly Lent 1) and Holy Week as bookends to the season that work cumulatively in terms of their annual recurrence, and focus primarily on Lent 1–5 (or Lent 2–5) in developing a cumulative preaching strategy that deals with the height dimension. What follows, therefore, are separate potential strategies for the Sundays in Lent and for Holy Week.

For the Sundays in Lent B

The first two strategies proposed deal with the lections as ordered by the lectionary itself, while the ones that follow those two offer thematic options:

STRATEGY 1—During Lent the Lectionary for Mass structured the First Testament lections according to a salvation history schema: Lent 1—origins; Lent 2—Abraham; Lent 3—exodus; Lent 4—nation;

Lent 5—eschatological hope. The Revised Common Lectionary, for the most part, follows this schema. However, in Year B the reading for Lent 4 has been changed to support the Gospel lection's enigmatic reference to Moses lifting up the bronze snake, resulting in two Sundays taken from the exodus and none dealing with the nation. Nevertheless, the salvation history schema is still present and useful for cumulative preaching.

Moreover, the First Testament lections during Lent have a strong covenantal thematic focus, which also spills over into the Psalter readings at times.

Lent 1: Origins (Gen. 9:8–17, God's covenant with Noah).

Lent 2: Abraham (Gen. 17:1–7, 15–16, reiteration of God's covenant with Abram and Sarai, changing their names to Abraham and Sarah).

Lent 3–4: Exodus (Ex. 20:1–17, the Decalogue, which serves as the cornerstone of the covenant established with the Israelites in the wilderness; and Num. 21:4–9, Moses lifting up the bronze serpent to ward off the effects of poisonous serpents in the encampment).

Lent 5: Eschatological hope (Jer. 31:31–34, the prophet's vision of God making a new postexilic covenant that will be written on the people's hearts).

To preach this schema in continuity with the pattern established in Year A, one may wish to bring the Lectionary for Mass reading back into the mix for Lent 4. It is 2 Chronicles 36:14–23. This passage concludes the chronicler's narrative by speaking of the exile and then of Cyrus following God's directive to rebuild the Jerusalem temple. The text specifically refers to Jeremiah and serves well to lead into the lection from Jeremiah 31 for Lent 5.

STRATEGY 2—Even though the Revised Common Lectionary designates a psalm or portion of a psalm for every Sunday of the three-year lectionary cycle, preachers give the Psalter short shrift. Indeed, the lectionary use of the Psalms is not directed toward homiletical goals. Instead, they are chosen as responses to the First Testament reading. But it would be a shame if the Psalms receive no attention in the pulpit. Lent is an ideal time to correct this deficiency. With Lent's emphasis on the discipline of prayer, a congregation will be well served by a series of sermons focusing on *praying the psalms* offered by the Revised Common Lectionary for the season. In Year B, the psalms chosen for Lent overlap with themes of God's trustworthiness and the call to adhere to God's word/teachings. Unlike the Psalter readings for Year A, most of those chosen for Year B do not include the whole psalm. Preachers may wish to preach on the whole psalm nevertheless; or they may focus on the assigned passage but invite the congregation to study and pray the whole psalm during the week as part of their Lenten discipline.

STRATEGY 3—The Gospel and Epistle lections for Lent focus, in a variety of ways, on interpreting *the death of Jesus.* These different interpretations can serve a congregation well as it prepares for Holy Week and Easter.

Lent 1: 1 Peter 3:18–22 interprets Jesus as suffering once-for-all for the sins of the unrighteous. This is especially evident in the claim that while dead in the flesh but alive in the spirit, Jesus preached the good news to those who died in the days of Noah.

Lent 2: Mark 8:31–38 is Jesus' first passion prediction in Mark. According to Mark, each time Jesus predicts his passion, his disciples respond inappropriately. Here that dynamic is found in Peter's attempt to rebuke Jesus, who responds to the rebuke by claiming that his death has radical implications for discipleship.

OR: Romans 4:13–25 is an exegetical approach to unpacking the meaning of justification by faith. Paul says that as God "reckoned" to Abraham righteousness, so through Christ, who was handed over to death for our trespasses, will it be reckoned to us.

Lent 3: 1 Corinthians 1:18–25 is part of much longer passage in which Paul defends the foolishness of his cross-centered gospel.

OR: John 2:13–22 tells of Jesus "cleansing the temple." But when interpreting the act for the religious authorities, Jesus refers to the destruction and rebuilding of the temple as a metaphor for his death and resurrection.

Lent 4: John 3:14–21 opens with a reference to the lifting up of the Son of Man, i.e., of Jesus' crucifixion. This lection is part of a much longer dialogue between Jesus and Nicodemus. A preacher would do well to consider the larger context to offer a stronger reading of 3:16 than is often proffered in the pulpit (or in football stadiums) and to help the congregation better understand John's theology of the cross.

Lent 5: Hebrews 5:5–10 offers an interpretation of Jesus' suffering as that which perfected him and through which he became the source of salvation.

OR: John 12:20–33 is the point at which Jesus turns from his public ministry to his private conversations with his disciples before his death. Setting the tone for much of that private discourse, this final public statement describes Jesus' imminent death in a number of different ways.

STRATEGY 4—Since Lent leads into the remembrance and celebration of Christ's crucifixion and resurrection, it is not surprising that the lections for the season have strong soteriological tones. A number of texts deal with the *forgiveness of sins.* This strategy allows for a connection between the lections for Ash Wednesday and those for the Sundays that follow.

Ash Wednesday: Joel 2:1—2, 12–17 is a call to repent and return to the Lord who is gracious.

OR: Psalm 51:1–17 is a penitential prayer in which the psalmist seeks forgiveness.

OR: 2 Corinthians 5:20b—6:10 is Paul's plea that his readers seek reconciliation with God.

Lent 1: 1 Peter 3:18–22 speaks of Christ's suffering for sins as bringing us to God and goes on to declare how that message was taken by the crucified Christ to the spirits in prison.

OR: Psalm 25:1–10 is a prayer seeking deliverance from sin, which will come in the form of instruction in God's way.

OR: Genesis 9:8–17 is the story of the covenant that follows the Deluge. While the text does not refer to forgiveness of sins explicitly, the reasons for God flooding the earth in the first place are implied, and God's resolve to never destroy the earth again in the same manner points to divine mercy.

Lent 2: Romans 4:13–25 is a key passage in Paul's theological argument. Here he interprets what he means by justification in light of the biblical example of Abraham.

Lent 3: While 1 Corinthians 1:18–25 does not speak explicitly of forgiveness of sins, it certainly deals with the issue of salvation. The passage opens with a description of believers as those "being saved"; and, if the passage is extended to the end of chapter 1, Christ is described as our wisdom, righteousness, sanctification, and redemption.

OR: Psalm 19 is a celebration of creation and torah. Torah is described as that which revives the soul and can correct our errors.

Lent 4: Ephesians 2:1–10 speaks of the radical change that came with the conversion of the Gentile readers, a change from death through sin to life in Christ.

OR: In John 3:14–21 Jesus speaks of God sending the Son to save the world. Placed in the context of the longer dialogue with Nicodemus in which Jesus describes being born from above, this can be a powerful Lenten text from which to preach.

OR: Psalm 107:1–3, 17–22 is a small portion of a lengthy prayer for deliverance. In the prayer, illness and sin are seen as related, and the Lord saves from both.

Lent 5: Hebrews 5:5–10 is part of a longer passage (4:14—5:10) that speaks of Christ as the high priest who can sympathize with our sinfulness because Christ has been tempted as we are. As such, through his self-sacrifice, Christ becomes the source of eternal salvation.

OR: Jeremiah 31:31–34 offers a vision of a new covenant that need not be taught because it will be written on human hearts, a covenant established by God forgiving and forgetting the sins of the people.

OR: Psalm 51:1–12 can be read on this day if it was not read on Ash Wednesday, or it can be read again (and serve as the biblical basis for the sermon) to emphasize the penitentiary nature of Lent.

OR: Psalm 119:9–16, a short portion of the longest psalm in the Bible, which speaks of God's word as protection against sin.

For Holy Week, Year B

Many Protestant congregations do not have Holy Week services on the weekdays of Holy Week, or only have services on Holy/ Maundy Thursday and/or Good Friday. Moreover, congregations that do have services throughout the week may well not have a service on Holy Saturday due to celebrating the Easter Vigil on Saturday night. Because of these varying practices it is difficult, and likely not helpful, to offer preaching strategies to be used for the entire week. Nevertheless, noting some of the broad cumulative patterns exhibited during the week will help preachers adapt them to whatever liturgical practices their congregations follow.

STRATEGY 1—The first pattern concerns the *juxtaposition of John and Mark's versions* of the Jerusalem narratives. Beginning with Palm/Passion Sunday, all of the lectionary readings for Holy Week are the same for all three years of the lectionary cycle, with the exception of the Gospel lections for Palm/Passion Sunday. The Gospel readings for the Liturgy of the Palm and the Liturgy of the Passion come from the Synoptic Gospel for the year. The gospel texts for the rest of Holy Week proceed from John. Thus in Year B, preachers who have been preaching through the gospel of John for the last three Sundays in Lent will be able to return to the lengthy Jerusalem narrative from Mark on Palm/Passion Sunday before preaching on portions of the passion narrative in John through the week. This allows the congregation to experience two different perspectives on Jesus' suffering and death.

STRATEGY 2—The *Suffering Servant* oracles from Isaiah dominate the First Testament lections. While preachers must avoid eisegetical errors of the past in which the church read these oracles as predictions about Christ, they can nevertheless be used to discuss the complex and confusing relation of vicarious suffering and redemption that is reiterated throughout much of the Judeo-Christian tradition and which is central to the Christ Event.

STRATEGY 3—In spite of the fact that the *Epistle readings* are not drawn from the same author or school and are subordinate to the Gospel lections for the week, they have some cohesion. They all interpret the death of Jesus from different theological perspectives and by using a range of metaphors. Although the liturgical emphasis for the week is on the story of Jesus' passion, preaching through various interpretations of his death has much homiletical potential.

EASTER

Year B

(See pp. 17–21 for an overview of the three-dimensional character of the Revised Common Lectionary's approach to Easter.)

Lectionary Readings

	FIRST TESTAMENT	PSALTER	EPISTLE	GOSPEL
Easter Day	Acts 10:34–43 (abc) Peter's sermon to Cornelius…"but God raised him on the third day"	118:1–2, 14–24 (abc) Rejoicing in God's providence: "I shall not die, but I shall live,…but he did not give me over to death"	1 Cor. 15:1–11 The tradition of Jesus' resurrection appearances	Jn. 20:1–18 (abc) Empty tomb OR Mk. 16:1–8 Empty tomb
Easter Evening (abc)	Isa. 25:6–9 Salvation of the LORD: will wipe away tears	114 Creation trembles at God's power exhibited in the exodus	1 Cor. 5:6b–8 Clean out the old yeast	Lk. 24:13–49 Emmaus & appearance to disciples
Easter 2	Acts 4:32–35 Church holding everything in common	133 How very good and pleasant it is when kindred live together in unity	1 Jn. 1:1—2:2 We declare what we have heard, seen, touched	Jn. 20:19–31 Resurrected Jesus breathes the Spirit on disciples; doubting Thomas
Easter 3	Acts 3:12–19 Peter's sermon after healing the paralytic: God did this	4 For you alone, O LORD, make me lie down in safety	1 Jn. 3:1–7 We are God's children now; what we will be has not yet been revealed	Lk. 24:36b–48 Resurrected Jesus teaches disciples scripture
Easter 4 Good Shepherd	Acts 4:5–12 Peter's defense before the Jewish council	23 The LORD is my shepherd	1 Jn. 3:16–24 We ought to lay down our lives for one another	Jn. 10:11–18 The good shepherd lays down his life for the sheep
Easter 5	Acts 8:26–40 Philip & the Ethiopian eunuch	22:25–31 Dominion belongs to the LORD	1 Jn. 4:7–21 Let us love one another, because love is from God	Jn. 15:1–8 I am the vine
Easter 6	Acts 10:44–48 The Spirit comes upon Cornelius' household	98 O sing to the LORD a new song	1 Jn. 5:1–6 By this we know that we love the children of God, when we love God and obey his commandments	Jn. 15:9–17 Love one another as I have loved you

Ascension (abc)	Acts 1:1–11 Opening of Acts: Ascension	47 The Lᴏʀᴅ is king		Eph. 1:15–23 God seated Christ at the right hand in the heavenly places	Lk. 24:44–53 Ending of Luke: Ascension
Easter 7	Acts 1:15—17, 21–26 Peter declares the need to replace Judas	1 Happy are those who do not follow the advice of the wicked		1 Jn. 5:9–13 This is the testimony: God gave us eternal life, and this life is in his Son	Jn. 17:6–19 Jesus' prayer for his disciples
Pentecost	Acts 2:1–21 (abc) Giving of Holy Spirit and Peter's Pentecost sermon	104:24–34, 35b (abc) O Lᴏʀᴅ, the earth is full of your creatures—when you send forth your Spirit		Rom. 8:22–27 We who have the first fruits of the Spirit, groan inwardly while we wait for adoption	Jn. 15:26–27; 16:4b–15 The coming of the Advocate

Cumulative Preaching Strategies

As noted in the overview of the Revised Common Lectionary's approach to Easter in the Introduction, multiple, competing cumulative patterns are at play in the choices of lections for this season that complicate developing cumulative preaching strategies. These patterns are further complicated by the fact that three holy days—Easter, Ascension, and Pentecost—occur within the season and give it its unique character. Indeed, Easter and Pentecost (or, in some sense, Easter on the one hand and Ascension/Pentecost on the other hand) serve as bookends to the season. These different dynamics lead to cumulative preaching strategies that can be combined or divided up in different ways to work through the season.

Easter Sunday

STRATEGY 1—On Easter Sunday, preachers will almost surely preach (and usually should preach) on the *Gospel lection.* The Epistle reading is from 1 Corinthians 15 and its focus on the tradition of resurrection appearances certainly supplies fitting material for homiletical consideration on this holy day. In Acts 10:34–43, Peter preaches the resurrection to a Gentile household—also a fitting text for the day. But Easter Sunday is the day people come to church to hear the story they know by heart, the story of the empty tomb.

However, lectionary preachers who follow this traditional route must still choose between Mark 16:1–8 and John 20:1–18. Choosing the Markan passage allows the preacher to connect the Easter sermon to the extended reading from Mark on Passion/Palm Sunday and to the "Messianic Secret" highlighted on the Sundays after Epiphany. Choosing John 20, on the other hand, allows preachers to connect with Johannine themes that they may have explored while preaching the Gospel lections during the Sundays in Lent or Holy Week or that they will explore on Easter 2 and 4–7.

Easter Sunday, Ascension, Pentecost

STRATEGY 2—The *three holy days* during Eastertide provide much of the continuity of the season by drawing a conclusion to the liturgical half of the year. Although the celebrations are spaced according to Lukan narrative chronology (forty days from Easter Sunday to Ascension and ten more days to Pentecost), they express different dimensions of the same theological reality and form a cumulative whole. That is, they call the church to remember that its very being rests upon the paradox of Christ's exaltation (transcendence) and the divine spiritual presence (immanence). Regardless of which texts preachers focus their sermons on for the rest of the season, preaching on the empty tomb in the Gospel lection and on the ascension and gift of the Spirit in Acts can and should give cohesion to the season as a whole. For churches that do not gather to celebrate Ascension on Thursday, Ascension can (and perhaps should) be celebrated on Easter 7. This shift creates a sense of the season having bookends: Easter Sunday at the start and Ascension/Pentecost at the end.

Gospel Lections in Eastertide

STRATEGY 3—As noted in the Introduction, Eastertide offers three thematic movements that are focused by the *Gospel lections.* These movements can serve to focus the preacher's attention. The first three Sundays—Easter Sunday through Easter 3—deal with *resurrection appearances.* Each of these, especially if one chooses to preach from the Markan text on Easter Sunday, offers a different perspective on and interpretation of the resurrection. On Easter Sunday, the focus is the initial news of the empty tomb and the failed response to the news (Mk. 16:1–8); on Easter 2, the focus is on Jesus giving the Spirit to his disciples and of Jesus revealing himself to Thomas (Jn. 20:19–31); and on Easter 3 the focus is on the story of Jesus appearing to the disciples and interpreting his death and resurrection as the fulfillment of the scriptures (Lk. 24:36b–48).

Easter 4 divides the season in half. It is *Good Shepherd Sunday,* and the Gospel reading is always drawn from the mixture of shepherding metaphors found in John 10. In Year B, the reading comes from a portion in which Jesus actually refers to himself as the "good shepherd" who lays his life down for his sheep (10:11–18). (Note also the shepherd language in Psalm 23 and the language of laying one's life down in 1 John 3.)

Gospel lections for Easter 5–7 proceed from *the Johannine farewell discourse.* As noted earlier, while it may, at first glance, seem odd to preach from texts in which Jesus prepares his disciples for his departure during Eastertide, two things are important to recognize. First, when John speaks of Jesus' departure or glorification he is speaking of the whole of Jesus' crucifixion, resurrection, and exaltation. Thus in this discourse, Jesus interprets not only his pending death, but also his being raised from the dead. Second, the theme of preparing for Jesus' departure fits the latter part of Eastertide in terms of preparing for Ascension. In the Gospel lessons for Year B, the thematic focus is on the intimate relationship between God and Jesus, and thus between God and Jesus on the one hand and the disciples on the other.

Semicontinuous Readings

STRATEGY 4—As noted in the overview, during Eastertide the Revised Common Lectionary substitutes readings from *Acts of the Apostles* for the First Testament lection. Broadly speaking, by examining narrative moments in the life of the early church that flowed out of the resurrection and gift of the Holy Spirit, a congregation prepares for the celebration of Pentecost that closes liturgical time before Ordinary Time begins.

However, when preachers first glance at the Acts readings for Eastertide, Year B, they will likely experience some level of frustration. Certainly the lectionary committee could have made choices that were better connected together. Nevertheless, this series of texts has homiletical potential. The pattern of pairing lessons from Acts can be discovered and used for cumulative effect:

Easter 1–2—Peter preaches the resurrection to Cornelius' household (10:34–43) and the early church gathers around the apostles' witness of the resurrection (4:32–35).

Easter 3–4—After Peter and John heal a crippled beggar at the temple, Peter preaches the resurrection to the crowd of witnesses (3:12–19) and to the religious authorities who arrest them (4:5–12).

Easter 5–6—The Holy Spirit is connected with baptism in two different ways in the stories of Philip preaching to the Ethiopian eunuch (8:26–40) and of Peter preaching to Cornelius' household (10:44–48; this reading follows immediately after the Acts lesson for Easter Sunday).

Ascension & Easter 7—The story of Jesus' departure (1:1–11) and the disciples replacing Judas afterward (1:15—17, 21–26).

STRATEGY 5—The Epistle lections for Eastertide come from *1 John.* This is an appropriate choice for the season of Easter given that most scholars think the anonymous essay or sermon (1 John is not actually a letter) was written near the end of the first or the beginning of the second century c.e. in response to a group splitting from the church over the issue of whether Jesus was truly human or simply a spirit (i.e., some form of Docetism). The story of Jesus' death and resurrection mean something quite different if Jesus' humanity (i.e., the Incarnation) is rejected. The author of 1 John opposes the splinter group and calls them "antichrists" and "liars" as well as accusing them of failing to keep the commandment to love one another. Of course, the author is not primarily addressing the antichrists but those whom he wants not to be influenced by the antichrists' false teachings, those whom he urges to remain faithful to the traditions they were originally taught.

The problem with the lectionary choices for Eastertide, however, is that none of them highlight this church schism. Instead the commandment to love one another (echoing the new commandment in the Gospel of John) is the primary focus of the lections. This is, indeed, a central theme for 1 John, but it needs to be understood in the original historical and theological context of the essay before being applied analogously to our contemporary circumstances. The preacher, therefore, must name the conflict behind 1 John for the congregation if preaching the lections cumulatively and interpreting the communal ethic and the references to sin are to be understood fully.

Thematic Approaches

Because Eastertide is thematically divided in half by the manner in which the Gospel lections focus the season, it is difficult to find thematic emphases that stretch across the whole season.

STRATEGY 6—One approach to preaching cumulatively, therefore, is simply to make use of that thematic division. For the first half of the season, focus on the theme that grows out of the beginning of the season *(resurrection)*, and for the second half, focus on the theme that leans toward the end of the season *(Holy Spirit)*.

RESURRECTION

Easter 1: Both of the Gospel choices (Mk. 16:1–8; Jn. 20:1–18) narrate the story of the women finding the empty tomb.

OR: In 1 Corinthian 15:1–11, Paul reminds the church of the tradition of Jesus' resurrection appearances in a manner that contradicts the stories in the gospels.

OR: Peter's sermon in Acts 10:34–43, like all of the sermons in Acts, is anchored to a witness to the resurrection.

OR: Psalm 118:1–2, 14–24 is an excerpt of a psalm of thanksgiving in which an individual faithfully proclaims, "I shall not die, but I shall live" (v. 17).

Easter 2: The reading from John 20:19–31 presents the resurrected Jesus appearing to the majority of the disciples on Easter evening and to Thomas a week later.

OR: The Lukan summary in Acts 4:32–35 presents the early church as gathered around the apostolic witness to the resurrection.

Easter 3: Luke's version of Easter evening (24:36b–48) tells of the resurrected Jesus' appearance to the crowd of disciples after he had appeared to the two on the way to Emmaus. Now he offers them peace, proves he is not a ghost, and teaches them how the resurrection fulfills scripture.

OR: In Acts 3:12–19, Peter preaches after the healing of the crippled beggar. In the sermon, Luke presents the apostle as using the formulaic expression in Acts, You killed Jesus, and God raised him from the dead.

Easter 4: Acts 4:5–12 recounts Peter's defense after being arrested for the healing and sermon referred to in the previous week's lesson from Acts. The same formula is used again: "Jesus Christ of Nazareth, whom you crucified, whom God raised from the dead." For Luke, this message is clearly at the center of the church's proclamation.

HOLY SPIRIT

Easter 4: As the theme of resurrection becomes less prominent on Good Shepherd Sunday, the theme of the Holy Spirit begins to appear. In the passage from 1 John 3:16–24, the author claims that we know Jesus abides in us by the Spirit he has given us.

Easter 5: Acts prefigures later church debates concerning the relation of baptism and reception of the Holy Spirit. It is clear that Luke finds a significant connection between the two, but the exact nature of that connection is somewhat vague. For instance, in Acts 8:4–24, Philip preaches, heals, and baptizes in Samaria, but the apostles must follow to lay on hands so that converts can receive the Spirit. In an odd contrast, our lection for today (8:26–40) presents Philip as converting and baptizing an Ethiopian eunuch. Then Philip is caught up in the Spirit and carried away.

OR: Characteristic of 1 John is a literary technique of repeating themes in different contexts to advance different claims. In the passage from 1 John 4:7–21, we read the same line we highlighted from 1 John 3:16–24 for the previous week—we know that we abide in Christ and Christ in us because Christ has given us the Spirit.

Easter 6: As with last week's reading from Acts 8:26–40, the lesson from Acts 10:44–48 connects baptism and the gift of the Holy Spirit. Here, however, Peter baptizes the Gentile converts (see the Acts lesson for Easter Sunday) in response to the fact that they have already received the Spirit.

OR: 1 John 5:1–6 ends with a reference to the Spirit. The text presents the Spirit as confirming (i.e., testifying to) the author's claim about Jesus Christ coming by water and the blood. It is by this Spirit, therefore, that those who believe in Christ conquer the world.

Ascension: In Acts 1:1–11, even as Jesus is leaving, he instructs the disciples to remain in Jerusalem to receive the promise from God, which is the Holy Spirit.

OR: Luke 24:44–53 offers a different version of the ascension than Luke's second narrative. Nevertheless, it presents the same view of Jesus instructing the disciples to wait in Jerusalem for the gift of the Holy Spirit.

Easter 7: Acts 1:15–17, 21–26 follows the story of the ascension and tells of the disciples choosing a replacement for Judas. In formulaic fashion, Peter speaks of the Holy Spirit working through David (i.e., the Psalter) to foretell Judas' demise.

Pentecost: Acts 2:1–21 is Luke's story of the gift of the Spirit to the church.

OR: The Gospel lection actually involves two passages from Jesus' farewell discourse (John 15:26–27; 16:4b–15) in which he foretells of the coming of the *Paraclete.*

OR: In Romans 8:22–27, Paul speaks eschatologically of the Spirit using the harvest metaphor of "first fruits," which serve as a sign of the full harvest to come. The already/not yet of Christian existence is never expressed more poignantly than when Paul speaks of our continued human suffering: "We do not know how to pray as we ought, but that very Spirit intercedes with sighs too deep for words."

OR: The portion taken from Psalm 104 read every year on Pentecost (vv. 24–34, 35b) speaks of God creating and renewing creation through God's Spirit.

STRATEGY 7—A final theme for Easter B that holds some promise for cumulative preaching is that of ***community.*** Ecclesiological sermons that look at the church as the post-resurrection community of the faithful have significance beyond the individualized way many hear the Easter proclamation in terms of individual persons of faith being delivered from death.

As noted above under strategy 5, 1 John is written to undergird a church from which some (whom the author considers antichrists) have split. Thus all of the lections from 1 John relate to this theme. The theme is most pronounced when the author uses familial metaphors to refer to the community's inner relationships and relationship with God and when the author reminds the readers of the command to love one another.

The theme of community also lies behind the Johannine readings for Easter 5–7. Taken from Jesus' farewell discourse, these Gospel lections present Jesus as shaping the post-glorification (passion, resurrection, exaltation) church.

Likewise, a number of the readings from Acts deal with community existence: inclusion of Gentiles (Easter 1 and 6), the community's approach to common possessions in response to the proclamation of the resurrection (Easter 2), and of course the spiritual birth of the church (Pentecost).

Finally, on Easter 2, Psalm 133 (which serves as a response to the summary in Acts 4) offers a beautiful image of community as one anointed.

ORDINARY TIME

Year B

(See pp. 21–23 for an overview of the three-dimensional character of the Revised Common Lectionary's approach to the Season after Pentecost.)

Lectionary Readings

	FIRST TESTAMENT	PSALTER	EPISTLE	GOSPEL
Trinity Sun.	Isa. 6:1–8 Calling of Isaiah: heavenly court	29 Ascribe to the LORD, O heavenly beings: voice of God in the thunderstorm	Rom. 8:12–17 When we call Abba, it is by the Spirit that we testify to our adoption, and being heirs with Christ	Jn. 3:1–17 Nicodemus: born of the Spirit; Son of Man lifted up
Proper 4 5/29–6/4	1 Sam. 3:1–10 (11-20) Calling of Samuel	139:1–6, 13–18 Omnipresence of God	2 Cor. 4:5–12 We proclaim Jesus Christ as Lord and ourselves as your slaves for Jesus' sake	Mk. 2:23—3:6 Sabbath controversies
Proper 5 6/5–6/11	1 Sam. 8:4–11 (12–15) 16–20; (11:14–15) Israel asks Samuel for a king	138 Thanksgiving for deliverance: All the kings of the earth shall praise you, O LORD	2 Cor. 4:13—5:1 Even though our outer nature is wasting away, our inner nature is being renewed day by day	Mk. 3:20–35 Jesus' true family; Accusations of casting out by Beelzebul
Proper 6 6/12–6/18	1 Sam. 15:34—16:13 Samuel anoints David	20 Prayer asking for God's help for the king	2 Cor. 5:6–10 (11–13) 14–17 We are always confident; even though we know that while we are at home in the body we are away from the Lord	Mk. 4:26–34 End of the parables discourse
Proper 7 6/19–25	1 Sam. 17:(1a, 4–11, 19–23), 32–49 David & Goliath OR 1 Sam. 17:57—18:5, 10–16 Saul brings David into his household but then turns against him	9:9–20 God protects the oppressed and punishes the wicked OR 133 How good and pleasant it is when kindred dwell together	2 Cor. 6:1–13 We are putting no obstacle in anyone's way…	Mk. 4:35–41 Jesus calms the sea

Proper 8 6/26–7/2	2 Sam. 1:1, 17–27 David laments over dead Saul and Jonathan	130 Penitential psalm: Out of the depths I cry to you	2 Cor. 8:7–15 Paul's request for relief aid	Mk. 5:21–43 Jairus's daughter and the woman with the hemorrhage
Proper 9 7/3–7/9	2 Sam. 5:1–5, 9–10 The beginning of David's reign	48 Praise of God for Zion	2 Cor. 12:2–10 Paul is content in weakness	Mk. 6:1–13 Jesus rejected in Nazareth; the sending of the Twelve
Proper 10 7/10–7/16	2 Sam. 6:1–5, 12b–19 David brings the ark to Jerusalem	24 Liturgy for entering the temple	Eph. 1:3–14 Doxology celebrat- ing blessings in Christ	Mk. 6:14–29 Martyrdom of John the Baptist
Proper 11 7/17–7/23	2 Sam. 7:1–14a The LORD instructs Nathan to tell David not to build a temple	89:20–37 Praise for God; the covenant with David	Eph. 2:11–22 Unity in Christ	Mk. 6:30–34, 53–56 Frame of the feeding of the five thousand
Proper 12 7/24–7/30	2 Sam. 11:1–15 David, Bathsheba, and Uriah	14 They have all gone astray, they are all alike perverse	Eph. 3:14–21 Prayer for the reader's formation	Jn. 6:1–21 Jesus feeds the crowd and walks across the sea
Proper 13 7/31–8/6	2 Sam. 11:26— 12:13a Nathan's parable revealing David's sin toward Uriah	51:1–12 Psalm of David when Nathan came to him	Eph. 4:1–16 One Lord, one faith, one baptism; but many gifts	Jn. 6:24–35 I am the bread of life
Proper 14 8/7–8/13	2 Sam. 18:5–9, 15, 31–33 The death of Absalom	130 Penitential psalm: Out of the depths I cry to you	Eph. 4:25—5:2 Put away false- hood, stealing, evil talk…	Jn. 6:35, 41–51 Whoever eats of this bread will live forever
Proper 15 8/14–8/20	1 Kings 2:10–12; 3:3–14 The beginning of Solomon's reign: Solomon asks for wisdom	111 Great are the works of the LORD studied by all who delight in them	Eph. 5:15–20 Be careful then how you live, not as unwise people but as wise	Jn. 6:51–58 Those who eat my flesh and drink my blood abide in me, and I in them
Proper 16 8/21–8/27	1 Kings 8:(1, 6, 10–11), 22–30, 41–43 Solomon's prayer of dedication for the temple	84 Pilgrimage psalm: How lovely is your dwelling place	Eph. 6:10–20 Put on the whole armor of God	Jn. 6:56–69 Some disciples depart offended, but the Twelve remain loyal
Proper 17 8/28–9/3	Song 2:8–13 Solomonic love poetry	45:1–2, 6–9 Psalm for a royal wedding	Jas. 1:17–27 Doers of the word: be quick to listen, slow to speak, slow to anger	Mk. 7:1–8, 14–15, 21–23 "There is noth- ing…that by going in can defile, but the things that come out are what defile"

Proper 18 9/4–9/10	Prov. 22:1–2, 8–9, 22–23 Solomonic wisdom concern- ing economic justice/generosity	125 Those who trust in the LORD are like Zion and cannot be moved	Jas. 2:1–10 (11–13) 14–17 Faith by itself, if it has no works, is dead: show no partiality for the rich	Mk. 7:24–37 Jesus heals the Syrophoenecian woman's daughter and the mute man
Proper 19 9/11–9/17	Prov. 1:20–33 Solomonic wisdom: wisdom cries out in the street	19 The torah of the LORD is perfect, reviving the soul	Jas. 3:1–12 Taming the tongue	Mk. 8:27–38 Confession at Caesarea Philippi; first passion pre- diction: take up your cross
Proper 20 9/18–9/24	Prov. 31:10–31 Solomonic wis- dom: a capable wife is more pre- cious than jewels	1 Happy are those who do not fol- low the advice of the wicked	Jas. 3:13—4:3, 7–8a Wisdom from above	Mk. 9:30–37 Second passion prediction: whoever wants to be greatest...
Proper 21 9/25–10/1	Esth. 7:1–6, 9–10; 9:20–22 Queen Esther saves the Jews	124 The LORD is on our side—saved us from our enemies	Jas. 5:13–20 The prayer of faith	Mk. 9:38–50 Competing exorcists and related sayings
Proper 22 10/2–10/8	Job 1:1; 2:1–10 Satan's wager with the Lord	26 Prayer for vindication against false accusation	Heb. 1:1–4; 2:5–12 In these last days, God has spoken to us by a Son	Mk. 10:2–16 Jesus discusses divorce and children
Proper 23 10/9– 10/15	Job 23:1–9, 16–17 Job desires to make his case before God	22:1–15 Prayer for help: My God, my God, why have you forsaken me?	Heb. 4:12–16 The word of God is living and active, sharper than any two-edged sword	Mk. 10:17–31 What must I do to inherit eternal life?—"Go, sell what you own, and give the mon- ey to the poor"
Proper 24 10/16– 10/22	Job 38:1–7, (34–41) The LORD answers Job out of the whirlwind	104:1–9, 24, 35c Praise for God the Creator	Heb. 5:1–10 Christ was desig- nated by God a high priest accord- ing to the order of Melchizedek	Mk. 10:35–45 James and John's request following the third passion prediction
Proper 25 10/23– 10/29	Job 42:1–6, 10–17 The LORD restores Job	34:1–8, (19–22) The LORD deliv- ered me from all my fears	Heb. 7:23–28 Christ's permanent priesthood and his once-for-all sacrifice	Mk. 10:46–52 Healing of Bartimaeus
Proper 26 10/30– 11/5	Ruth 1:1–18 Tragic introduction to the story of Naomi and Ruth	146 Praise for God's providence: the LORD upholds the orphan and widow	Heb. 9:11–14 The completeness of Christ's sacrificial blood	Mk. 12:28–34 Which commandment is first of all?

Proper 27 11/6–11/12	Ruth 3:1–5; 4:13–17 Naomi and Ruth catch Boaz and Obed is born	127 The blessing of children	Heb. 9:24–28 Christ has appeared once-for-all at the end of the age to remove sin by the sacrifice of himself	Mk. 12:38–44 Beware of the scribes
Proper 28 11/13–11/19	1 Sam. 1:4–20 Hannah petitions the LORD	1 Sam. 2:1–10 Hannah's Song	Heb. 10:11–14 (15–18) 19–25 Let us hold fast to the confession of our hope without wavering	Mk. 13:1–8 Eschatological discourse: prediction of the destruction of the temple
Proper 29 *Reign of Christ* 11/20–11/26	2 Sam. 23:1–7 David's last words: concerning God's everlasting covenant with him	132:1–12 (13–18) The LORD swore to David: one of your sons, I will sit on the throne	Rev. 1:4b–8 Opening of letter to the seven churches: Christ, the ruler of kings; lo, he is coming; Alpha & Omega	Jn. 18:33–37 Jesus before Pilate: my kingdom is not from this world

Cumulative Preaching Strategies

After Pentecost, the function of the readings of the Revised Common Lectionary changes significantly, and so must also one's cumulative preaching strategies. The lections chosen for liturgical time are determined by seasonal themes related to the remembrance and celebration of various aspects of the Christ Event. Thus the four readings assigned to a particular Sunday are chosen to relate to or interact with one another in such a way as to shape the church's experience of the liturgical occasion. In other words, the scripture lessons are subordinate to the liturgical theme, and a preacher's interpretation of a particular lection within the set of readings is influenced by that liturgical context.

In Ordinary Time, with the exception of a few Solemnities here and there (see below), no liturgical themes are at work. Neither the season nor individual Sundays are thematically determined. Instead, the scripture readings shape the season and the individual Sundays instead of the liturgical occasion determining the choice of scripture. Indeed, apart from the Psalter reading serving as a response to the First Testament, the lections for each Sunday are not related at all.[3] The three-dimensional lectionary of the liturgical season gives way to a two-dimension lectionary during Ordinary Time. Put differently, a predominant width dimension gives way to a strong height (connection from week to week) and depth (relation of each of the three years).

This means that there will be no reason at all to look for thematically oriented cumulative preaching strategies for the Sundays after Pentecost. Because the series of First Testament, Epistle, and Gospel lessons are each structured in a semicontinuous fashion, preachers should look for ways to preach in ways that allow congregations to experience significant segments of the canon. In other words, the flow of the lections themselves will provide a cumulative quality to sermons throughout Ordinary Time as long as preachers do not hop from one kind of lection to another Sunday after Sunday. Preachers must have the patience to stay with a particular series (i.e., the Gospel, First Testament, or Epistle series) long enough to allow the connections across time to influence the congregation's experience of the biblical writing being explored.

Before we consider specific strategies for dealing with the semicontinuous flow of the different series of lections, it will be helpful to name a few overarching issues related to the Season after Pentecost.

First, preachers should remember that the Season after Epiphany also utilized semicontinuous readings for the New Testament texts. They should recall what strategy they used during that season and reflect on whether and to what extent that strategy should influence the approach during the Season after Pentecost, or, at least, the beginning of the Season after Pentecost. For example, preachers who focused on the Markan lections dealing with the miracles during Jesus' Galilean ministry may or may not want to return to a focus on Mark at this point, following the use of John in Lent and Easter. Likewise, the Season after Epiphany ended with three readings from the opening of 2 Corinthians (if the Season after Epiphany extended to its fullest possible length). The series from 2 Corinthians is picked up again after Trinity Sunday.

Second, although Ordinary Time is not shaped by liturgical themes related to the Christ Event, a few thematic celebrations occur during the season. The lections for these days break from the semicontinuous pattern of the readings for all other Sundays.

> **Trinity Sunday** follows on the heels of Pentecost and opens the season. Since the doctrine of the Trinity represents a post-biblical theological development, the readings for this Sunday are usually related to the doctrine in a tentative or formulaic fashion. During Year B, there is no connection between the lections for this celebration and the Sundays that follow.

Although it is not recognized by the Revised Common Lectionary, many congregations and denominations celebrate **World Communion Sunday** on the first Sunday of October. For some preachers, this will cause no problem because they will still follow the lectionary. For others who use thematically oriented scripture lessons, this day will also force a break in a cumulative strategy based on the semicontinuous readings of the Revised Common Lectionary.

All Saints' Day falls in the middle of the Season after Pentecost on November 1. Since many churches celebrate this day on the first Sunday of November and since November 1 occasionally falls on a Sunday for churches that celebrate it on the first day of November, this day may force the preacher to take a break in the pattern of preaching through semicontinuous readings.

The **Reign of Christ** (also referred to as Christ the King) closes the season and indeed the whole year. This day has a strong eschatological tone, which connects thematically with Advent and the lections late in Ordinary Time. Nevertheless, the readings for Reign of Christ are not in literary continuity with the readings for the Sundays leading up to it.

Third, because Easter is a movable feast (it can occur as early as March 22 or as late as April 25), the opening of the season will vary greatly year to year. Easter must occur very early for all of the readings assigned to Ordinary Time to be available. It is more likely that a couple or more sets of readings assigned to the Sundays after Trinity Sunday will be dropped at the beginning of the season.

Fourth, the "semi" in the semicontinuous readings presents significant challenges to preachers and congregations during the Season after Pentecost. The semicontinuous approach to reading through sections of the canon in worship is a modification of lectio continua. Lectio continua (or "continual reading") works through a biblical work verse by verse, passage by passage, while the semicontinuous approach works through a biblical work in order by reading key and representative passages from the work. Preachers will often find themselves frustrated at the significant gaps between the semicontinuous readings. Therefore, preaching during Ordinary Time can be greatly enhanced by inviting congregations to read and study the materials that fall between the lections in group Bible studies and/or private devotion. More to the homiletical point, preachers must fill in something of these gaps in their sermons. They should think of their sermons as having a dual focus in relation to the biblical text. First, as with all Sundays, sermons should grow out of exegesis of an individual lection of choice. This, of course, should be the primary focus. Second, however, sermons should also deal in some sense with the entire section of the biblical writing that extends from the previous week's reading through the current week's lesson. Thus the preacher should offer a message that moves from a wide-angle glance at the broad sweep of a narrative to a zoom lens view of a particular moment within that narrative.

Finally, while the First Testament, Epistle, and Gospel lections for the Season after Pentecost work through different portions of the canon in a semicontinuous fashion, pastors who desire to preach cumulatively are not forced to choose one route (e.g., the Gospel lections) and stay with that route through the whole season. While jumping from one type of lection to another from week to week fails to utilize the cumulative potential of the Revised Common Lectionary, many pastors will consider half the calendar year too long a period to stay with a single strategy. Certainly preachers can stay with one such route for the whole season and enter into a portion of the canon with more depth than is allowed when they jump around in the canon. The lections in a series vary enough over time that preaching the series need not become stale or repetitive. Nevertheless, the series have natural breaks (e.g., the shift from one epistle to another or from one narrative section of a Gospel to the next) that allow preachers to move from one series to another and thus utilize more than one cumulative strategy. However, the shifts that occur in, say, the First Testament series of readings will not necessarily coincide with the shifts in the Epistle or Gospel lections. One way to manage the gaps between ending one strategy and starting the next is to preach from the Psalter readings during the gap. We read from the Psalms more than from any other writing in the Bible, but preach on it less than most.

Given these general opening comments, let us turn to specific cumulative strategies inherent in the semicontinuous structure of the readings through the Season after Pentecost. For each type of lection (i.e., First Testament, Epistle, and Gospel), we will begin with an overview of how the readings work as a whole throughout the season and then we will consider smaller units that lend themselves to a cumulative approach.

First Testament Lections

In Year B, the First Testament lessons for Ordinary Time begin where they left off the previous year. In Year A, the readings for the Season after Pentecost stretched from the beginning of the world to the rule of the judges over the confederacy of the twelve tribes of Israel. This year the readings start with Samuel, the last judge, who anointed Saul and David, the first two kings of Israel. The lections then proceed through the reigns of Saul, David, and Solomon, with David's story receiving the primary focus. These narrative readings carry the church through the first half of the Season after Pentecost.

The focus for the second half of the First Testament series spins off of the end of the first. The first half closes with Solomon, and the second begins with excerpts from wisdom literature attributed to him. This move into the Song of Solomon and Proverbs opens an exploration of various books that are found in the section of the Hebrew Bible known as *Kethuvim,* or The Writings (in contrast to The Torah and the *Nevi'im* or The Prophets).

This division means that no unified narrative schema covers the whole of Ordinary Time in Year B as there was for Year A. Moreover, by stopping the first half of the season with narrative bits drawn from Solomon's reign, the church never gains a sense of the narrative of the divided kingdom that follows from Solomon's oppressive use of his subjects in building the temple. While it is important that The Writings not be ignored by the Revised Common Lectionary, this narrative gap in the history of Israel and Judah's monarchies will create a problem for the beginning of Ordinary Time Year C when the semicontinuous approach to the First Testament focuses on the prophets who respond to the historical period (see pp. 193–94).

When we turn to discuss specific cumulative strategies for preaching through the First Testament series of readings, we are really asking questions about different ways of slicing the pie of Ordinary Time, and which pieces to select.

STRATEGY 1—As already named, the most obvious division in the First Testament series is to split the season in half. One cumulative approach is to preach through the *narrative passages* that make up the first half of Ordinary Time (Propers 4–16). These are primarily drawn from 1 and 2 Samuel, which in the Hebrew text is a single book of the Bible, with a couple of readings taken from 1 Kings at the end of the series. This is a key section of the Deuteronomistic history, which has as some of its major themes the establishment of the nation, the Davidic covenant, and the rationale for the Babylonian exile. This section from which our lections are drawn deals primarily with the first two of these themes. Nevertheless, the lections do not deal only with these central themes. While working through the stories of Samuel, Saul, David, and Solomon will give the week-to-week movement a sense of a continuing plot, preachers will find a wide range of political and theological issues as well as perspectives on the human condition with which to deal in the pulpit.

STRATEGY 2—If preachers do not wish to stay with the approach for the whole of approximately three months, this half of the First Testament series can be divided into sections that focus on the *different main characters: Samuel* (Propers 4–6), *David* (Propers 6–14), and *Solomon* (Propers 15–16). (Saul is present in Propers 6–8, but his story is not well represented in the Revised Common Lectionary. He is only present to pave the way for David's appearance in the series.) If one is willing to massage the Revised Common Lectionary at points, any of these subsections can be expanded a bit to allow the congregation to get a fuller understanding of the saga surrounding the reign of the main character.

STRATEGY 3—A third strategy is to preach through The Writings during the second half of the season. This series of readings does not have the same level of unity as the First Testament narrative series in the first half of the season. Nevertheless, the preacher will be able to highlight the nature of this portion of the canon to emphasize the connection.

STRATEGY 4—A fourth strategy (or group of strategies) is to deal with any of the *individual writings* highlighted in the second half of Ordinary Time. We will comment on each one of these briefly.

Only one lection comes from *Song of Solomon* (Proper 17). Indeed this is the only passage from Song of Solomon that is used as a First Testament lection in the three-year cycle of the Revised Common Lectionary.[4] Nevertheless, as a work traditionally attributed to Solomon, this is an interesting choice for setting the tone for the other readings to follow from The Writings. As a love poem with erotic themes and no mention of God, Song of Solomon offers the congregation an introduction to a world of biblical literature that shows a concern for all aspects of life, not just explicitly religious aspects of life. Preachers who explore the worldview implied in this text will have a chance to revisit that worldview when reading in Esther and Ruth. Preachers should consider the appearance of Song 2:8–13 as an opportunity to preach on the whole work, highlighting the dialogue between the lovers and exploring romantic love as a gift from God, and overcoming unwieldy and illegitimate allegorical interpretations.

Three readings (Propers 18–20) come from *Proverbs* for Year B. The materials in Proverbs were likely composed, collected, and edited over centuries. This long transmission history translates into a complex book, and, certainly, three lections cannot do justice to the diversity of materials found in the book. Nevertheless, they will offer preachers the chance to explore with their congregation some of the core elements of the worldview of the biblical wisdom tradition. Before turning to do exegesis on the specific passages offered by the lectionary, therefore, preachers will do well to spend some time reading about the wisdom tradition and wisdom literature in general in a good Bible dictionary.

The Revised Common Lectionary turns to *Esther* only once (Proper 21). The fact that the lection is drawn from more than one passage in the book (7:1–6, 9–10; 9:20–22) implies an invitation to preach on the whole story of the book, or at least the central storyline. As with Song of Solomon, Esther is not a theological book. Nevertheless, it does deal with issues of religious identity and ethnic oppression in a theologically significant manner. Preachers may well want to focus on the passages chosen by the Revised Common Lectionary, but they will also need to offer an overview of the narrative to place the scenes in context and to introduce the characters of Vashti, Ahasuerus, Esther, Mordecai, and Haman.

The Revised Common Lectionary directs the church's attention to *Job* for four Sundays (Propers 22–25). The first and last of the readings come from the narrative frame of the book, while the second and third readings proceed from later portions of the poetic bulk of the book. While four passages cannot do justice to a complex forty-two chapter parable, they will allow preachers to raise serious questions about righteousness, suffering, and God's justice (i.e., theodicy).

The final First Testament work to which the Revised Common Lectionary turns in its romp through the Kethuvim is the book of *Ruth*, which, chronologically speaking, takes us full circle back to the beginning of the Season after Pentecost, since Ruth was David's great-grandmother. However, while Ruth's story ends with David's genealogy, this narrative is more than just a prelude to the story of David. As with the book of Esther, this book tells of strong, bright women (Naomi and Ruth) dealing with a crisis. Since narratives about men dominate the first half of the season, preachers will do well at the end of the season to lift up women of the Bible.

Epistle Lections

Year B offers an odd mixture of semicontinuous Epistle lections for Ordinary Time. The season opens by continuing the series of readings from Paul's Second Letter to the Corinthians that was started during the Season after Epiphany. Next, readings are drawn from the Deutero-Pauline letter to the Ephesians. After Ephesians, the Revised Common Lectionary directs our attention to the general Epistle of James. The season then closes with readings from chapters 1–10 of the general Epistle of the Hebrews—readings from chapters 11–13 are reserved for the middle of Ordinary Time, Year C (Propers 14–17).

There are a few general things to keep in mind and, indeed, to offer to the congregation if one chooses a cumulative preaching strategy that involves Epistles. Unlike the undisputed Pauline Epistles of Ordinary Time Year A, the New Testament readings for Year B are not letters in the true sense of the word. Second Corinthians is likely a composite made up of portions from several Pauline letters to the house churches at Corinth. Ephesians was probably not written by Paul to a specific recipient but by a disciple of Paul as a "general" circulating letter. Although James and Hebrews are referred to as "general Epistles" in the New Testament, neither are actually letters. James is moral exhortation, and Hebrews seems to be a written sermon. Nevertheless, the writings did arise out of specific contexts to address specific perceived needs that can be determined, at least in part, through the words of the writings themselves. Preachers need to discover these contexts and convey some sense of them to their congregations if the fullest understanding of the writings is to be grasped.

Second, in preaching passages from these writings, not only should preachers (and congregations) be clear about the circumstances that necessitated the writing of the documents, they must also ascertain how individual lections function within the structure of the document. Ephesians, and to some degree 2 Corinthians, follow the standard structure of ancient letters (see pp. 82–83). James, though like much Wisdom literature, is difficult to discern. Hebrews has a complex sermonic argument built on a structure of alternating biblical exposition, theological reflection, and moral exhortation.

Finally, it is important to remember that the Revised Common Lectionary often sets the boundaries for Epistle lections inappropriately. Texts divide in the middle of logical developments and thus arguments are skewed. Preachers who are following a cumulative strategy of preaching through a New Testament letter should be willing, at times, to designate different beginnings and endings to lessons.

Given these broad insights into preaching from the epistle readings for Ordinary Time, Year B, what potential strategies are available for the season?

STRATEGY 5—The first possible cumulative preaching strategy is to focus on the whole series of Epistle readings throughout the whole season. The strength of this approach for Year B is that it offers great diversity in the readings. The weakness of the approach is that so much diversity in theological perspective will make it difficult to build a sense of connection from one writing to the next.

STRATEGY 6—If one wants to build a cumulative approach connecting the different Epistles, another possibility is to focus on the "general" writings. This could include Ephesians, James, and Hebrews, or simply James and Hebrews in contrast to the Pauline milieu found in 2 Corinthians and Ephesians. There will still be a variety of contextual situations addressed and theological perspectives, but there will also be a sense of unity in that these documents address broad situations instead of narrow, specific pastoral concerns.

STRATEGY 7—The most obvious cumulative strategy for preaching the Epistle lections during the Season after Pentecost is to focus on the semicontinuous readings for a particular individual New Testament writing. If one preached from the Epistle texts during the Season after

Epiphany Year B (Proper 2–Transfiguration, see pp. 81–83), the themes and issues of 2 Corinthians can be picked up again at the beginning of Ordinary Time (Propers 4–9).

As mentioned earlier, *2 Corinthians* is probably a composite of parts of different letters. Paul wrote these different letters to address a conflict that arose in the house churches at Corinth. It seems that rival missionaries arrived while Paul was gone and challenged his interpretation of the gospel. They evidently succeeded in turning some Christians away from Paul's theology and from Paul himself. Throughout 2 Corinthians the way Paul speaks of the conflict shifts dramatically: from condemning his rivals and chastising those who would follow their teaching to defending his apostolic ministry; from imploring the church for reconciliation to a tone of reconciliation achieved. These differences account for much of why scholars argue for viewing the writing as a redacted composite.

It is difficult to preach cumulatively through this disjointed document—a difficulty compounded by the Revised Common Lectionary dividing the text between the seasons after Epiphany and after Pentecost. Nevertheless, there is potential for cumulative preaching through 2 Corinthians. The potential resides in the core thematic unity of the document that is due to the consistent, albeit evolving, situation Paul is addressing. Keeping the controversy in the minds of the congregation while preaching on these lections will help hearers keep from getting lost in the dramatic rhetorical shifts in the Epistle from week to week. Moreover, the lections invite the preacher to explore some significant topics in the area of ecclesiology, congregational conflict management, leadership/ministry in the church, and measuring the truth claims of competing attempts to interpret the good news of Jesus Christ.

STRATEGY 8—*Ephesians* comprises the Epistle readings for Propers 10–16. Seven weeks is a significant amount of time to give to preaching this letter. The letter reads as one written by Paul, while he was in prison, to house churches in Ephesus. Most scholars agree, however, that a Pauline disciple composed the letter in the last third of the first century C.E. This judgment is due to differences between this letter and undisputed Pauline letters in terms of style, use of metaphors, and theology. Add to these elements that Ephesians gives signs of literary dependence upon Colossians, and pseudonymity is assured.

To complicate matters further, some significant ancient manuscripts do not have any reference to Ephesus in the opening verse. Thus neither author nor recipient is known.

The occasion for the letter is likewise unclear. No obvious theological issue, social crisis, or pastoral need precipitates the letter. Nevertheless, some central themes of the letter reveal something of the author's view of his audience as well as the potential for cumulative preaching. The theological foundation of the letter is a cosmic view of God's work/plan through Christ. The central argument of the letter that grows out of this view is one for the unity of the church rooted in the cosmic Christ. Inclusion in the church meant, for the Gentile audience of the letter, a radical contrast between life before and after entering the faith—as radical as the contrast between death and resurrection. As the body of Pauline letters is followed by a section of ethical exhortation, so in Ephesians is this view of new life in Christ brought to bear on the lives of the readers. The connections between christology, ecclesiology, soteriology, and ethics just laid out offers preachers the opportunity to explore the issues in existentially relevant ways.

STRATEGY 9—The Revised Common Lectionary focuses the church's attention on the Epistle of *James* for five Sundays during Ordinary Time of Year B (Propers 17–21). James is actually a letter only in terms of its opening lines functioning as a greeting. Otherwise, it has none of the standard structures of epistolary literature, nor is it clear who is being referenced in the name of James as sender or the twelve tribes of the dispersion as recipients. Nevertheless, particular circumstances described in the document (e.g., the privilege granted to the rich) give the sense that the author is addressing a specific congregation. Thus the lections from James should not be read as abstract, general instruction.

But instruction it is. It explores no grand theological foundation, contrary to Ephesians. Moreover, the document has no clear flow of argumentation to it. Often a piece of instruction has little or no relation to the instruction that follows. James is less concerned with defining a Christian worldview and more with shaping the Christian life.

This concern should be the basis of a cumulative preaching strategy on James. The lections vary greatly in terms of topic, but all are concerned with Christian behavior—Christian actions, speech, and piety. As the document addresses a specific situation, it also offers concrete admonitions for that situation. Preaching on the lections from James will invite preachers to offer similar specific claims on Christian behavior. Pastors should approach the task by exegetically reflecting on the rationale behind the instruction offered in the ancient pericope and the author's intended result in order to draw homiletical analogies to needs for individual and communal Christian behavior today.

STRATEGY 10—The Season after Pentecost closes its cycle of semicontinuous readings through New Testament epistolary literature by focusing on *Hebrews*. Like James, Hebrews is not a letter. Instead, it reads more like a sermon. Indeed, it is like a complex argument built out of short sermonettes, each of which includes exposition of a First Testament passage, theological (i.e., christological and soteriological) interpretation, and moral exhortation.

Hebrews is a difficult read. It is an intriguing mixture of alien (to us) first-century hermeneutics for the Christian reading and appropriation of First Testament literature and images with Hellenistic philosophical concepts. The Revised Common Lectionary makes reading Hebrews even more difficult in two significant ways. First, as noted above, the lectionary divides the book into two sets of lessons read a year apart—lessons from chapters 1—10 are read during Propers 22–28 of Ordinary Time, Year B, and those from chapters 11—13 are read during Propers 14–17 of Year C. Making a break where the Revised Common Lectionary does is not entirely inappropriate—because themes shift. Nevertheless, it is not correct to assume (as the Revised Common Lectionary structure implies) that chapters 11—13 do not flow out of the earlier chapters. Second, the sermonic sections from which the lections for Year B come from are built, to a great degree, on a hermeneutical contrast between an image or concept found in the First Testament (e.g., the high priest offering an annual sacrifice on the Day of Atonement) and Christian theology (Christ as the great high priest who offers himself as a sacrifice of atonement once for all). Yet the lections often offer only a reading from the second half of the contrast.

These problems may be enough to scare preachers away from attempting to develop a cumulative preaching strategy from the lectionary's presentation of Hebrews. However, there are also some good reasons to consider preaching from this series of semicontinuous readings. In Year B, the readings are, for the most part, focused on a christology/soteriology of sacrifice. Hebrews reiterates this theme a number of times with different nuances. This invites a cumulative look at a Christian understanding of salvation. Moreover, the dominance of the metaphor of sacrifice in Hebrews has had a significant impact on Christian soteriology throughout its two millennia history. The result has been substitution and satisfaction theories of atonement that many Christian traditions find troubling today. Taking time to reexamine the metaphors of Hebrews cumulatively will likewise give preachers the opportunity to re-image atonement in an extended manner.

Gospel Lections

Mark is the Gospel that anchors Year B of the lectionary. As one considers a cumulative preaching strategy for the Sundays after Pentecost, however, it is important to remember that Mark has been absent for a while. Mark was the focus during the Sundays after Epiphany, in which the beginning of Jesus' Galilean ministry—healing and conflict stories—was presented in a semicontinuous fashion. The Second Gospel then also started off Lent, but after two weeks made way for John to dominate through the rest of the season and all of Easter, with the exceptions of Palm/Passion Sunday and perhaps the Easter Vigil/Easter Sunday. Thus when Mark appears on the first Sunday following Trinity Sunday, preachers will need to remind the congregation of what they heard from Mark earlier in the year.

Preachers should have a couple of recent, critical commentaries on Mark to use as conversation partners while working through Year B as a whole, but especially through Ordinary Time. Given the amount of time spent in Mark, preachers will need the level of detail offered in introductions to the Gospel and comments on the various pericopae that relate to a sense of the whole. (Although no lectionary year as a whole focuses on John and all three years give some attention to John during Lent and Easter, the Fourth Gospel plays its strongest role during Year B due to the fact that Mark is shorter in length than Matthew or Luke.)

While preachers will need to use commentaries to refresh their memories concerning the various theological and narrative nuances of Mark, especially in terms of the significant gaps in the lectionary choices, a few items of introduction can be offered here in passing to give a sense of how the Second Gospel can be presented over time for the sake of a deeper, cumulative hearing on the part of the congregation.

Although we know nothing of the author or the location in which the Gospel was written, it seems fairly likely that Mark was written just before or just after 70 C.E., in response to the impending or recent destruction of Jerusalem and fall of the temple. How were Christians, now a mixture of Jewish and Gentile Christians, to respond to the razing of the symbol of the God's presence and of the Jewish cultus? Mark replaces a theology of victory associated with the resurrection and the expectation that the Messiah would return to protect Jerusalem with a focus on the cross. Indeed, the whole of Mark has been referred to as a passion narrative with an extended introduction.

This christological focus on the cross plays out in several ways. Two ways are especially significant for the Revised Common Lectionary's approach to Ordinary Time, and they are closely related. The first is structural. Three major sections of Mark lead to a narrative climax at the cross: the Galilean ministry (1:1—8:26), the "way" to Jerusalem (8:27—10:52), and the Jerusalem narrative (11:1—16:8). The second deals with the revelation of Jesus' identity. The opening of the narrative makes clear to the reader that Jesus is the Son of God (1:1). A heavenly voice confirms this at Jesus' baptism (1:11) and transfiguration (9:7). But the characters consistently fail to recognize this. The religious authorities, crowds, family, and even disciples interpret Jesus in various, yet inadequate, ways because the basis of their interpretations are only Jesus' teachings, conflicts, healings, or exorcisms. This misunderstanding lies behind the "Messianic Secret" motif in which Jesus repeatedly instructs people to tell no one about him. (See the earlier discussion of Mark for the Season after Epiphany, Year B, pp. 106–8.)

Using great literary irony, Mark demonstrates that Jesus' full identity can only be known through the crucifixion by having the centurion who executes Jesus be the only human to call him God's Son (15:39). This consistent focus on the cross means that preachers should read every Markan lection in Ordinary Time from the shadow of the cross. They should ask, "How does this passage lead to the cross?" Indeed, preachers will need to be explicit about this perspective given that the passion narrative will not be read during the Season after Pentecost (see Palm/Passion Sunday, Year B). It will be a sound hermeneutical/homiletical approach to read these lections as if the community is returning to read them a second time, after having read Mark's story of the cross and the empty tomb. Many scholars suggest that, in the young man's message that the resurrected Jesus will meet the disciples back in Galilee, Mark invites a reevaluation of the Galilean section of the narrative, since the narrator never tells of that meeting (Mk. 16:1–8).

One final characteristic of Mark that is worth noting is that scholars commonly hold that Matthew and Luke used Mark and "Q" (a hypothetical sayings source) as their primary sources. Because only a very small percentage of Mark was not used by either Matthew or Luke, there is almost always either one or two parallel passages with which to compare a Markan lection. While noticing differences between Mark on the one hand and Matthew and/or Luke on the other, one must be careful about not jumping to too strong of an assumption about Mark's intentions. In other words, one cannot necessarily work backward from a piece of derivative literature to a better understanding of the source. Nevertheless, the differences will point to unique characteristics of Mark's presentation of Jesus as the Son of God.

Given these broad insights into preaching from Mark, what particular strategies are available during Ordinary Time, Year B?

STRATEGY 11—There is a nice balance of thematic overlap and variation in Mark (and John 6) that would justify preaching on *the whole series of Gospel lections* throughout the whole season. But given the predominance of the Gospel readings throughout the year, it is more likely that preachers may want to focus on sections of the Gospel series. The series is best divided in terms of narrative structures.

STRATEGY 12—As noted above, the opening section of Mark is 1:1—8:26. Thus Propers 4–18 come from *the Galilean ministry*, with Propers 12–16 functioning as a Johannine interlude (see the following strategy). This section connects well to the readings for the Sundays after Epiphany and can reinforce themes drawn out if one preached on the Gospel lections during that season. Although not the focus of the individual periciopae, the misunderstanding of Jesus' identity by a range of characters is a significant sub-theme that preachers should draw out as they deal with the main foci to help congregations get a sense of Mark's own cumulative strategy.

STRATEGY 13—As mentioned earlier, in Propers 12–16 the Revised Common Lectionary shifts from Mark to *John 6.* The narrative connection is the feeding of the five thousand, but beyond that John's theology and narrative style are radically different than Mark's. Moreover, the lectionary pace itself shifts from racing through Galilee in Mark to a long, deliberate pause over one extended scene in John.

Preachers and congregations are likely to experience this series of texts as repetitive from week to week, since John spends the chapter unpacking the metaphor of Jesus as the bread of life in detail. We find, however, logical progression from lection to lection. There are especially significant differences in nuance depending on the characters with whom Jesus is engaging—crowd (Propers 12–13), religious authorities (Propers 14–15), or disciples (Proper 16).

STRATEGY 14—The next section of Mark explored in Ordinary Time is the *journey to Jerusalem* (Propers 19–25). Although it is not as evident in the choice of lections as it might be, throughout this section the Markan narrator repeatedly reminds the readers that Jesus and the disciples are "on the way"—a metaphor for discipleship rooted in Christ's suffering and death.

What is more evident in the lections is the disciples' misunderstanding of Jesus' identity. Since the travel narrative consists primarily (but not solely) of teaching to the disciples as opposed to crowds, it is not surprising that the broad view of everyone misunderstanding found in the Galilean sections gives way to a focus on the disciples' lack of faith in this section. This lack of understanding is epitomized in the scenes in which Jesus tells of his impending death (again relating his identity as Son of God to the cross). Each time, the disciples respond inappropriately to the news that Jesus is heading to Jerusalem to die (Propers 19–20, 24). There is also a significant contrast between the disciples' response and that of blind Bartimaeus. When he gains his sight and Jesus tells him to "go," he follows Jesus "on the way" (Proper 25). The next scene in Mark is the entry into Jerusalem.

STRATEGY 15—Indeed, the last set of lessons from Mark come from the *Jerusalem narrative* (Propers 26–28). To be precise, the three lections present Jesus' teaching in and about the temple. Last year, the Revised Common Lectionary spent a great deal of time in Matthew's version of the temple controversies, so this year we only take a brief glance at the section. The main purpose (structurally speaking) is to get to the eschatological discourse in Mark 13 (Proper 28), thus returning to the point of origin for Year B and setting up the beginning of Year C in Luke's version of the eschatological discourse (Advent 1).

Cumulative
Preaching
Strategies for
Year C

ADVENT

Year C

(See pp. 8–9 for an overview of the three-dimensional character of the Revised Common Lectionary's approach to Advent.)

Lectionary Readings

	FIRST TESTAMENT	PSALTER	EPISTLE	GOSPEL
Advent 1	Jer. 33:14–16 Days are coming: righteous branch of David	25:1–10 Don't let those who wait on you be put to shame	1 Thess. 3:9–13 Be blameless at the coming of our Lord Jesus Christ with all the saints	Lk. 21:25–36 Eschatological discourse – coming of Son of Man
Advent 2	Mal. 3:1–4 Messenger of the coming of the Lord	Lk. 1:68–79 Zechariah's canticle	Phil. 1:3–11 The one who began a good work among you will bring it to completion by the day of Jesus Christ	Lk. 3:1–6 Introduction to John's ministry
Advent 3	Zeph. 3:14–20 Rejoice—the day of the Lord is coming.	Isa. 12:2–6 Sing praises for God's salvation	Phil. 4:4–7 Rejoice in the Lord always; the Lord is near	Lk. 3:7–18 John's preaching
Advent 4	Mic. 5:2–5a From Bethlehem shall come a ruler of Israel	Lk. 1:47–55 The Magnificat OR Ps. 80:1–7 O Shepherd of Israel, come to save us	Heb. 10:5–10 Christ's sacrifice— when Christ came into the world	Lk. 1:39–45 (46–55) Mary & Elizabeth— the Magnificat

Cumulative Preaching Strategies

Advent is the liturgical season in which the church expectantly awaits God to come *(vent)* to *(ad)* us. While the season prepares us for the celebration of the Incarnation, the advent of God-in-Christ toward which the season looks includes more than the past coming of Christ (Christmas). It also involves the present (the claim that God comes to us in our current lives) and the future (the eschatological claim that God is always before us). Liturgical preaching that works cumulatively through this season needs to recognize that the season is structured in reverse chronological order by moving from the eschatological claims about the coming of the Son of Man through

John the Baptist's foreshadowing of the ministry of "the one who is to come," to the coming of the Christ child.

The lections for the season suggest a number of such potential cumulative preaching strategies:

STRATEGY 1—Since the liturgical year is rooted in the plot of the Christ Event, an obvious strategy for preaching through every season will be focusing on the *Gospel readings.* Indeed, the Gospel themes for Advent date back at least five hundred years in worship practice and are the same each year of Revised Common Lectionary cycle, regardless of which Synoptic Gospel anchors the year. Preaching these texts allows the congregation to experience variations found in each Gospel on themes found in all three. The themes deal specifically with different chronological expectations concerning the coming of Christ:

Advent 1 – Jesus describes the coming of the Son of Man in the eschatological discourse

Advent 2 & 3 – John the Baptist as a precursor to Jesus' ministry

Advent 4 – Joseph & Mary's preparation for the birth of Jesus

During Year C, Luke is the Synoptic Gospel that anchors the lectionary calendar. The beginning of the liturgical year is a good time to buy a new commentary or two on the Third Gospel, since preachers will return to this biblical text repeatedly throughout the year. Especially helpful at the beginning of the year is to read the introductory material on Luke in a couple of commentaries to remind ourselves of the major themes and narrative emphases/ structures in the Gospel. This will help preachers keep in mind Luke's cumulative presentation of the Christ Event while focusing on individual Lukan pericopae. (See also the introductory notes for preaching the semicontinuous reading of Luke during Ordinary Time on pp. 204–6.)

A particular element of the Lukan narrative is the way Luke explicitly and repeatedly subordinates John the Baptist to Jesus. For instance, throughout the infancy narrative, Luke tells the stories of John and Jesus' birth in parallel fashion but in a way that makes clear the two children are not at all equals. This shows up in the Benedictus (Lk. 1:68–79, substituted for the Psalter reading on Advent 2), in which

Zechariah prophesies about Jesus before he speaks of his own son. It is also evident in the scene in which Mary and Elizabeth meet and John leaps in Elizabeth's womb (Lk. 1:39–45, Advent 4). Since three Gospel lections and two canticles from Luke that can be substituted for Psalter readings deal with the relationship of John and Jesus, it is important to keep this dynamic in mind. The contrast between the two is the starting point of Luke's narrative christology.

STRATEGY 2—As the first strategy focuses on the Gospel lections, a second option would be to preach on the *First Testament lections* through the whole season. (To preach a full and appropriate passage, one will need to change the boundaries of some of these readings.) While these lections are primarily chosen to support the New Testament readings, preaching on them in their original historical and literary contexts can serve well to elucidate Advent themes. Indeed, the sermons for Advent 1, 2, and 4 could almost begin with a structure that states, "The early church interpreted this text in reference to Christ in such-and-such manner. While such an interpretation makes sense in the context of the first Christians shaping their preaching about Christ in ways that showed continuity with the ancient scriptures of Israel, it is also important to hear these texts in their own right..." This approach is the other side of the coin of option 6 below, dealing with New Testament hermeneutics.

Moreover, the lections all represent an eschatological worldview, which is fitting for the following strategy.

STRATEGY 3—The remaining strategies are thematic in nature. One such approach to cumulative preaching in Advent would be to deal with *eschatology* all four Sundays. Mainline Protestants tend to avoid eschatology because we do not want to sound like bedfellows with those on TV and in print who interpret biblical apocalyptic material in nonsensical ways. But this odd, "literal" reading of such texts is exactly why preachers whose training has been informed by biblical criticism should preach about the eschatological emphases in scripture. Preachers need to unpack ancient eschatological expressions of living in the "already/not yet" as descriptions of religious experience in all times and places in contrast to linear, temporal interpretations of eschatology.

As the liturgical year opens with eschatology, so also it ends with eschatology. Thus the last couple of Sundays in Ordinary Time, Year B, and especially the Reign of Christ, have already raised the themes that take central focus in Advent. Some Advent texts to consider follow:

Advent 1: Luke 21:25–36 is an excerpt from the Third Gospel's version of Jesus' eschatological discourse.

> **OR:** Jeremiah 33:14–16 is a vision of a ruler in the line of David who will establish justice in the land.

> **OR:** In 1 Thessalonians 3:9–13, Paul foreshadows the apocalyptic description of the coming of the Lord in chapters 4—5 with a prayer that God may strengthen the readers to be blameless when the day of the Lord comes.

> **OR:** Psalm 25:1–10, while not explicitly eschatological, this prayer well expresses the sentiment of one with an eschatological worldview, i.e., that of awaiting God's salvation.

Advent 2: Malachi 3:1–4 offers a vision of the Lord coming to purify worship.

> **OR:** Philippians 1:3–11, as with the passage from 1 Thessalonians 3 for Advent 1, the foundational eschatological view of Paul permeates his giving thanks for his readers.

> **OR:** Luke 1:68–79, which is substituted for a Psalter reading, is the Benedictus in which Zechariah speaks eschatologically about the birth of Jesus and John. (See the use of the Magnificat on Advent 4.)

> **OR:** In Luke 3:1–6, the Lukan narrator presents John the Baptist as the eschatological forerunner of the coming of the Lord.

Advent 3: Zephaniah 3:14–20 is an oracle from the period of Josiah's reforms, which proclaims that God will restore Jerusalem and bring about salvation.

> **OR:** Luke 3:7–18, the eschatological preaching of John the Baptist.

> **OR:** Philippians 4:4–7 calls the readers to rejoice and is rooted in the eschatological claim that the Lord is near.

Advent 4: Micah 5:2–5a is an eschatological vision of the restoration of Israel's throne (and thus of the nation) to a place of prominence.

OR: Luke 1:47–55, the Magnificat, can be read either in place of the Psalter reading or as part of the Gospel lection. It is Mary's prophetic speech that eschatologically describes the effects of the coming of her child, Jesus. So confident is Mary in God's promises that she describes these effects (a salvific reversal of the status quo) in the past tense.

STRATEGY 4—The eschatological outlook named in the previous strategy relates to another potential cumulative approach. One could preach through Advent highlighting the *ethical demands* the texts make. In other words, one of the ways we prepare for the coming of God-in-Christ is to live out a certain type of ethic of expectation.

Advent 1: Luke 21:25–36, the passage from the eschatological discourse, ends with a call to be on guard against dissipation, drunkenness, and worries.

OR: Jeremiah 33:14–16 lifts up a vision of a ruler who executes righteousness and justice.

OR: Psalm 25:1–10 is a prayer that the psalmist might know God's way.

OR: In 1 Thessalonians 3:9–13, Paul prays that his readers abound in love and be found blameless at the coming of the Lord.

Advent 2: Philippians 1:3–11, Paul's opening thanksgiving, includes a prayer that his recipients' love overflow and that they may be able to determine what is best so that they are found blameless in the day of Christ and produce a harvest of righteousness (compare the 1 Thess. 3:9–13 lection for Advent 1).

OR: Malachi 3:1–4, an oracle that speaks of God purifying temple worship, has ethical implications when one reads the lection in its broader literary context.

OR: Luke 1:68–79, the Benedictus, ends with Zechariah naming that John is to lead the people in the way of peace.

Advent 3: Luke 3:7–18 presents the preaching of John the Baptist which calls for repentance manifested in charity and honesty.

OR: Zephaniah 3:14–20 calls hearers to rejoice for the restoration God is bringing to Jerusalem. This restoration involves the removal of oppression, illness, marginalization, and shame.

Advent 4: Luke 1:47-55, the Magnificat, offers a vision of a salvation that reverses the status quo of oppressed and oppressor, rich and poor. In the context of the Third Gospel, this view of divine initiative cannot be separated from the call to enact an ethic that imitates it.

STRATEGY 5—Many congregations use wreaths to mark time during Advent. Often liturgical and devotional materials assign themes for each candle/week. Except for the third week (joy), these themes often have little to do with the lectionary texts for the year. During Year C, some potential *weekly sub-themes* flow out of the broader theme of awaiting the coming of the Lord.

Advent 1: Be alert (Lk. 21:25–36)

Advent 2: Prepare the way (Lk. 3:1–6; Mal. 3:1–4)

Advent 3: Rejoice (Phil. 4:4–7; Zeph. 3:14–20; Isa. 12:2–6)

Advent 4: Magnify the Lord (Lk. 1:47–55).

STRATEGY 6—The early church used the First Testament to support its claims about and interpretation of Jesus as the Christ. This causes two problems for the contemporary church: (1) it leads to a misunderstanding of the function of those First Testament texts in their original literary and historical contexts; and (2) a confusion concerning the hermeneutic behind the use of these texts in the New Testament. Therefore, an appropriate strategy for preaching Advent could be to examine *the use of the First Testament in the New Testament* as a means of appreciating both the power of the texts originally, and the creativity of the early church in their appropriation of these texts. Three of the four Sundays of Advent offer texts that invite this strategy:

Advent 1: Jeremiah 33:14–16 envisions the advent of a ruler in the Davidic line that will reestablish justice and righteousness in the land. This text was originally addressed to postexilic Judah. The early church interpreted Jesus as the righteous branch of David.

OR: Luke 21:25–36 echoes numerous prophetic text presenting apocalyptic cosmic signs. However, central to the text is the use of Daniel 7:13–14 in describing the coming of a son of man. The original context of the reference was the oppression of the Jews at the hands of Antiochus Epiphanes.

Advent 2: Luke 3:1–6 follows early Christian practice in applying Isaiah 40:3–5 (originally an exilic oracle proclaiming God's coming deliverance of the Jews from Babylon) to John the Baptist.

OR: Malachi 3:1–4 speaks of the sending of a messenger to prepare the way of the Lord who will purify temple worship. It is unclear whether the prophet refers to himself, but the early church interpreted the forerunner as John the Baptist.

Advent 4: Micah 5:2–5a is used in Matthew 2:6 to explain why Jesus is born in Bethlehem. In its original context, it deals with the restoration of Israel's ruler.

CHRISTMAS

Year C

(See pp. 10–11 for an overview of the three-dimensional character of the Revised Common Lectionary's approach to Christmas.)

Lectionary Readings

	FIRST TESTAMENT	PSALTER	EPISTLE	GOSPEL
Christmas Eve/Day Proper 1 (abc)[1]	Isa. 9:2–7 A child has been born for us	96 Sing a new song: the Lord is king	Titus 2:11–14 The grace of God has appeared	Lk. 2:1–14 (15–20) Birth story
Christmas Eve/Day Proper 2 (abc)	Isa. 62:6–12 See, your salvation comes…	97 The Lord is king! Let the earth rejoice	Titus 3:4–7 When the goodness and loving kindness of God our Savior appeared…	Lk. 2:1–7 (8–20) Birth story
Christmas Eve/Day Proper 3 (abc)	Isa. 52:7–10 The return of the Lord to Zion	98 Make a joyful noise to the Lord	Heb. 1:1–4 (5–12) God has spoken to us through a Son, through whom God created the worlds	Jn. 1:1–14 John's Prologue— Incarnation of the Word
Christmas 1	1 Sam. 2:18–20, 26 The boy Samuel in the temple	148 (abc) Praise the Lord who has raised up a horn for the people	Col. 3:12–17 Let Christ dwell in you	Lk. 2:41–52 Jesus at age 12 in the temple
Christmas 2 (abc)	Jer. 31:7–14 God will save a remnant	147:12–20 Praise God for divine providence	Eph. 1:3–14 God chose us in Christ before the foundation of the world	Jn. 1:(1–9) 10–18 John's Prologue— the Word
Epiphany (abc)	Isa. 60:1–6 Nations shall come to your light: camels, gold, frankincense	72:1–7, 10–14 Give the king your justice, O God	Eph. 3:1–12 Paul, a prisoner of Christ for Gentiles	Mt. 2:1–12 Magi

Cumulative Preaching Strategies

Proposing a variety of concrete, cumulative preaching strategies for the season of Christmas is difficult because the season takes a couple of different forms depending on which days of the week Christmas and Epiphany fall and what congregational practice is.

For congregations that celebrate Epiphany on January 6, regardless of what day of the week it falls on, there will always be at least one Sunday after Christmas and sometimes there will be two (a little more than half the time). However, in congregations that celebrate Epiphany Sunday on the Sunday before January 6 when Epiphany falls on a day other than Sunday, there will never be a Second Sunday after Christmas. If Christmas falls on a Sunday or Monday (with Epiphany falling on a Friday or Saturday), there will be no Sunday "after Christmas" at all—only Christmas Eve or Christmas Day followed a week later by Epiphany Sunday. Thus, approximately four of every six years will have one Sunday between Christmas and Epiphany Sunday, with the other two having none.

The brevity of the season and the dominance of the Gospel lections limit our strategies. In the proposals below are suggestions for each possibility—no Sunday after Christmas, one Sunday, and two Sundays. Each proposal builds on the one that precedes it. Note, also, that the dominance of the liturgical themes of the nativity and Incarnation and the ways the First Testament texts were chosen to be subordinate to those New Testament themes has led me not to offer proposals for preaching from the First Testament or Psalter lections for this short, focused season.

Christmas and Epiphany Sunday only:

STRATEGY 1—On Christmas and Epiphany, preachers will usually want to focus their sermons on the Gospel readings, since the accounts of Jesus' birth in Luke and Matthew anchor the liturgical remembering of the Christ Event. Placing Luke's version next to Matthew's is a great way to highlight the theological and narrative differences between the two accounts and undo the harmonizing misinterpretation of the texts that has occurred through centuries of using nativity scenes that place the shepherds and the magi side by side. Note some of the differences:

LUKE (Christmas)	MATTHEW (Epiphany)
Joseph and Mary forced to go to Bethlehem by the emperor's census	Joseph and Mary presumably live in Bethlehem
Setting is a stable	Setting is a house
Angel(s) reveal the birth	Star reveals the birth
Shepherds receive the revelation	Magi receive the revelation
Shepherds proclaim what they have seen	Magi depart in secret

But pointing out the differences between the two versions should also lead a preacher to claim a root similarity: God does not reveal the birth of the Christ child to those in power (Augustus in Luke or Herod in Matthew), but to outsiders (shepherds who are economically marginalized in Luke and Gentile astrologers [i.e., magicians] in Matthew). Thus both present a soteriological understanding of the Incarnation that has sociopolitical implications that could be unpacked in two related but distinct sermons.

STRATEGY 2—Another option is to follow a Christmas sermon on Luke 2:1–14 (15–20) with an Epiphany sermon on the Epistle lection (Eph. 3:1–12). The Ephesians text actually speaks more directly to the liturgical theme of revelation to the Gentiles than does the traditional Matthean lesson. Similar to strategy 1 above, the preacher could highlight the outsider character of the recipients of the revelation of the God of Israel: poor shepherds in Luke on Christmas and Gentiles in Ephesians on Epiphany.

One Sunday after Christmas:

STRATEGY 3—If the season has one Sunday in between Christmas and the congregation's celebration of Epiphany, the preacher may still want to focus on the Gospel lections. For Year C, the Gospel reading for Christmas 1 is the story of Jesus' visit to Jerusalem at age twelve. Focusing on Jesus' childhood extends the sense of incarnation established in the story of the nativity.

STRATEGY 4—The earlier Common Lectionary recommended that if the second alternate set of lections for Christmas (Christmas Proper 3) were not used on Christmas Eve or Day, they should be used later during the Christmas season due to the importance of John's prologue for the New Testament understanding of incarnation.[2] A similar option is to *substitute the readings for Christmas 2* (which include Jn. 1:[1–9], 10–18) for Christmas 1 in years and worshiping traditions where there is only one Sunday after Christmas. John 1:1–18 serves well to follow the Christmas focus on the nativity by inviting us to step back and reflect on the meaning of the Incarnation in a broader way. Likewise, the text's language of light overcoming darkness sets up the move toward the emphasis on revelation on Epiphany and during the Season after Epiphany.

Two Sundays after Christmas:

STRATEGY 5—See STRATEGY 4 on page 163.

STRATEGY 6—For congregations that celebrate Epiphany on January 6 and not on the Sunday before, the lectionary provides more possibilities for cumulative preaching. But the best option is still for the preacher to focus on the Gospel lections for the entire season. The themes mentioned in strategies above all still work together. On Christmas Eve/Day the focus is on the birth. On Christmas 1, it is on Jesus at age twelve. On Christmas 2, it is on John's understanding of the Incarnation. On Epiphany, Matthew tells of the revelation of the Christ child to foreign magi.

SUNDAYS after EPIPHANY

Year C

(See pp.11–13 for an overview of the three-dimensional character of the Revised Common Lectionary's approach to Epiphany.)

Lectionary Readings

	FIRST TESTAMENT	PSALTER	EPISTLE	GOSPEL
Epiphany (abc)	Isa. 60:1–6 Nations shall come to your light: camels, gold, frankincense	72:1–7, 10–14 Give the king your justice, O God	Eph. 3:1–12 Paul, a prisoner of Christ for Gentiles	Mt. 2:1–12 Magi
Epiphany 1 Baptism of the Lord	Isa. 43:1–7 I have redeemed you…when you pass through the waters	29 (abc) Voice of the LORD is over the waters	Acts 8:14–17 Apostles pray that those baptized in Samaria will receive the Holy Spirit	Lk. 3:15–17, 21–22 Baptism of Jesus
Epiphany 2	Isa. 62:1–5 Your land shall be called Married	36:5–10 Expanse of God's love: "drink from the river of your delights"	1 Cor. 12:1–11 Varieties of gifts of the Spirit	Jn. 2:1–11 Wedding at Cana
Epiphany 3	Neh. 8:1–3, 5–6, 8–10 Reading and interpretation of the Law of Moses	19 The Law of God is perfect	1 Cor. 12:12–31a Diversity of spiritual gifts: one body with many members	Lk. 4:14–21 First half of inaugural address in Nazareth
Epiphany 4	Jer. 1:4–10 Call of Jeremiah: "Before I formed you in the womb I knew you"	71:1–6 God as refuge: "You…took me from my mother's womb"	1 Cor. 13:1–13 Greatest gift is love	Lk. 4:21–30 Second half of inaugural address in Nazareth
Epiphany 5	Isa. 6:1–8 (9–13) Call of Isaiah—heavenly court	138 Before the gods I praise you…	1 Cor. 15:1–11 Resurrection appearance traditions	Lk. 5:1–11 Call of Peter, James, & John
Epiphany 6 Proper 1	Jer. 17:5–10 Woe to those who trust in mortals, blessed are those who trust in God	1 Blessed are those who delight in the torah…The wicked are not so…	1 Cor. 15:12–20 Christ has been raised from the dead, the first fruits of those who have died	Lk. 6:17–26 Beginning of Sermon on the Plain: Blessings & Woes

Epiphany 7 Proper 2	Gen. 45:3–11, 15 Joseph reconciles with his brothers	37:1–11, 39–40 Refrain from anger	1 Cor. 15:35–38, 42–50 It is sown a physical body, it is raised a spiritual body	Lk. 6:27–38 Middle of Sermon on the Plain: love your enemies, turn the other cheek
Epiphany 8 Proper 3	Isa. 55:10–13 My word does not return empty— sows fruitful seed, trees of the field	92:1–4, 12–15 Good to sing praises to God— righteous flourish like palm trees	1 Cor. 15:51–58 I tell you a mystery: we will not all die, but we will all be changed	Lk. 6:39–49 End of Sermon on the Plain: blind leading the blind, tree known by its fruit, house's foundation
Epiphany Last Transfiguration	Ex. 34:29–35 I have redeemed you…when you pass through the waters	99 (ac) Lord is King— worship at holy mountain	2 Cor. 3:12—4:2 We act with great boldness, not like Moses, who put a veil over his face	Lk. 9:28–36 (37–43) Transfiguration

Cumulative Preaching Strategies

As we consider a variety of cumulative preaching strategies for the Season after Epiphany, we need to keep two challenging considerations in mind. First, the season's length varies year to year depending first on the date of Easter, which can fall anywhere from March 22 to April 25, and second on which day of the week Epiphany falls—the later in the week that January 6 falls, the earlier in January the Baptism of the Lord occurs. In other words, including Baptism of the Lord and Transfiguration Sunday, the season can last from four to nine Sundays after Epiphany, although the minimum and maximum are quite rare and most years fall between five and eight Sundays.

The second consideration involves the tension between the bookends of the season and the Sundays in between. On the Solemnities of the Lord at both ends of the season (Baptism on the first Sunday after Epiphany and Transfiguration on the last Sunday after Epiphany) the liturgical themes will focus the sermon. During the two to seven weeks in between, however, the Epistle and Gospel lections take on the form of semicontinuous readings found during the Sundays after Pentecost, with the First Testament and Psalter lection being chosen to support the Gospel.

With these two complications in mind, let us consider possible cumulative strategies for preaching through the Sundays after Epiphany.

STRATEGY 1—Since the ecumenical lectionary has its roots in the Lectionary for Mass, which considers the Sundays between Baptism of the Lord and Ash Wednesday to be Ordinary Time, during the Season after Epiphany the Revised Common Lectionary has us begin reading through the Gospel of Luke in a semicontinuous fashion that will be picked up again after Pentecost. (See also the introductory notes for preaching the semicontinuous reading of Luke during Ordinary Time on pp. 204–6.) This pattern begins after Baptism of the Lord and Epiphany 2, which is always drawn from John. Thus one obvious cumulative preaching strategy for this season is to focus one's sermons on the *Gospel lections.* The pattern is as follows:

Epiphany 1: Baptism (Luke 3:15–17, 21–22)

Epiphany 2: Jesus' first sign at the wedding in Cana (John 2:1–11)

Epiphany 3–4: Jesus' inaugural sermon at Nazareth (Luke 4)

Epiphany 5: Jesus calls the first disciples (Luke 5:1–11)

Epiphany 6 through the next to last Sunday after Epiphany:
The Sermon on the Plain (Luke 6)

It is important to notice the thematic shift from Epiphany 3–5 and 6–8. The first deals with *vocation* (Jesus' mission and the call of the disciples—see strategy 3 below) and the second with *ethics.*

STRATEGY 2—Another straightforward strategy for cumulative preaching on the Sundays in between Baptism of the Lord and Transfigurations is to focus on the semicontinuous readings from *Paul's First Letter to the Corinthians.* As with the Gospel series, this semicontinuous approach to the Epistles is again a reflection of the Lectionary for Mass's view of this season as Ordinary Time. The Epistle lessons from 1 Corinthians for Year C are more closely related than they were in Year B, although the lections fall into two sections. The first section, taken from chapters 12—14, deal with the division in the community over *spiritual gifts.* The second section, from chapter 15, deals with the division in the community over *resurrection of the body.*

This cumulative approach has two downsides, both of which should be taken into consideration, but neither of which should be prohibitive. The first is that these semicontinuous readings have no explicit connection with Epiphany themes or the other three lections for each Sunday. However, a liturgical balance can be created in which the language of much of the worship service grows out of the thematic core of the other lections, while the sermon draws on Paul's writing.

The second problem is that the semicontinuous reading of 1 Corinthians is limited to the seasons of Epiphany across the three-year cycle. The congregation will not return to 1 Corinthians until January of the following year. This means that each Epiphany when preaching from 1 Corinthians, the congregation will need to be reintroduced to the significant social, theological, and ecclesiological struggles facing the church at Corinth. Certainly this can and should be done as part of the sermons themselves by referring to, citing, and quoting from earlier parts of the letter. But outside of worship, individuals and groups within the congregation should be invited to read through and study the whole of 1 Corinthians while the pastor preaches through the closing chapters—historically, sociologically, and theologically contextualizing what they are reading.

STRATEGY 3—As noted under strategy 1, a thematic focus of one section of the Gospel lections has to do with Jesus announcing the nature of his ministry and the call of the first disciples. Combined with the supporting readings from the First Testament, we find a strong emphasis on *calling* that will serve well for a cumulative strategy through at least part of this season.

> **Epiphany 1:** Luke 3:15–17, 21–22 is the story of John's witness to Jesus' eschatological ministry and of Jesus' baptism. Both parts of the lection speak of the nature Jesus' ministry as well as the church's understanding of the ministry of the baptized.

> **Epiphany 2:** John 2:1–11 is the story of Jesus' first sign and involves a dialogue between Jesus and his mother concerning whether his hour has come.

> **OR:** 1 Corinthians 12:1–11 is part of Paul's discourse concerning spiritual gifts. This passage deals with various ministries of the church.

Epiphany 3: In Luke 4:14–21, Jesus reads from Isaiah and declares that his ministry is a fulfillment of its vision. This is the first part of two readings from Jesus' inaugural sermon in his hometown.

OR: 1 Corinthians 12:12–31a continues Paul's discussion of spiritual gifts and God's appointment of ministries.

Epiphany 4: Luke 4:21–30 continues the account of Jesus' inaugural sermon in Nazareth begun on Epiphany 3. However, in this passage, Jesus makes it clear that the focus of his ministry will bring him into conflict with his hometown's self-interests.

OR: In 1 Corinthians 13:1–13, Paul continues discussing spiritual gifts (see Epiphany 2–3). In contrast to chapter 12, in which Paul speaks of the diversity of gifts, here he claims that all gifts of ministry must be grounded in the greatest spiritual gift: love.

OR: Jeremiah 1:4–10, the prophet's description of his call expressed in terms of being known before he was born.

Epiphany 5: In Luke 5:1–11, Jesus calls Simon, James, and John as his first disciples (in a version quite different from the other gospels).

OR: Isaiah 6:1–8 (9–13), a description of the prophet's call, expressed in terms of a vision of the heavenly court.

STRATEGY 4—Another cumulative theme worth exploring for part of the season is that of the *moral/ethical life.* This is a natural extension of the thematic focus of calling described in the previous strategy.

Epiphany 2: 1 Corinthians 12:1–11, Paul's discourse about spiritual gifts involves an ecclesiological ethic.

Epiphany 3: Luke 4:14–21, Jesus' inaugural sermon presents a view of salvation in terms of social justice—good news for the poor, the imprisoned, the infirmed, and the oppressed.

OR: Nehemiah 8:1–3, 5–6, 8–10 brings the reading and reinstitution of the Mosaic torah to fruition when the people are told to feast and to share their feast with those for whom nothing is prepared.

OR: Psalm 19 celebrates the Lord's torah.

OR: 1 Corinthians 12:12–31a, a continuation of Paul's discourse about spiritual gifts in which he grounds his discussion in a view of a community ethic.

Epiphany 4: 1 Corinthians 13:1–13, Paul's elevation of love as the greatest gift serves as an exclamation point to his view of a church ethic.

OR: Luke 4:21–30 is a continuation of Jesus' inaugural sermon in Nazareth, in which he makes clear that his ministry will be to the marginalized.

Epiphany 6: Luke 6:17–26 opens the Sermon on the Plain with the Beatitudes and Woes. In contrast to Matthew's spiritualized Beatitudes, Luke's version expresses a view of salvation that is a reversal of the social status quo.

OR: Jeremiah 17:5–10 and Psalm 1 are similar wisdom poems. Both contrast the life of righteousness with the life of wickedness.

Epiphany 7: Luke 6:27–38 continues the Sermon on the Plain. Here Jesus proclaims an ethic of loving one's enemy.

OR: Although the Psalter reading for the day is Psalm 37:1–11, 39–40, one might want to preach on Psalm 37 as a whole. It is a wisdom poem in acrostic (i.e., alphabetical) form that lifts up the virtues of patience, obedience, and piety.

OR: Genesis 45:3–11, 15, the story of Joseph's reception of his brothers, exemplifies forgiveness instead of wrath.

Epiphany 8: Luke 6:39–49 is a final reading from the Sermon on the Plain. This passage deals with the issue of hypocrisy.

OR: Psalm 92:1–4, 12–15 is an excerpt from a wisdom hymn of thanksgiving contrasting the wicked and the righteous. As with Psalm 37 on Epiphany 7, one would do well to preach on the whole psalm.

LENT and HOLY WEEK

Year C

(See pp. 13–17 for an overview of the three-dimensional character of the Revised Common Lectionary's approach to Lent.)

Lectionary Readings

	FIRST TESTAMENT	PSALTER	EPISTLE	GOSPEL
ASH WEDNESDAY				
Ash Wed. (abc)	Joel 2:1–2, 12–17 Blow the trumpet —call to repentance	51:1–17 Penitential prayer, confessing sin and asking forgiveness	2 Cor. 5:20b—6:10 Ambassadors of Christ commended in every way	Mt. 6:1–6, 16–21 Practice your righteousness
SUNDAYS IN LENT				
Lent 1	Deut. 26:1–11 First fruits— a wandering Aramean	91:1–2, 9-16 Profession of confidence in God's protection	Rom. 10:8b–13 Professing Christ	Lk. 4:1–13 Temptation of Christ
Lent 2	Gen. 15:1–12, 17–18 God makes covenant with Abram	27 Profession of trust in God as basis of prayer for help	Phil. 3:17—4:1 Stand fast	Lk. 13:31–35 Prophet must die in Jerusalem
Lent 3	Isa. 55:1–9 Call to repentance	63:1–8 Seeking God's presence as sustenance for life	1 Cor. 10:1–13 Mosaic rock: God will not test beyond strength	Lk. 13:1–9 Repent—fig tree parable
Lent 4	Josh. 5:9–12 Transition from manna to eating fruits of promised land	32 Thanksgiving for deliverance from sin and its effects	2 Cor. 5:16–21 New creation in Christ	Lk. 15:1–3, 11b–32 The parable of prodigal son
Lent 5	Isa. 43:16–21 Past—path in sea; future—path in desert	126 Song of Ascent: restore the fortunes of Zion	Phil. 3:4b–14 Count gains as loss	Jn. 12:1–8 Anointing by Mary
HOLY WEEK				
Palm	Isa. 50:4–9a (abc) Suffering Servant	118:1–2, 19–29 (abc) Hallel Psalm: festal procession with branches		Lk. 19:28–40 Triumphant entry OR Jn. 12:12-16 Triumphant Entry
Passion		31:9–16 (abc) Lament in the face of bodily suffering	Phil. 2:5–11 (abc) Christ Hymn	Lk. 22:14—23:56 Last Supper–Burial

Holy Mon. (abc)	Isa. 42:1–9 Suffering Servant	36:5–11 God's steadfast love	Heb. 9:11–15 Christ's blood of the new covenant	Jn. 12:1–11 Mary anoints Jesus; leaders seek his & Lazarus' death
Holy Tue. (abc)	Isa. 49:1–7 Suffering Servant	71:1–14 Prayer for deliverance from enemies	1 Cor. 1:18–31 Foolishness of Christ crucified	Jn. 12:20–36 Jesus withdraws from public ministry & announces the hour of his glorification has arrived
Holy Wed. (abc)	Isa. 50:4–9a Suffering Servant	70 Prayer for deliverance from enemies	Heb. 12:1–3 Jesus, pioneer & perfecter of faith thru endurance of cross	Jn. 13:21–32 Jesus predicts Judas' betrayal
Holy Th. (abc)	Ex. 12:1–4 (5–10) 11–14 First Passover	116:1–2, 12–19 Thanksgiving— cup of salvation	1 Cor. 11:23–26 Institution of Lord's supper	Jn. 13:1–17, 31b–35 New commandment—Footwashing
Good Fri. (abc)	Isa. 52:13—53:12 Suffering Servant	22 Lament: My God, my God…	Heb. 10:16–25 Blood of Jesus	Jn. 18:1—19:42 Arrest–Burial
Holy Sat.	Job. 14:1–14 Lament concerning human mortality OR Lam. 3:1–9, 19–24 Suffering God's wrath	31:1–4, 15–16 Petition for refuge	1 Pet. 4:1–8 Prepare to suffer in the flesh as Christ did	Mt. 27:57–66 Jesus' burial OR Jn. 19:38–42 Jesus' burial

Cumulative Preaching Strategies

When developing cumulative preaching strategies for Lent, one must take into account a few factors. First, the season is initiated on Ash Wednesday, for which the Revised Common Lectionary offers the same readings every year. Ash Wednesday creates a strong depth dimension, defining the liturgical season in the same manner every year by focusing on themes of mortality, confession, repentance, and Christian disciplines. Beyond this general emphasis, the lessons for Ash Wednesday, however, do not lead into the lections that follow throughout the rest of the season. Therefore the lections for Ash Wednesday should not be strongly considered when developing a cumulative preaching strategy for Lent.

Second, the liturgical focus of the first Sunday in Lent every year is the temptation of Jesus in the wilderness, based on the Synoptic

Gospel of the year. This lection is offered as a rationale for the forty-day length of the season as well as to reinforce the Lenten practices of fasting and prayer. Again, this lectionary pattern serves the depth dimension of the three-year liturgical cycle more than the height dimension. Thus the connection between Lent 1 and the following Sundays in Lent, especially in terms of the Gospel readings, may be weak.

Third, while many of the texts for Lent, Year C, offer significant homiletical potential, the lections as a group do not offer as many strong cumulative options as the other two years. In other words, the height dimension for this season is not as well defined as it might have been. Thus preachers may want to combine a couple of the options proposed below. Or those who follow the Revised Common Lectionary but do not feel tied to it may wish to take one of the options suggested below and supplement it by changing a reading here or there.

Finally, the season concludes with Holy Week, which begins on Palm/Passion Sunday. In some sense, Holy Week (leading to the Easter Vigil on Saturday night or to Easter Sunday) represents a season in and of itself, although most Protestant churches worship only on Holy Thursday and/or Good Friday. Therefore, preachers should develop a cumulative preaching strategy for Lent 1–5 and deal with Ash Wednesday and Holy Week as bookends that are separate cases.

For the Sundays in Lent C

The first two strategies proposed deal with the lections as ordered by the lectionary itself, while the ones that follow offer thematic options:

STRATEGY 1—In Years A and B, the Synoptic Gospel (Matthew and Mark, respectively) give way to John. But in Year C, John only appears on Lent 5. Thus one cumulative strategy appropriate to the year is to preach on the *Lukan texts for Lent 1–4.* This will set up a strong hearing of the texts for Palm/Passion Sunday and Easter Sunday (if the Lukan version of the empty tomb story is chosen). While there is not a clear flow to the choice of Lukan passages, they are all fitting for the themes associated with Lent— temptation, fasting, prayer, crucifixion, repentance, and forgiveness.

STRATEGY 2—The Lectionary for Mass structures the First Testament lections for Lent according to a *salvation history schema:* Lent 1—origins; Lent 2—Abraham; Lent 3—exodus; Lent 4—nation; Lent 5—eschatological hope. The Revised Common Lectionary, for the most part, follows this schema. Two factors in Year C, however, complicate this pattern.

The first concerns the reading for Lent 1. During Years A and B, the focus on origins relates to the garden of Eden and the recreation of humanity after the flood, respectively. In Year C, however, the First Testament lection is Deuteronomy 26:1–11. This passage does deal with the origin of the nation of Israel's existence in the promised land and involves a creedal-like statement that looks back further, but nevertheless it chronologically follows the reading for Lent 2 (Gen. 15:1–12, 17–18), which deals with Abraham. This different approach to origins does not break the salvation history pattern, but it does realign it somewhat.

Second, in Year C, the reading for Lent 3 changes from a focus on the exodus to Isaiah 55:1–9 in order to support the Gospel lection's focus on repentance. In the Lectionary for Mass, the First Testament assignment is Exodus 3:1–8, 13–15 (extended to Ex. 3:1–15 in the original New Common Lectionary), which is the story of Moses and the burning bush. Unlike the first factor, this substitution breaks the salvation history pattern. Part of this pattern, however, remains in the Epistle lection (1 Cor. 10:1–13). In it, Paul offers a midrashic interpretation of the story of Moses getting water from the rock. To preach this pattern, one may wish to bring Exodus 3 back into the mix, or simply switch from the First Testament lections to the Epistle reading on Lent 3. As it stands, the pattern in the Revised Common Lectionary looks like this:

Lent 1: Origins (Deut. 26:1–11, "a wandering Aramean was my ancestor").

Lent 2: Abraham (Gen. 15:1–12, 17–18, God's covenant with Abram).

Lent 3: Exodus (1 Cor. 10:1–13, Paul refers to Moses getting water from the rock).

Lent 4: Nation (Josh. 5:9–12, the Israelites cease to eat manna and begin to eat from the fruits of the land).

Lent 5: Eschatological hope (Isa. 43:16–21, recalling the exodus through the Red Sea, the prophet envisions a new path through the desert).

STRATEGY 3—Even though the Revised Common Lectionary designates a psalm or portion of a psalm for every Sunday of the three-year lectionary cycle, preachers give the Psalter short shrift. Indeed, the lectionary use of the Psalms is not directed toward homiletical goals. Instead, they are chosen as responses to the First Testament readings. But it would be a shame if the Psalms receive no attention in the pulpit. Lent is an ideal time to correct this deficiency. With Lent's emphasis on the discipline of prayer, a congregation will be well served by a series of sermons focusing on *praying the psalms* offered by the Revised Common Lectionary for the season. In Year C, the psalms chosen share a common theme of the trustworthiness of God's providence and salvation.

STRATEGY 4—Turning to thematic options, the most obvious one to be found in the readings concerns *salvation.* Since Lent leads into the remembrance and celebration of Christ's crucifixion and resurrection, it is not surprising that the lections for the season have such a soteriological focus.

> **Ash Wednesday:** Joel 2:1–2, 12–17 is a call to repent and return to the Lord who is gracious.
>
> **OR:** Psalm 51:1–17 is a penitential prayer in which the psalmist seeks forgiveness.
>
> **OR:** 2 Corinthians 5:20—6:10 is Paul's plea that his readers seek reconciliation with God.
>
> **Lent 1:** Deuteronomy 26:1–11, as part of a liturgy of tithing the first fruits of harvest, calls the Israelites to reflect on God's deliverance of the people from Egypt.
>
> **OR:** Psalm 91:1–2, 9–16— or, better, when the whole psalm is read—speaks of God's deliverance with powerful metaphors.
>
> **OR:** Romans 10:8b–13 describes the relationship between salvation and confession of Christ.

Lent 2: Psalm 27 is a prayer of confidence in which salvation is imaged as divine protection.

OR: Philippians 3:17—4:1 contrasts living as enemies of the cross with living out one's salvation in Christ.

OR: Luke 13:31–35 presents Jesus using a feminine metaphor to describe the salvation he wished to offer Jerusalem.

Lent 3: Isaiah 55:1–9 understands salvation as God's restoration of the postexilic nation. The passage uses the powerful metaphor of a royal banquet to image this restoration.

OR: Psalm 63:1–8 is a prayer for help that ends with an expression of confidence in God's providence.

Lent 4: Joshua 5:9–12, as the Israelites enter the promised land, the disgrace of their enslavement in Egypt is finally removed.

OR: Psalm 32 is a psalm of penitence, but it celebrates God's forgiveness.

OR: 2 Corinthians 5:16–21 discusses salvation in terms of those in Christ becoming a new creation.

OR: Luke 15:1–3, 11b–32, the parable of the prodigal son, joins the parables of the lost sheep and lost coin, to offer the image of salvation as finding the lost.

Lent 5: Isaiah 43:16–21, a Second Isaiah vision of Israel's restoration in terms of God doing such a new thing that it is like a river running through the desert.

OR: Psalm 126 is a prayer for restoration rooted in the memory of God having restored Jerusalem.

OR: Philippians 3:4b–14, Paul's contrast of his own achievements with the salvation only God can effect.

STRATEGY 5—While soteriology is the dominant thematic option present in the Lenten lections, it is not the only one. Two other options are not so much theologically explicit discourses as they are clusters of images that have theological import. Thus a preacher using these images to shape a cumulative preaching strategy for the season must be sure to look through the images to the central theological purposes of the texts. The first cluster of images involves *food and drink*. Given that the church calls for a fast on Ash Wednesday, remembers Jesus' last supper on Maundy Thursday, and celebrates the risen Christ eating in front of and with his disciples during Easter, this is no mean cluster of images to highlight and explore in the pulpit.

Lent 1: Luke 4:1–13, the story of Jesus being tested in the wilderness, opens with Satan tempting Jesus to turn stones into bread.

OR: Deuteronomy 26:1–11 is a harvest liturgy involving an offering of the first fruits of produce and a celebration of God bringing the Israelites into the land of milk and honey.

Lent 2: Philippians 3:17—4:1 does not mention eating or drinking explicitly, but Paul does refer to enemies of the cross who have "the belly" as their god.

Lent 3: Isaiah 55:1–9 offers a vision of divine restoration of Judah in terms of God inviting the hearers to a royal banquet.

OR: Psalm 63:1 8 speaks of the soul thirsting for God and being satisfied as with a rich feast.

OR: In 1 Corinthians 10:1–13, Paul uses imagery of eating and drinking in contrasting ways: first he recalls the image of God's gifts of heavenly manna and water from the rock in a typological fashion; then he turns the image on its head to portray idolatry and immorality.

Lent 4: Luke 15:1 3, 11b–32, the parable of the prodigal son, is part of Jesus' response to the religious leaders who protested Jesus eating with sinners. The parable ends with a feast of the fatted calf.

Lent 5: John 12:1–8 is the scene in which Mary anoints Jesus. The setting is a dinner given in Jesus' honor.

OR: Isaiah 43:16–21 presents a vision of restoration in terms of water in the desert, water that God will provide for the people to drink.

OR: Psalm 126 ends with harvest imagery.

STRATEGY 6— A second cluster of images involves *Jerusalem* and specifically the *temple*. Shaping a cumulative strategy around these images is appropriate given that Lent culminates in the passion narrative that is set in Jerusalem.

Lent 1: Luke 4:1–13, the story of Jesus being tested in the wilderness, ends with Satan tempting Jesus to throw himself down from the pinnacle of the temple.

OR: Psalm 91 likely served as a liturgy for entering the temple.

OR: Deuteronomy 26:1–11 is a liturgy for making an offering of the first fruits of the harvest at the sanctuary.

Lent 2: Luke 13:31–35 presents Jesus heading toward Jerusalem and declaring that he will die a prophet's death there. A lament concerning how he had wished to save Jerusalem follows his announcement.

OR: Psalm 27 is a prayer of distress from one who comes to the temple seeking an oracle from the Lord.

Lent 3: Psalm 63:1–8 is a prayer of one who comes to the temple seeking help, in the form of a sign of God's presence, from persecution.

OR: In Luke 13:1–9, Jesus refers to a tragedy in Jerusalem to argue that such events are not caused by God's wrath for sinfulness, but instead all are sinful and need to repent.

Lent 4: While no text on this Sunday refers to Jerusalem or the temple, the passage from Joshua 5:9–12 does describe the first Passover celebration at Gilgal, which was a significant political and religious center of premonarchial Israel.

Lent 5: Psalm 126 opens by remembering the restoration of Jerusalem after the exile as the basis for praying for future restoration.

For Holy Week, Year C

Many Protestant congregations do not have Holy Week services on the weekdays of Holy Week, or only have services on Holy/Maundy Thursday and/or Good Friday. Moreover, congregations that do have services throughout the week may well not have a service on Holy Saturday due to celebrating the Easter Vigil on Saturday night. Because of these varying practices, it is difficult, and likely not helpful, to offer preaching strategies to be used for the entire week. Nevertheless, noting some of the broad cumulative patterns exhibited during the week will help preachers adapt them to whatever liturgical practices their congregations follow.

STRATEGY 1—The first pattern concerns *the juxtaposition of John and Luke's versions of the Jerusalem narratives.* Beginning with Palm/Passion Sunday, all of the lectionary readings for Holy Week are the same for all three years of the lectionary cycle, with the exception of the Gospel lections for Palm/Passion Sunday. The Gospel readings for the Liturgy of the Palm and the Liturgy of the Passion come from the Synoptic Gospel for the year. The Gospel texts for the rest of Holy Week proceed from John. While this is the same throughout all three years of the lectionary cycle, the dynamic for Year C differs. Unlike in Years A and B, this year Luke has remained the dominant Gospel for Lent, instead of being replaced by John. John only appears on Lent 5. Therefore, the readings for Palm/Passion Sunday are not a return to Luke after a significant absence but a culmination of the Gospel readings for the season. The use of John in Holy Week, therefore, breaks into the dominance of Luke and offers a different perspective on Jesus' suffering and death.

STRATEGY 2—The *Suffering Servant oracles* from Isaiah dominate the First Testament lections. While preachers must avoid eisegetical errors of the past in which the church read these oracles as predictions about Christ, they can nevertheless be used to discuss the complex and confusing relation of vicarious suffering and redemption that is reiterated throughout much of the Judeo-Christian tradition and which is central to the Christ Event.

STRATEGY 3—In spite of the fact that the *Epistle readings* are not drawn from the same author or school and are subordinate to the Gospel lections for the week, they have some cohesion. They all interpret the death of Jesus from different theological perspectives and by using a range of metaphors. Although the liturgical emphasis for the week is on the story of Jesus' passion, preaching through various interpretations of his death has much homiletical potential.

EASTER

Year C

(See pp. 17–21 for an overview of the three-dimensional character of the Revised Common Lectionary's approach to Easter.)

Lectionary Readings

	FIRST TESTAMENT	PSALTER	EPISTLE	GOSPEL
Easter Day	Acts 10:34–43 (abc) Peter's sermon to Cornelius…"but God raised him on the 3rd day"	118:1–2, 14–24 (abc) Rejoicing in God's providence: "I shall not die, but I shall live…but he did not give me over to death"	1 Cor. 15:19–26 Resurrection: Christ is the first fruits	Jn. 20:1–18 Empty tomb OR Lk. 24:1–12 Empty tomb
Easter Evening (abc)	Isa. 25:6–9 Salvation of the Lord: God will wipe away tears	114 Creation trembles at God's power exhibited in the exodus	1 Cor. 5:6b–8 Clean out the old yeast	Lk. 24:13–49 Emmaus & appearance to disciples
Easter 2	Acts 5:27–32 Peter's response to high priest: God exalted Jesus	118:14–29 Stone rejected has become cornerstone: "I shall not die, but I shall live…" OR 150 Praise the Lord	Rev. 1:4–8 Opening of letter to seven churches: Jesus is coming; alpha and omega	Jn. 20:19–31 (abc) Giving of the Spirit; Thomas
Easter 3	Acts 9:1–6 (7–20) Paul's call/ conversion	30 The Lord restored me from Sheol	Rev. 5:11–14 Singing to the one on the throne, and the Lamb	Jn. 21:1–19 Resurrection appearance: miraculous catch of fish; Peter, do you love me?
Easter 4 Good Shepherd	Acts 9:36–43 Peter heals Dorcas in Joppa	23 (abc) The Lord is my shepherd	Rev. 7:9–17 The Lamb will be their shepherd	Jn. 10:22–30 My sheep hear my voice
Easter 5	Acts 11:1–18 In Jerusalem, Peter recounts the giving of the Spirit to Gentiles	148 Praise the Lord	Rev. 21:1–6 New Jerusalem	Jn. 13:31–35 Glorification of the Son of Man; new commandment

Easter 6	Acts 16:9–15 Paul dreams of going to Mace-donia; baptizes Lydia's household	67 Let the nations be glad, for you judge with equity	Rev, 21:10, 22—22:5 New Jerusalem	Jn. 14:23–29 Promise of the Advocate OR Jn. 5:1–9 Healing of lame man at pool of Beth-zatha
Ascension (abc)	Acts 1:1–11 Opening of Acts: Ascension	47 The LORD is king OR 93 The LORD is king, robed in majesty.	Eph. 1:15–23 God seated Christ at the right hand in the heavenly places	Lk. 24:44–53 Ending of Luke: Ascension
Easter 7	Acts 16:16–34 Paul & Silas beaten/arrested for disturbing city; and opening of prison doors	97 The LORD is king: let the earth rejoice	Rev. 22:12–14, 16–17, 20–21 Come, Lord Jesus	Jn. 17:20–26 The glory you have given me, I have given them
Pentecost	Acts 2:1–21 (abc) Giving of Holy Spirit and Peter's Pentecost sermon	104:24–34, 35b (abc) O LORD, the earth is full of your crea-tures—when you send forth your Spirit	Rom. 8:14–17 All led by the Spirit of God are children of God	Jn. 14:8–17, (25–27) The Advocate, the Spirit of Truth

Cumulative Preaching Strategies

As noted in the overview of the Revised Common Lectionary's approach to Easter (in the Introduction), multiple, competing cumulative patterns are at play in the choices of lections for this season that complicate developing cumulative preaching strategies. These patterns are further complicated by the fact that three holy days—Easter, Ascension, and Pentecost—occur within the season and give it its unique character. Indeed, Easter and Pentecost (or, in some sense, Easter on the one hand and Ascension/Pentecost on the other hand) serve as bookends to the season. These different dynamics lead to cumulative preaching strategies that can be combined or divided up in different ways to work through the season.

Easter Sunday

STRATEGY 1—On Easter Sunday, preachers will almost surely preach (and usually should preach) on the *Gospel lection.* The Epistle reading from 1 Corinthians 15:19–26 and its focus on the resurrection of the body certainly supplies fitting material for homiletical consideration on this holy day, especially given the focus on 1 Corinthians 15 during the Season after Epiphany. In Acts 10:34–43, Peter preaches the resurrection to a Gentile household—also a fitting text for the day. But Easter Sunday is the day people come to church to hear the story they know by heart, the story of the empty tomb.

However, lectionary preachers who follow this traditional route must still choose between Luke 24:1–12 and John 20:1–18. Choosing the Lukan passage allows the preacher to connect the Easter sermon to the use of Luke during Lent and especially the extended reading from Luke on Passion/Palm Sunday. Choosing John 20, on the other hand, allows preachers to connect with Johannine themes that they have explored while preaching the Gospel lections during Holy Week or that they will explore throughout Easter.

Easter Sunday, Ascension, Pentecost

STRATEGY 2—The *three holy days* during Eastertide provide much of the continuity of the season by drawing a conclusion to the liturgical half of the year. Although the celebrations are spaced according to Lukan narrative chronology (forty days from Easter Sunday to Ascension and ten more days to Pentecost), they express different dimensions of the same theological reality and form a cumulative whole. That is, they call the church to remember that its very being rests upon the paradox of Christ's exaltation (transcendence) and the divine spiritual presence (immanence). Regardless of which texts preachers focus their sermons on for the rest of the season, preaching on the empty tomb in the Gospel lection and on the ascension and gift of the spirit in Acts can and should give cohesion to the season as a whole. For churches that do not gather to celebrate Ascension on Thursday, Ascension can (and perhaps should) be celebrated on Easter 7. This shift creates a sense of the season having bookends: Easter Sunday at the start and Ascension/Pentecost at the end.

Gospel Lections in Eastertide

STRATEGY 3—As noted in the Introduction, Eastertide offers three thematic movements focused by the *Gospel lections*. These movements can serve to focus the preacher's attention.

The first three Sundays—Easter Sunday through Easter 3—deal with *resurrection appearances*. Preaching on John for all three Sundays will allow the congregation to hear most of John's extensive resurrection narrative (from Jn. 20—21) in its literary order.

Easter 4 divides the season in half. It is *Good Shepherd Sunday* and the gospel reading is always drawn from the mixture of shepherding metaphors found in John 10. In Year C, the reading is taken from the portion in which Jesus speaks of his followers knowing his full identity as sheep know the voice of their shepherd. (Note also the shepherd language in Ps. 23 and the metaphor of Lamb for Christ in Rev. 7.)

Gospel lections for Easter 5–7 proceed, as always, from the *Johannine farewell discourse*. While it may, at first glance, seem odd to preach from texts in which Jesus prepares his disciples for his departure during Eastertide, two things are important to recognize. First, when John speaks of Jesus' departure or glorification he is speaking of the whole of Jesus' crucifixion, resurrection, and exaltation. Thus in this discourse, Jesus interprets not only his pending death, but also his being raised from the dead. Second, the theme of preparing for Jesus' departure fits the latter part of Eastertide in terms of preparing for Ascension.

Semicontinuous Readings

STRATEGY 4—As noted in the Introduction, during Eastertide the Revised Common Lectionary follows the ancient practice of substituting readings from **Acts of the Apostles** for the First Testament lection. Broadly speaking, by examining narrative moments in the life of the early church that flowed out of the resurrection and gift of the Holy Spirit, a congregation prepares for the celebration of Pentecost that closes liturgical time before Ordinary Time begins.

However, a glance at the Acts readings for Year C will likely raise some level of frustration in preachers. Certainly the lectionary committee could have made choices that were better connected. The lections are in narrative order, but they jump wide spans of text as well as jumping back and forth between Peter and Paul. Nevertheless, this series of texts has homiletical potential. A number of the texts deal with God's response to religious, social, and political persecution of the church.

STRATEGY 5—The Epistle lections for Eastertide come from **The Revelation to John**. While Revelation is an apocalypse and not an epistle, the heavenly vision opens with seven letters to seven church in Asia Minor (chapters 2 3), as well as opening and closing with literary structures found in ancient letters (1:4–6; 22:21).

The apocalyptic worldview of Revelation is certainly appropriate to engage in the pulpit during Easter given the New Testament's view that the resurrection is an eschatological event. Indeed, it serves as a nice parallel to liturgical time opening with an eschatological emphasis back in Advent. However, preachers will experience a great deal of frustration if they hope the semicontinuous reading through Revelation in Easter C will give the congregation a chance to experience the major movements of the apocalyptic narrative. The Revised Common Lectionary avoids the texts that deal with judgment and cataclysmic battles (e.g., there are no readings taken from 7:18—20:15) and thus misses the religio-political context of the book's message (which is primarily a call to endure through trials of persecution because God will ultimately be victorious). Instead, they focus primarily on the exaltation of Christ and visions of salvation. While these images are certainly thematically appropriate for Eastertide, they have been disembodied from the specific trouble that the original readers were facing. Preachers will do well to spend time in the pulpit to counter the range of illegitimate allegorical readings that are popular. But to guide a congregation through a critical hearing of the work, preachers must highlight the original circumstances of persecution that gave rise to the apocalyptic vision. Otherwise, no serious homiletical analogies can be drawn.

Preachers who wish to engage Revelation in a serious cumulative fashion during Easter have two main options. The first is to begin with the assigned lections but use them as a diving board into the broader scope of the writing. The second, which is only available to those whose tradition allows them to break from the lectionary, is to follow the lead of the Revised Common Lectionary in reading from Revelation but to choose a different semicontinuous series of readings that better represent the full span of the book while at the same time relate to themes of Eastertide.

Thematic Approaches

STRATEGY 6—A final cumulative strategy for Easter C is the possibility of exploring the *inclusiveness of God's reign and salvation* through the lens of the Easter faith.

> **Easter 1:** Acts 10:34–43 is Peter's sermon to the first Gentile converts to the Christian faith. The speech opens with the claim that God shows no partiality.

Easter 2: Revelation 1:4–8, a passage taken from the opening of the Revelation in which John offers a greeting to the seven churches in Asia Minor, describes Jesus Christ as ruler of the kings of the earth.

Easter 3: In Acts 9:1–6 (7–20), Saul the persecutor becomes Paul the apostle to the Gentiles.

    OR: Revelation 5:11–14 presents a view of the entirety of creation being included in the heavenly worship of the Lamb.

Easter 4: Revelation 7:9–17 is the vision of a multitude, drawn from every nation, worshiping the Lamb. This scene of inclusivity follows on the heels of the vision of 144,000 of Israel only being protected from God's judgment on the earth.

Easter 5: In Acts 11:1–18 Peter reports to the Jerusalem church concerning the conversion and baptism of the first Gentiles.

    OR: Revelation 21:1–6 offers a vision of a new heaven and a new earth.

Easter 6: Revelation 21:10, 22—22:5, the vision of the New Jerusalem, encompasses all nations.

    OR: Psalm 67 is a call for all nations to glorify God.

Ascension: In Acts 1:1–11, the risen Jesus commands his followers to be his witnesses "in Jerusalem, in all Judea and Samaria, and to the ends of the earth." This instruction serves as the basis for the spread of the gospel throughout the narrative of Acts.

Pentecost: In Acts 2:1–21, when the disciples receive the Holy Spirit, pilgrims from around the world are gathered in Jerusalem. Thus when Peter preaches the good news to and baptizes the three thousand, it is a group representative of humankind.

ORDINARY TIME

Year C

(See pp. 21–23 for an overview of the three-dimensional character of the Revised Common Lectionary's approach to the Season after Pentecost.)

LECTIONARY READINGS

	FIRST TESTAMENT	PSALTER	EPISTLE	GOSPEL
Trinity Sun.	Prov. 8:1–4, 22–31 Wisdom created first	8 Praise God for the place of humans in glorious creation	Rom. 5:1–5 We have peace with God through Christ… God's love has been poured into our hearts through the Holy Spirit	Jn. 16:12–15 Spirit will guide you in all truth…All that the Father has is mine
Proper 4 5/29–6/4	1 Kings 18:20–21 (22–29) 30–39 Elijah vs. prophets of Baal	96 Sing to the LORD a new song…all the gods of the people are idols	Gal. 1:1–12 Opening of the letter—setting the themes	Lk. 7:1–10 Healing the centurion's slave
Proper 5 6/5–6/11	1 Kings 17:8–16 (17–24) *Elijah (ca.859–850 B.C.E.)* Elijah & the widow at Zarephath	146 Praise for God's providence: the LORD upholds the orphan and widow	Gal. 1:11–24 Autobiographical defense	Lk. 7:11–17 Raising the widow's son
Proper 6 6/12–6/18	1 Kings 21:1–10 (11–14) 15–21a Elijah pronounces judgment on Ahab/Jezebel for Naboth's vineyard	5:1–8 You are not a God who delights in wickedness	Gal. 2:15–21 Autobiographical defense continued	Lk. 7:36—8:3 Anointing by a sinful woman; women following Jesus
Proper 7 6/19–25	1 Kings 19:1–4 (5–7) 8–15a Elijah flees to Mt. Horeb	42 and 43 Prayer for help by one seeking the face of God	Gal. 3:23–29 Law as slave-teacher; but heirs through faith	Lk. 8:26–39 Healing of the Gerasene demoniac
Proper 8 6/26–7/2	2 Kings 2:1–2, 6–14 *Elisha (ca. 849–815 B.C.E.)* Elisha succeeds Elijah—strikes the water with the mantle	77:1–2, 11–20 Recounting the mighty deeds of God…Your path was through the seas	Gal. 5:1, 13–25 Called to freedom	Lk. 9:51–62 Turning toward Jerusalem; rejection by the Samaritan village; would-be followers
Proper 9 7/3–7/9	2 Kings 5:1–14 Elisha heals Naaman	30 Thanksgiving for healing	Gal. 6:(1–6) 7–16 Closing exhortations	Lk. 10:1–11, 16–20 Sending out of the 70

Proper 10 7/10–7/16	Am. 7:7–17 (ca. 760 B.C.E.) Amos's calling —plumbline, accusation by Amaziah	82 Prayer for justice	Col. 1:1–14 Opening of the letter	Lk. 10:25–37 Love God and neighbor; parable of good Samaritan
Proper 11 7/17–7/23	Am. 8:1–12 Judgment like a bowl of summer fruit	52 Judgment against the wicked	Col. 1:15–28 Christ Hymn	Lk. 10:38–42 Martha and Mary
Proper 12 7/24–7/30	Hos. 1:2–10 (mid 8th c.—721 B.C.E.) Hosea's call— marriage to a har- lot and children	85 Prayer for restoration of the community	Col. 2:6–15 (16–19) Against heretics	Lk. 11:1–13 Teach us to pray
Proper 13 7/31–8/6	Hos. 11:1–11 God as idolatrous Israel's loving parent	107:1–9, 43 Thanksgiving for deliverance from distress	Col. 3:1–11 Closing exhortations	Lk. 12:13–21 Parable of rich fool
Proper 14 8/7–8/13	Isa. 1:1, 10–20 Prologue—choice of obedience or rebellion against God	50:1–8, 22–23 Call to live righ- teously, not just make correct sacrifices	Heb. 11:1–3, 8–16 By faith, Abraham…	Lk. 12:32–40 Parable of slaves awaiting the master's return
Proper 15 8/14–8/20	Isa. 5:1–7 (First Isaiah, ca. 742–700 B.C.E.) Judgment on the vineyard/Israel	80:1–2, 8–19 Prayer for res- toration: you brought a vine out of Israel	Heb. 11:29—12:2 Cloud of witnesses	Lk. 12:49–56 I came to bring division
Proper 16 8/21–8/27	Jer. 1:4–10 (622–586 B.C.E.) Jeremiah's calling	71:1–6 Prayer for protec- tion: it was you who took me from the womb	Heb. 12:18–29 Warning against rejecting God's grace (preaching on Ex. 19)	Lk. 13:10–17 Healing of crippled woman
Proper 17 8/28–9/3	Jer. 2:4–13 Accusation of Idolatry	81:1, 10–16 I brought you out of Egypt, but you Israel would not submit to me	Heb. 13:1–8, 15–16 Closing exhortations	Lk. 14:1, 7–14 Dinner with the Pharisees
Proper 18 9/4–9/10	Jer. 18:1–11 Potter-God shapes evil against Judah—call to repentance	139:1–6, 13–18 Omnipresence of God—it was you who knit me together in my mother's womb	Philem. 1–21 Appeal for Onesimus	Lk. 14:25–33 Cost of discipleship
Proper 19 9/11–9/17	Jer. 4:11–12, 22–28 Utter judgment	14 They have all gone astray	1 Tim. 1:12–17 Opening biograph- ical gratitude for mercy	Lk. 15:1–10 Parables of lost sheep & coin

Proper 20 9/18–9/24	Jer. 8:18—9:1 Lament over coming destruction (no balm in Gilead)	79:1–9 Prayer for help following the destruction of the temple	1 Tim. 2:1–7 Pray for the authorities so that we might have peace	Lk. 16:1–13 Parable of dishonest steward
Proper 21 9/25–10/1	Jer. 32:1–3a, 6–15 Jeremiah buys a field—hope of restoration	91:1–6, 14–16 God will protect you	1 Tim. 6:6–19 Fight the good fight	Lk. 16:19–31 Parable of Lazarus & rich man
Proper 22 10/2–10/8	Lam. 1:1–6 Lament over desolate Jerusalem	137 Lament over the destruction of Jerusalem and the exile	2 Tim. 1:1–14 Greeting and thanksgiving	Lk. 17:5–10 Sayings: faith, slaves of God
Proper 23 10/9–10/15	Jer. 29:1, 4–7 Letter to exiles	66:1–12 Recalling the exodus and judgment as testing	2 Tim. 2:8–15 Theological foundation for endurance	Lk. 17:11–19 Healing of ten lepers
Proper 24 10/16–10/22	Jer. 31:27–34 New covenant	119:97–104 How I love your torah, your commandment makes me wiser than my enemies	2 Tim. 3:14—4:5 Closing charge	Lk. 18:1–8 Parable of the widow & unjust judge
Proper 25 10/23–10/29	Joel 2:23–32 *(prob. postexilic, between 500 and 350 B.C.E.)* Salvation from locust plague	65 Harvest thanksgiving	2 Tim. 4:6–8, 16–18 Closing instructions	Lk. 18:9–14 Parable of the Pharisee and the tax collector
Proper 26 10/30–11/5	Hab. 1:1–4; 2:1–4 *(ca. 609–597 B.C.E.)* How long shall I cry out?	119:137–144 You are righteous, O LORD, and your judgments are right	2 Thess. 1:1–4, 11–12 Letter opening	Lk. 19:1–10 Salvation of Zacchaeus
Proper 27 11/6–11/12	Hag. 1:15b—2:9 *(520 B.C.E.)* The splendor of the temple God will rebuild	145:1–5, 17–21 Hymn of praise: I will extol you, O God…the LORD is near to all who call OR 98 Thanksgiving for salvation: God has remembered God's steadfast love for Israel	2 Thess. 2:1–5, 13–17 The parousia	Lk. 20:27–38 Sadducees ask about resurrection
Proper 28 11/13–11/19	Isa. 65:17–25 *(Third Isaiah, after 539 B.C.E.)* Eschatological redemption—wolf and the lamb	Isa. 12 Thanksgiving for deliverance: though you were angry, you comforted me	2 Thess. 3:6–13 Exhortation against idleness	Lk. 21:5–19 Eschatological discourse

Proper 29 Reign of Christ 11/20–11/26	Jer. 23:1–6 Raise up for David a righteous branch	Lk. 1:68–79 Benedictus—God has raised up a mighty Savior for us in the house of David	Col. 1:11–20 Christ Hymn	Lk. 23:33–43 Crucifixion— "king of the Jews"

CUMULATIVE PREACHING STRATEGIES

After Pentecost, the function of the readings of the Revised Common Lectionary changes significantly, and so must one's cumulative preaching strategies. The lections chosen for liturgical time are determined by seasonal themes related to the remembrance and celebration of various aspects of the Christ Event. Thus the four readings assigned to a particular Sunday are chosen to relate to or interact with one another in such a way as to shape the church's experience of the liturgical occasion. In other words, the scripture lessons are subordinate to the liturgical theme, and a preacher's interpretation of a particular lection within the set of readings is influenced by that liturgical context.

In Ordinary Time, with the exception of a few solemnities here and there (see below), no liturgical themes are at work. Neither the season nor individual Sundays are thematically determined. Instead, the scripture readings shape the season and the individual Sundays. Indeed, apart from the Psalter reading serving as a response to the First Testament, the lections for each Sunday are not related at all.[3] The three-dimensional lectionary of the liturgical season gives way to a two-dimension lectionary during Ordinary Time. Put differently, a predominant width dimension gives way to a strong height (connection from week to week) and depth (relation of each of the three years).

This means that there will be no reason at all to look for thematically oriented cumulative preaching strategies for the Sundays after Pentecost. Because the series of First Testament, Epistle, and Gospel lessons are each structured in a semicontinuous fashion, preachers should look for ways to preach through in ways that allow congregations to experience significant segments of the canon. In other words, the flow of the lections themselves will provide a cumulative quality to sermons throughout Ordinary Time as long as preachers do not hop from one kind of lection to another Sunday after Sunday. They must have the patience to stay with a particular series (i.e., the Gospel, First Testament, or Epistle series) long enough to allow the connections across time to influence the congregation's experience of the biblical writing being explored.

Before we consider specific ways to shape the semicontinuous flow of the readings into specific cumulative strategies, it will be helpful to review a few overarching issues related to the Season after Pentecost.

First, preachers should remember that the Season after Epiphany also utilized semicontinuous readings for the New Testament texts. They should recall what strategy they used during that season and reflect on whether and to what extent that strategy should influence the approach during the Season after Pentecost, or, at least, the beginning of the Season after Pentecost. For example, preachers who focused on the Lukan lections for the Sundays after Epiphany would have dealt with the inauguration of Jesus' ministry, the call of the first disciples, and the Sermon on the Plain. (During Lent the focus stayed primarily on Luke—primarily chapters 13 and 15—instead of shifting to John as in Years A and B. However, in Easter, the Gospel readings shifted to John.) At the beginning of Ordinary Time, the Gospel readings return to where the semicontinuous readings ended during the Season after Epiphany. There is significant continuity between the semicontinuous Gospel readings of the two seasons.

In contrast, the semicontinuous Epistle readings for the Season after Epiphany drew the three-year cycle of reading from 1 Corinthians to a close. After Trinity Sunday, the Revised Common Lectionary begins a series of readings from Galatians. Thus, we find no connection with the Epistle readings from the Sundays after Epiphany as there was for Year B.

Second, although Ordinary Time is not shaped by liturgical themes related to the Christ Event, as noted earlier, a few thematic celebrations occur during the season. The lections for these solemnities break from the semicontinuous pattern of the readings for all other Sundays.

> **Trinity Sunday** follows on the heels of Pentecost and opens the season. Since the doctrine of the Trinity represents a post-biblical theological development, the readings for this Sunday are usually related to the doctrine in a tentative or formulaic fashion.
>
> Although it is not recognized by the Revised Common Lectionary, many North American mainline congregations

and denominations celebrate World Communion Sunday on the first Sunday of October. For some preachers, this will cause no problem because they will still follow the lectionary. For others who use thematically oriented scripture lessons chosen for the day, **World Communion Sunday** will force a break in a cumulative strategy based on the semicontinuous readings of the Revised Common Lectionary.

All Saints' Day falls in the middle of the Season after Pentecost on November 1. Since many churches celebrate this day on the first Sunday of November and since November 1 occasionally falls on a Sunday for churches that celebrate it on the first day of November, this day may force the preacher to take a break in the pattern of preaching through semicontinuous readings.

The **Reign of Christ** (also referred to as Christ the King) closes the season and indeed the whole liturgical year. This day has a strong eschatological tone, which leads well into Advent and for which the lections late in Ordinary Time begin to prepare. Nevertheless, with the exception of the Gospel lections, the readings for Reign of Christ are not in literary continuity with the readings for the Sundays leading up to it.

Third, because Easter is a movable feast (it can occur as early as March 22 or as late as April 25), the opening of the season will vary greatly year to year. Easter must occur very early for all of the readings assigned to Ordinary Time to be available, but this is rare. It is more likely that a set of readings or two assigned to the Sundays after Trinity Sunday will be dropped at the beginning of the season.

Fourth, the "semi" in the semicontinuous readings presents significant challenges to preachers and congregations during the Season after Pentecost. The semicontinuous approach to reading through sections of the canon in worship is a modification of the lectio continua approach to choosing biblical texts for worship. Lectio continua (or "continual reading") works through a biblical writing verse by verse, passage by passage. The semicontinuous approach, on the other hand, works through a biblical work in its literary order by reading key and representative passages from the work, but not by examining the entire writing. Preachers will often find themselves frustrated at the significant gaps between the semicontinuous readings assigned by the Revised Common Lectionary. Therefore, preaching during Ordinary Time can be greatly enhanced by inviting congregations to read and study the materials that fall between the lections in group Bible studies and / or private devotion. More to the homiletical point, preachers must fill in something of these gaps in their sermons. Indeed, they should think of their sermons as having a dual focus in relation to the biblical text. First, as with all Sundays, sermons should focus on the individual lection of choice. This, of course, should be the primary focus. Second, however, sermons should also deal in some sense with the entire section of the biblical writing that extends from the previous week's reading through the current week's lesson. Thus the preacher is invited to offer a message that takes a wide-angle glance at the broad sweep of a section of a biblical work, but that ultimately zooms in on a particular moment within it.

Finally, while the First Testament, Epistle, and Gospel lections for the Season after Pentecost work through different portions of the canon in a semicontinuous fashion, pastors who desire to preach cumulatively are not forced to choose one route (e.g., the Gospel lections) and stay with that route through the whole season. Since the season comprises approximately half of a calendar year, many pastors will think this is too long to stay with a single strategy. Certainly preachers can stay with one such route for the whole season and enter into a portion of the canon with more depth than is allowed when they jump around in the canon. The lections in a series vary enough over time that preaching the series need not become stale or repetitive. Nevertheless, natural breaks occur in the series (e.g., the shift from one epistle to another or from one narrative section of a gospel to the next) that allow preachers to move from one series to another and thus utilize more than one cumulative strategy. However, the shifts that occur in, say, the First Testament series of readings will not necessarily coincide with the shifts in the Epistle or Gospel lections. One way to manage the gaps between ending one strategy and starting the next is to preach from the Psalter readings during the gap. We read from the Psalms more than from any other writing in the Bible, but preach on it less than most. An occasional sermon on the Psalter, especially on texts that vary thematically and rhetorically, will help a congregation better understand the Psalter as its canonical hymnal and prayer book.

Given these general opening comments, let us turn to specific cumulative strategies inherent in the semicontinuous structure of the readings through the Season after Pentecost. For each type of lection (i.e., First Testament, Epistle, and Gospel), we will begin with an overview of how the readings work as a whole throughout the season and then we will consider smaller units that lend themselves to a cumulative approach.

First Testament Lections

In Year A, the First Testament readings for the Season after Pentecost stretched from the beginning of the world to the rule of the judges over the confederacy of the twelve tribes of Israel. The first half of Year B continued working through this sacred narrative, starting with Samuel, the last judge, and proceeding through the reigns of Saul, David, and Solomon. The second half of the season then explored various books that are found in the section of the Hebrew Bible known as Kethuvim (The Writings). This Year, the First Testament lections all focus on *prophets*, starting with the narrative selections focusing on Elijah and Elisha, and then working chronologically from the eighth-century prophets through the post-exilic prophets.

This schema has much to offer a congregation: an examination of portions of each section of the Hebrew canon (Torah, Writings, and Prophets), an overview of a significant part of the salvation history present in the First Testament (especially in Genesis/Exodus and 1 and 2 Samuel), and a range of theological and existential issues with which to struggle. However, the schema presents significant problems as well. Two are especially important to keep in mind while preaching on the First Testament lections for Year C. The first is that the historical sections of readings for Years A and B have not prepared a congregation to understand the circumstances addressed by the prophets being read this year. The history in Year B stopped with Solomon, so a lectionary-oriented congregation has heard no scripture lessons from 1 and 2 Kings that discuss the divided kingdom, the threats of Assyria and Babylon, the destruction of the Northern Kingdom, Josiah's reforms, the fall of the temple, the exile of the Southern Kingdom, the ascendancy of Persia, or the return from exile to a desolate land. The preacher must fill out these details while preaching on the prophetic texts addressing them. The Revised Common Lectionary promotes this role of the preacher by arranging the prophetic texts in chronological order. (See chart of Lectionary Readings at beginning of chapter.)

The second problem facing one who would preach the prophetic lections in Year C is the way in which the Revised Common Lectionary curtails prophetic voices. A few examples are necessary to show the significance of this problem. (A) Isaiah barely appears during Ordinary Time because it gets so much attention during the liturgical seasons. This means that Isaiah is rarely heard on its own terms but instead is read as subordinate to the Gospel lesson. (B) Year C presents readings from eight of the fifteen prophetic writings of the First Testament. Of those not represented, Obadiah, Nahum, and Zechariah never show up in the lectionary, while Daniel, Jonah, Zephaniah, and Malachi only show up once.[4] The only way preachers can correct this problem is by breaking from the lectionary to give attention to these Minor Prophets. (C) Even for those prophetic writings represented in Ordinary Time, the congregation gets only a quick glance at most of the literary works. The Revised Common Lectionary only offers one lection from Lamentations, Joel, Habakkuk, Haggai, and Third Isaiah. Amos, Hosea, and First Isaiah each have two. The focus of the series is primarily on Jeremiah, as seen by its eight readings (Propers 16–21, 23–24). The reason for this arrangement is the chronological approach taken by the Revised Common Lectionary, which works well. Nevertheless, preachers will need to offer an overview of each of the prophetic writings on which they preach in order to fill out the full literary, theological, and historical context.

When we turn to discuss specific cumulative strategies for preaching through the First Testament series of readings, we are really asking questions about different ways of combining and separating the different prophets.

STRATEGY 1—One approach is to preach the *First Testament lections* through the whole season. This strategy allows a congregation to consider slowly what it means to be heirs to a prophetic religion and come to understand that prophets less predicted the future and more analyzed sociopolitical circumstances with a theological lens. While maintaining that focus through the season, however, the semicontinuous approach also allows a congregation to move through a variety of different historical periods and theological perspectives at a fairly quick pace.

Preachers usually use the historical circumstances that gave rise to a biblical text as the backdrop for preaching that text. This approach certainly fits with this strategy. However, given the three-century span of materials considered during Year C, preachers may choose to reverse this approach. In other words, one could use individual lections to provide the foreground for preaching on the circumstances addressed by the prophets. Preachers will not have to look far to find homiletical analogies between ancient circumstances of economic inequity, injustice, military violence, exile, and natural disaster.

STRATEGY 2—For pastors who do not wish to preach on the whole of the First Testament series during Year C, the series of readings from the prophetic books can be divided into *two large segments.* The first segment deals with the *preexilic prophetic vision of justice and God's judgment* (Propers 10–20). The second section deals with the *exilic and postexilic theme of eschatological hope of redemption and restoration* (Propers 21, 23–28). These themes are not, of course, mutually exclusive. We find preexilic prophetic visions of hope as well as postexilic calls for justice. Nevertheless, judgment thematically dominates the earlier period while hope dominates the later. Also, it is important to note that preachers may have to look to the broader context for the lection to fit the theme. For instance, the lection taken from Habakkuk 1 and 2 is a complaint seeking an answer to the question of theodicy. However, if preachers read the whole of the book of Habakkuk, they will find the book ends with an expression of hopeful expectation.

STRATEGY 3—In addition to the large division of the readings suggested in the previous strategy, preachers can divide the First Testament series into smaller sections in terms of *historical periods* being addressed. The first such section would be the materials taken from *1 and 2 Kings* (Propers 4–9). Set in the Northern Kingdom in the ninth century b.c.e., the stories of Elijah and Elisha provide a paradigm for what it means to be a prophet in Israel.

STRATEGY 4—The next section would include the *eighth-century prophets* Amos, Hosea and Isaiah. Here the themes of God's judgment upon injustice, corruption, and oppression are raised up. For many congregations today, it is difficult to understand a God of judgment. Nevertheless, without divine justice, divine grace makes no sense.

STRATEGY 5—After exploring the eighth-century prophets, the Revised Common Lectionary directs the church's attention to

Jeremiah for a lengthy eight weeks, nine if you count the appropriate interruption by Lamentations (Propers 16–24). The book of Jeremiah is a mixture of different poetic oracles and laments and prose biographical narratives and sermons. The history of its composition and redaction appears extremely complex, and the arrangement of the material is not always clear. Finally, Jeremiah's ministry spanned the course of the reigns of the last four kings of Judah. But even with the diversity of literary styles used, the confusing process of composition, and the different political powers addressed, the book of Jeremiah is, thematically speaking, fairly well focused.

Jeremiah focuses on the time leading up to the destruction of Jerusalem and the temple (587 B.C.E.) and into the early exilic period. The prophet interprets the defeat at the hands of the Babylonians as divine judgment upon Judah's unfaithfulness in its covenant with God. Nevertheless, Jeremiah assumes that God's faithfulness will result in restoration for the nation grounded in a new covenantal relationship. In other words, Jeremiah prophetically interprets the present circumstances of turmoil in light of the past but not as the final determinant for God's future.

It is difficult to overestimate the importance of this time period for the development of Judaism and of the First Testament. Moreover, the exile has become a metaphor that a number of biblical scholars, theologians, and preachers have turned to in describing the state of the church in North America in a post-Christendom society.[5] Yet the period with which Jeremiah deals is not well understood by most laity. Preachers will do well to pause in this period, examine it, reflect theologically about it, and draw analogies from it for today's Christians, church, and world.

STRATEGY 6—The final historical period explored in this series of First Testament readings is *the postexilic era.* The Revised Common Lectionary offers us only one lection from each of the following: Joel, Habakkuk, Haggai, and Third Isaiah. In truth, scholars are not in agreement that Joel and Habakkuk are postexilic, but they share an eschatological outlook with Haggai and Third Isaiah. Their focus on the day of the Lord serves well to draw the prophetic series to a close, to join with other lections at the end of Ordinary Time that share eschatological emphases, and to prepare for the eschatological emphasis of Advent. For the three Minor Prophets represented (Joel,

Habakkuk, and Haggai), preachers should, as part of the sermon, offer a broad view of the literary work as a whole.

Epistle Lections

In Year C, the New Testament lessons for Ordinary Time come from Galatians, Colossians, Hebrews 11—13, Philemon, 1 and 2 Timothy, and 2 Thessalonians. This is an odd progression of Epistle readings. The majority of the texts are taken from the Pauline corpus, but Hebrews breaks the sets of Pauline readings in two. However, it is not even the whole of Hebrews, but only lections drawn from chapters 11—13 (Propers 14–17), since chapters 1—10 are dealt with in Year B (Propers 22–28). To complicate matters further, the Pauline material is a mixture of letters with undisputed and disputed authorship, but the material is not separated into those two categories. For the most part, scholars agree that Paul wrote Galatians and Philemon, argue about whether he wrote Colossians and 2 Thessalonians, and agree that a Pauline disciple wrote 1 and 2 Timothy.

If we take Hebrews out of the equation for the sake of discussion, the other writings do have some broad commonalities. Being aware of these will aid a cumulative approach involving the Epistle lections.

First, even though the Deutero-Pauline letters come after the death of Paul and therefore address churches in very different circumstances than the churches Paul addressed, they do all have at their core a Pauline understanding of the good news of Jesus Christ. The very reason a disciple of Paul would write a letter in Paul's name is to extend and apply Paul's theology to new circumstances. This does not mean that there is no development of thought from the Pauline corpus to the Deutero-Pauline works in, say, the areas of christology, soteriology, and ecclesiology. There certainly is. Underneath those developments, however, is a foundational Pauline worldview.

Second, these epistles are letters in the true sense of the word. In other words, they are occasional in nature, written for a specific reason to address specific circumstances. In today's church, we often ignore this occasional nature of the letters because we read them from a great distance of time and claim them as scripture. The Revised Common Lectionary reinforces this ignorance by primarily choosing lections that exhibit theological dimensions of the letters instead of those that focus on pastoral and communal issues. This is not inappropriate in that in worship (in contrast to a Bible study in a setting of educational ministry), the church seeks from the Bible a word of good news to proclaim. However, viewing the reading of New Testament Epistles as a process of overhearing half of an ongoing pastoral conversation between author and ancient congregation enhances our theological reading of the texts, and indeed allows us to see with better focus the potential for drawing homiletical analogies between the Pauline context and our own.

Third, preachers need to teach congregations that letters were understood and functioned somewhat differently in antiquity than today. While it is important to recognize the occasional nature of the Pauline letters, it is also important that they served an official purpose in the life of the early church. The letters were epistles in the sense that they were not personal correspondence between friends or relatives but were public addresses to a community of faith. The letters were written to be read orally to the community as a whole. This includes those letters addressed to individuals (Philemon, 1 and 2 Timothy).

Moreover, in the ancient mind, writers were thought to be present in the letter, and thus they carried something of the sender's persona, social status, and authority. This means the Deutero-Pauline letters should be read, not as forgeries, but as authentic attempts to bring Paul's apostolic presence and authority to bear on a new day.

Fourth, in preaching passages from Pauline and Deutero-Pauline letters, not only should preachers (and congregations) be clear about the circumstances that necessitated the writing of the letter and of the relationship between the writer and the recipients, they must also ascertain how individual lections function within the structure of the letter. As is true of letters today, ancient letters were composed using set structural forms. Pauline letters have five parts: (a) the greeting, which names the sender and the recipient; (b) a prayer of thanksgiving for the recipients; (c) the body of the letter, in which Paul addresses the main pastoral and theological main issue(s); (d) ethical exhortation, which can flow out of the material in the body of the letter and/or grow out of formulaic ethical instruction found in the ancient Mediterranean world; and (e) closing greetings and blessing. By understanding the function of a passage within the structure of the letter, the preacher will be better able to evaluate the rhetorical strategy behind Paul's language and to shape the function of a sermon based on that text. As mentioned earlier, when preaching from semicontinuous readings, pastors will often need to fill in gaps to help congregations contextualize a pericope. This is especially important in terms of understanding how passages from epistles function in relation to the standard parts of ancient letters, given the Revised Common Lectionary's preference to avoid some of the parts that deal most directly with the conflict or controversy that necessitated the letters.

Finally, it is important to remember that the Revised Common Lectionary often sets the boundaries for Epistle lections inappropriately. It divides the texts in the middle of logical developments and thus arguments are skewed. Preachers who are following a cumulative strategy of preaching through an New Testament letter should be willing, at times, to designate different beginnings and endings to lessons.

Given these broad insights into preaching from epistolary materials, we are ready to consider particular cumulative strategies that are available during Ordinary Time of Year C.

STRATEGY 7—The first option is to preach on the *whole series of Epistle lections* for the Sundays after Pentecost. While this is certainly a viable homiletical option, preachers need to be aware that because of the Revised Common Lectionary's structuring of the Epistle series for Year C, the texts will not be experienced as a cumulative whole by the congregation. They can, however, be experienced as a collection of cumulative sections—in other words, as a combination of some of the cumulative strategies named below.

STRATEGY 8—Even though the height dimension of the Epistle readings is inconsistent across the whole of Ordinary Time, some cumulative tendencies in the lections extend beyond the individual writings. The first is that Galatians and Colossians both focus on *defending the Pauline faith* against rival interpretations. (Elements of this are found in 1 and 2 Timothy as well.) This focus is not always evident in the lections chosen, however, and must be brought out by the preacher. Nevertheless, it is worth the effort to fill in these gaps when there is a clear analogy between the struggle in the letter and the task of doing theology and proclaiming the faith today, when the church is fragmented into numerous denominations and theological orientations, but when laypeople are often confused or even ignorant about the differences.

STRATEGY 9—Another grouping of some of the letters relates to the fact that Philemon and 1 and 2 Timothy are *addressed to individuals.* (Note that the canonical arrangement of the Pauline corpus is based in part on whether the letters are addressed to communities or individuals.) As mentioned above, these letters were still clearly intended to be read aloud in the community of faith. Nevertheless, there is a more personal tone in the letters given that the primary recipients are individuals within the community as opposed to the community as a whole. This invites, at times, a more individualistic orientation of sermons.

STRATEGY 10—One other grouping is part of the previous group. First and Second Timothy are *Pastoral Letters.* (Titus, the third Pastoral Letter, appears in the Revised Common Lectionary only on Christmas.) They are called Pastorals because they are addressed to Christian leaders, or shepherds/pastors. The author(s) who wrote these letters in Paul's name was (were) concerned with influencing future leadership for the church as it became more of an institutional organization. These letters provide preachers the opportunity to reflect on leadership issues facing the church today.

The Revised Common Lectionary avoids some of the more difficult passages, e.g., those concerning the role of women in the church. While this omission is likely an attempt not to pass on the patriarchy of the texts, allowing them to stay in the text with silence in response from the pulpit fails to address patriarchy in the church today. Given the twentieth- and twenty-first–century church's moves to correct the ways it has oppressed women, and given that in most congregational circumstances and most Mainline seminaries today, women significantly outnumber men, how can preachers legitimately talk about the future of church leadership without dealing with the sexism inherent in our sacred texts?

STRATEGY 11—Beyond these different groupings, preachers can deal with each of the *individual writings* in a cumulative fashion. Given its significant role in shaping Protestant theology, spending up to six weeks (depending on when Pentecost occurs) on *Galatians* in the pulpit can be time well spent (Propers 4–9). As has perhaps always been the case, we live in a day when we love to speak of God's "amazing grace," but in reality think that, and act as if, we must earn salvation. Perhaps even more importantly, many people in the church today (and this has not always been the case) are unsure what "salvation" is from a Christian perspective. Preaching on Galatians and the ancient crisis Paul is addressing will offer preacher and congregation an opportunity to explore our contemporary dilemma.

Galatians is Paul's most polemical letter. He is so upset that he omits an opening prayer of thanksgiving for the recipients. This strong tone is due to the level of importance of what Paul thinks is at stake. While Paul is absent, Jewish Christian missionaries have arrived and begun teaching that for Gentiles to be fully Christian they must be circumcised. For Paul this teaching questions the center of the gospel proclaiming God's initiative *pro nobis*, for us, in the faithful death and resurrection of Jesus Christ. This sharp, focused argument has complexities (e.g., in the way Paul interprets the First Testament account of Abraham) that the Revised Common Lectionary choices skim over. The preacher will have to fill in some significant gaps without getting lost in the details if congregations are to understand the full weight of Paul's argument.

Pastors will also need to clarify a common misconception of the way Galatians is often read and preached. Contemporary readers hear the dichotomies of circumcision/justification and law/gospel in anti-Jewish terms. But Galatians is not about Jew versus Gentile. The struggle being addressed is not interreligious but intra-religious. It is about Jewish Christians and Gentile Christians. It is about competing Christian interpretations of the good news of Jesus Christ and the implications of how one should respond to that good news.

STRATEGY 12—Many preachers would not, on their own initiative, choose to spend a month preaching through *Colossians* (Propers 10–13). One of the strengths of lectionary preaching is that the Revised Common Lectionary often pushes the church into parts of the canon we might otherwise neglect (although the Revised Common Lectionary also neglects parts of the canon). With the rise of historical criticism and the dispute over Pauline authorship of much of the Pauline corpus, preachers have tended to prefer the undisputed letters over the Deutero-Pauline letters. During Year C, however, the Revised Common Lectionary sends us off to read Colossians, 1 and 2 Timothy, and 2 Thessalonians.

Colossians is most likely a Deutero-Pauline letter written primarily to confront "heretical" teachings that infiltrated the church after Paul's death. "False teachers" were encouraging asceticism and religious celebrations that resemble esoteric practices found in Hellenistic mystery religions. For the writer, supplementing the Christian faith in such ways is, essentially, a subversion of loyalty to Christ. The author asserts a cosmic christology and uses baptism metaphors to counter this teaching.

In the postmodern context of North America, most Christians (like almost everyone else) construct a worldview out of multiple ideological resources. Christian theology and practice are among those resources, perhaps are even the primary ones. But they are in conversation with others as well—political ideologies, economic theories, popular psychology, etc. Of course, other religions and spiritual practices are in the mix. Preachers would do well to think through how to preach from Colossians in this postmodern world.

STRATEGY 13—As noted above, the whole of Hebrews is not considered during Year C. Instead in Year B, *Hebrews 1—10* is offered in semicontinuous readings; and in Year C, the Revised Common Lectionary offers readings from Hebrews 11—13 (Propers 14–17). This is a clumsy and irresponsible division of the text. Nevertheless, we find something of a thematic shift between the two sets of readings that can serve a cumulative approach.

In the first part of book, the focus is on christology and soteriology; in the second, the focus is on *faith*. In 11:1 the author defines faith as "the assurance of things hoped for, the conviction of things not seen," and then he moves through the rest of the chapter to show how God approved this faith when it was found in the ancestors of the tradition. The climax of this movement, and indeed the epitome of exemplifying faith is Jesus (12:1ff). From this description of the faithfulness of Jesus proceeds a call to endurance (as Jesus endured his suffering) and various ethical exhortations. If preachers are able to keep this unfolding logic in mind while preaching Propers 14–17, the congregation will have a cumulative experience of the lections.

STRATEGY 14—Because *Philemon* is such a short letter, it can be read as a single lection (Proper 18). It is strange to consider a single lection in terms of cumulative preaching strategies. However, preaching through an entire Pauline letter can support cumulative preaching through other epistolary literature.

Because of the complex nature of biblical literature, it is rare that one gets the opportunity to preach on a whole biblical work in one sermon. In sermons on Philemon, preachers can talk about how Paul's letters functioned in general. In its focus as a letter of commendation for Onesimus, Philemon illustrates well the occasional nature of Paul's letters. Paul's call for Philemon to accept Onesimus back as a brother offers insight into Pauline theology, specifically his soteriology and ecclesiology. The way Paul highlights his relationship with Philemon shows something of the way ancient letters signified the presence and authority of the sender. Finally, the letter follows most of the structural elements of Pauline letters—missing only is the moral exhortation section. A preacher would do well to preach an expository sermon on Philemon, following the structure:

Greeting (1–3)

Thanksgiving (4–7)

Body (8–21)

Closing Greetings and Benediction (22–25).

STRATEGY 15—The lections for *1 Timothy* (Propers 19–21) do not serve a cumulative strategy well. The individual passages chosen, in and of themselves, do contain some homiletical potential, but we find neither an explicit thematic connection between them from week to week, a good representation of the flow of the letter (the readings skip from chapter 2 to chapter 6), nor a highlighting of the defining characteristics of the letter (e.g., the heretical teachings being attacked and the orders of ministry). If pastors truly want to preach through 1 Timothy in a cumulative fashion, they will be forced to break from the lectionary and choose better selections. Doing so, however, will also set up the readings from 2 Timothy better than do the lectionary assignments.

STRATEGY 16—Although preachers might wish the Revised Common Lectionary had chosen different texts from *2 Timothy* (Propers 22–25), and will certainly need to adjust the boundaries of the lections, the lectionary does a somewhat better job with the second Pastoral Letter than it does with 1 Timothy. This is due, in some sense, to the simple fact that more is read from 2 Timothy (four lections from four chapters) than from 1 Timothy (three lections from six chapters). Thus, it will not be too difficult for preachers to fill in the missing gaps (e.g., naming the false teaching being countered) and to convey the tone of the letter as a last will and testament ascribed to Paul by one of his disciples. Certainly the core of the writer's exhortation to a pastoral leader is presented in the lections and will serve a cumulative approach well.

STRATEGY 17—The shift from 2 Timothy to *2 Thessalonians* is not a natural one. But the choice of 2 Thessalonians is oriented toward what follows (Reign of Christ and Advent) instead of what precedes it. The end of the liturgical cycle (as well as the beginning that is just around the curve) has a strong eschatological tone. Second Thessalonians is an appropriate choice for this period given that Paul (or perhaps a Pauline disciple) wrote it to counter a misinterpretation of Paul's teaching concerning the parousia. Some in the church at Thessalonica evidently assumed the coming of Christ was so near that they needed no longer to work. Paul counters by arguing that signs that will accompany the day of the Lord have yet to come, and by exhorting idlers to get back to work.

Many preachers cringe at the thought that people sitting in their pews have read the Left Behind series with great interest. Works that proffer damaging, so-called "literal" readings of the apocalyptic visions of the New Testament have found a hearing in every generation. Pastors should consider preaching cumulatively through the readings from 2 Thessalonians (and on those Advent texts that call the church to wait for the coming of the Lord) in order to follow Paul's tactic of countering such misinterpretations. This will require thinking through a theology of "end-time" metaphors, which dominate so much of New Testament Christianity.

Gospel Lections

Luke is the Gospel that anchors Year C of the lectionary. As one considers a cumulative preaching strategy for the Sundays after Pentecost, it is important to remember how the Revised Common Lectionary has used Luke through the liturgical seasons. During Advent, Christmas, and Lent, Lukan texts were chosen for liturgical, thematic purposes. However, during the Season after Epiphany, Luke was read in a semicontinuous fashion that is continued after

Pentecost. Indeed, on the Sundays after Epiphany, we began working through the Galilean ministry in Luke, focusing on Jesus' inaugural sermon in Nazareth and the Sermon on the Plain. After Trinity Sunday, the Revised Common Lectionary begins where it paused—later in the Galilean ministry. But the lectionary soon progresses on to the travel narrative, in which Jesus makes his way from Galilee to Jerusalem (see below).

However, separating this semicontinuous reading is, of course, Lent and Easter. We have already mentioned that in Lent, Luke is used thematically. For most of Easter, the Gospel of John replaces Luke. Thus, when the semicontinuous reading of Luke restarts on the first Sunday following Trinity Sunday, preachers will need to help the congregation become reacquainted with the Third Gospel.

Preachers should have a couple of recent, critical commentaries on Luke to use as conversation partners while working through Year C as a whole, but especially through Ordinary Time. Given the amount of time spent in Luke, preachers will need the level of detail offered in introductions to the Gospel and comments on the various pericopae that relate to a sense of the whole. This is especially important since the lectionary choices for Ordinary Time do not highlight some of the most unique characteristics of Lukan theology and plot. The choices do highlight some materials—especially teachings of Jesus—that are found only in Luke. But harder to find throughout the season is Luke's view of the periodization of salvation history, the understanding of salvation as the reversal of the social status quo, the apologetic for the inclusion of the Gentiles, the prophetic characterization of Jesus and those who follow in his pattern of ministry, the delay of the parousia, and the manner in which elements in Luke foreshadow Acts. Understanding these Lukan elements will help preachers better make sense of the Lukan pericopae under consideration.

While preachers will need to use commentaries to refresh their memories and deepen their understanding of the various theological and narrative nuances of Luke, especially in terms of the function of the travel narrative and the gaps in the Revised Common Lectionary choices, a few items of introduction can be named here in passing to give a sense of how Luke can be presented over time for the sake of a deeper, cumulative hearing on the part of the congregation.

Although we know nothing of the author or the location in which the Gospel was written, it seems fairly likely that Luke was written in the 80s or 90s of the first century C.E. It was written as the first volume of a two-volume work (Luke-Acts) portraying the beginning of the Christian movement. This two-volume work was written to Gentile Christians, with a major purpose being the theological argument (in narrative form) of showing how the Gentile Church is a fulfillment of God's promises to Israel.

Scholars commonly hold that Luke used Mark and "Q" (a hypothetical sayings source) as his two main sources for adapting/ writing the story of Jesus for his community in its specific circumstances. But when compared to Matthew, Luke uses a lower percentage of Markan material in his Gospel, meaning that a higher percentage of the material in the Third Gospel is unique to Luke. Still, Luke follows Mark's narrative structure: Galilean ministry (Lk. 3:1—9:50), journey to Jerusalem (9:51—19:27), Jerusalem narrative (19:28—24:53). Luke adds to the beginning of this structure a prologue (1:1–4) and infancy narrative (1:5—2:52). Whereas Mark ends his narrative with an empty tomb and the promise that the risen Jesus will meet the disciples back in Galilee (Mark 16:1–8), Luke adds resurrection appearances that occur in and around Jerusalem (Lk. 24) in order to set up the addition of a second volume focusing on Jesus' followers (Acts). The end result is that Luke creates an "orderly account" (Lk. 1:1–4) of a salvation history extending backward through Israel, engaging the political world, centered in the person of Jesus and the place of Jerusalem, and extending forward through the church to the ends of the earth.

Another way Luke adapts Mark's outline that is more significant for a cumulative preaching approach through Ordinary Time, Year C, is that he greatly expands Mark's narrative section of Jesus traveling to Jerusalem. Both Matthew and Luke supplement Mark's text by adding significant amounts of Jesus' teaching. Whereas Matthew collects this material into five thematic sermons/discourses spread throughout the narrative, Luke collects a majority of the sayings material into the travel narrative. (See Strategy 20 below.)

In addition to these features, preachers should pay special attention to whom the different teachings are addressed. Is Jesus speaking to the disciples, the crowds, or opponents (religious leaders)? The tone and underlying intent of the teaching shifts based on the audience.

Given these broad insights into preaching from Luke, what particular strategies are available during Ordinary Time of Year C?

STRATEGY 10—One could certainly spend the entire season working through the *whole series of Gospel lections*. Indeed, Strategy 20 takes up most of the season, so to preach Luke for the whole Season after Pentecost is, in a sense, to follow Strategy 20 with an introduction (the Galilean texts) and epilogue (the temple pericopae).

STRATEGY 19—Ordinary Time opens with four Gospel lections from the *Galilean ministry* (Propers 4–7). Three of these passages are healing stories, but actually connecting all four is Luke's understanding of salvation as reversal of the person's situation, just as healing reverses one's illness. This series of texts invites a sermonic exploration of salvation as a gift from God in the here and now as opposed to some future afterlife. Of course, how well a cumulative approach can work with these texts depends upon when the season begins. The later Trinity Sunday occurs, the fewer of these readings that will be used. Indeed, if Easter occurs at its latest possibility, none of these readings will be used.

STRATEGY 20—As already noted, the largest collection of Gospel lections for the Sundays after Pentecost come from *Luke's travel narrative* (Propers 8–26). Because of the narrative material from Luke used in the liturgical seasons, the semicontinuous readings after Epiphany that covered a significant portion of Luke's version of the Galilean ministry, and the Revised Common Lectionary's tendency to minimize duplication of shared Synoptic material across the three-year lectionary cycle, Ordinary Time focuses primarily on Luke's travel narrative. Specifically, nineteen out of the twenty-five Gospel lections between Trinity and Reign of Christ (i.e., Propers 4–28) come from the travel narrative, and almost all of the material in these lections has no parallel in the other Synoptic Gospels.

It is difficult (if not impossible) to find in the travel narrative a geographical progression from Galilee to Jerusalem that makes sense. Nevertheless, what is clear is that by beginning the narrative section, with the expression that Jesus "set his face toward Jerusalem" (9:51, the entire section is to be understood as leading to Jesus' martyrdom as a prophet, to his coming "exodus" (9:31). This dynamic makes the Revised Common Lectionary's choice of the Lukan crucifixion scene in which Jesus is ironically named "king of the Jews" (Lk. 23:33–43) for the Reign of Christ especially appropriate.

STRATEGY 21—The series of texts drawn from the travel narrative divide easily neither in terms of Luke's narrative structure, nor thematically. However, several *groupings of parables* allow for shorter cumulative possibilities. We find parables or parabolic material in Propers 10, 12–14, 17, 19–21, 24–25. Unlike the majority of parables in Mark and Matthew, these Lukan parables are not varying metaphors for the reign of God. They deal with a range of theological and ethical themes.

STRATEGY 22—As is true of Years A and B, the Gospel lections for the end of Ordinary Time, Year C, proceed from *Jesus' eschatological teaching in Jerusalem* (Propers 27–28). While only two Gospel readings focus on the theme of eschatology, they work cumulatively with the eschatological themes that orient the Reign of Christ and Advent.

Notes

Preface

[1]The following discussion of cumulative preaching is excerpted and adapted from O. Wesley Allen Jr., *The Homiletic of All Believers* (Louisville: Westminster John Knox Press, 2005) 51–57, 59–64, 76–85.

Introduction: The Three Dimensional Lectionary

[1]The following survey of the evolution of Christian lectionaries draws on "Introduction," in *Lectionary for Mass* (Collegeville: Liturgical Press, 1970), xxvi–xli; *Common Lectionary: The Lectionary Proposed by the Consultation on Common Texts* (New York: Church Hymnal Corporation, 1983), 7–27; *The Revised Common Lectionary: The Consultation on Common Texts* (Nashville: Abingdon Press, 1992), 9–20; John Reumann, "A History of Lectionaries: From the Synagogue at Nazareth to Post-Vatican II," *Interpretation* 31 (1977): 116–30; "Introduction," in *Lectionary I: Proper of Seasons, Sundays in Ordinary Time* (London: Collins Liturgical Publications, 1983), xvii–lxvii; R.H. Fuller, "Lectionary," in *The New Westminster Dictionary of Liturgy and Worship*, ed. J.G. Davies (Philadelphia: Westminster Press, 1986), 297–99; Laurence Hull Stookey, *Calendar: Christ's Time for the Church* (Nashville: Abingdon, 1996); Fritz West, *Scripture and Memory: The Ecumenical Hermeneutic of the Three-Year Lectionaries* (Collegeville: Liturgical Press, 1997), 11–18.

[2]The text of the Constitution on the Sacred Liturgy Sacrosanctum Concilium Solemnly Promulgated by His Holiness Pope Paul VI on December 4, 1963, can be found online at http://www.vatican.va/archive/hist_councils/ii_vatican_council/documents/vat-ii_const_19631204_sacrosanctum-concilium_en.html (accessed on June 6, 2007).

[3]Many books offering overviews of the liturgical year begin with the Easter cycle, since, in terms of historical development, Easter was the first annual liturgical celebration and all others evolved from it. Since our overview is focused less on the history of the calendar and more on the potential for shaping current congregational experience of the Revised Common Lectionary, this chapter will proceed through the liturgical year from Advent to Pentecost.

[4]The Catholic Church actually considers the season to extend to the First Sunday after Epiphany, on which Baptism of the Lord is celebrated.

[5]For more on the commemoration of Epiphany, see the following section on the Sundays after Epiphany.

[6]The Revised Common Lectionary actually provides three propers for Christmas, but their use presumes three different services for the same group of congregants. Most churches only use the first set of readings (Proper 1), and that is our focus in this book as well.

[7]To be more precise, the Roman Catholic Church ends Christmastide on Baptism of the Lord and then the Sundays that follow are considered Ordinary Time.

[8]The number of Sundays after Epiphany varies from year to year because the fact that Easter is a movable feast.

[9]Adapted from a table entitled, "The Memory Pattern of the Old Testament Readings in the Season of Lent, Lectionary for Mass," in Fritz West, *Scripture and Memory*, 93.

[10]See O. Wesley Allen Jr., *Preaching Resurrection*, Preaching Classic Texts (St. Louis: Chalice Press, 2000), 95–106.

[11]While Revelation is not an epistle, the first reading for the season (1:4–8 – Easter 2) is the opening of the letter to the seven churches in Asia Minor.

Cumulative Preaching Strategies for Year A

[1]The RCL actually provides three propers for Christmas, but use of all three presumes three different services for the same group of congregants. Most Protestant churches only use the first set of readings (Proper 1), and that is our focus in this book as well.

[2]Dates refer to the year in which Advent begins; thus "2010" signifies the 2010–11 liturgial year.

[3]See note 1 above.

[4]The RCL includes two options for the First Testament lections during the Season after Pentecost. The only one considered in this work is the semicontinuous option. The alternate, however, offers First Testament lections (and corresponding Psalter readings) chosen to support (typologically) the gospel lections. While this approach is somewhat justified during the thematically controlled liturgical seasons, the approach during Ordinary Time inappropriately implies that the First Testament has sub-canonical status.

Cumulative Preaching Strategies for Year B

[1]The RCL actually provides three propers for Christmas, but use of all three presumes three different services for the same group of congregants. Most Protestant churches only use the first set of readings (Proper 1), and that is our focus in this book as well.

[2]See note 1 above.

[3]The Revised Common Lectionary includes two options for the First Testament lections during the Season after Pentecost. The only one considered in this work is the semicontinuous option. The alternate, however, offers First Testament lections (and corresponding Psalter readings) chosen to support (typologically) the gospel lections. While this approach is somewhat justified during the thematically controlled liturgical seasons, the approach during Ordinary Time inappropriately implies that the First Testament has sub-canonical status.

[4]Actually, this same passage is also offered as an alternative for the Psalter reading for Proper 9 Year A.

Cumulative Preaching Strategies for Year C

[1]The RCL actually provides three propers for Christmas, but use of all three presumes three different services for the same group of congregants. Most Protestant churches only use the first set of readings (Proper 1), and that is our focus in this book as well.

[2]See note 1 above.

[3]The RCL includes two options for the First Testament lections during the Season after Pentecost. The only one considered in this work is the semicontinuous option. The alternate, however, offers First Testament lections (and corresponding Psalter readings) chosen to support (typologically) the Gospel lections. While this approach is somewhat justified during the thematically controlled liturgical seasons, the approach during Ordinary Time inappropriately implies that the First Testament has sub-canonical status.

[4]This count changes if one includes the alternate (i.e., non-semicontinuous) First Testament readings for Ordinary Time.

[5]See, for example, the collection of essays edited by Erskine Clarke, *Exilic Preaching: Testimony for Christian Exiles in an Increasingly Hostile Culture* (Harrisburg, Pa.: Trinity Press International, 1998).